Resorts of the Raj

Resorts of the Raj

Hill Stations of India

Text and Photographs
by
Vikram Bhatt

Mapin Publishing Pvt. Ltd.
Ahmedabad

First published in the
United States of America in 1998 by
Grantha Corporation
80 Cliffedgeway
Middletown, NJ 07701

Simultaneously published in India by
Mapin Publishing Pvt.Ltd.
Chidambaram, Ahmedabad 380 013
Mapinpub@ad1.vsnl.net.in

Text & Photographs © Vikram Bhatt except otherwise noted
Editor: Shernaz Cama

ISBN: 0-944142-98-2 (Grantha)
       81-85822-41-7 (Mapin)
LC No: 96-79502

Design: Paulomi Shah / Mapin Design Studio
Typeset by Swift Graphics Pvt. Ltd., Ahmedabad
Processed by Reproscan, Mumbai
Printed in Singapore

Captions
Page 1:
The profusion of colours and flowers in the springtime in
the Himalayas is amazing.
Pages 2-3:
Sunset view, Pachmarhi. Every hill resort offers similar
spectacular views of sunrise and sunset.
Pages 4-5:
Government Guesthouse, Ootacamund.
Pages 6-7:
Wrap-around veranda of a fine bungalow, Mahabaleshwar.

**The corporations concerned with
the preservation of India's heritage, who have
made this book possible are:**

Rajshree Group of companies
Coimbatore

Reliance Industries Ltd
(Textile Division)

Tiger Tops Mountain Travel
India and Nepal

Air India

Acknowledgments

When I started working on this book, I did not realise how much I would have to rely on others to produce it: several institutions and many individuals have helped me at various stages of the project. A major part of the study was conducted during my 1993-94 sabbatical year. I would like to thank McGill University for this opportunity, also my colleagues at the School of Architecture who took up the slack during my absence. The study was also supported by grants from two organisations: The Graham Foundation for the Arts, Chicago and the Shastri Indo-Canadian Institute. I would also like to thank the staff of the Shastri Institute in New Delhi, particularly Ronald Neufeldt and P.N. Malik for their outstanding cooperation during my research in India.

Krishan Chugh, Chairman of the ITC, made the facilities of its guesthouses available to me during my research trips throughout India. Special thanks are also due to Ramesh Khosla and Debasish Guha of ARCOP Associates, New Delhi for co-ordinating my research visits. Rekha Khosla, Department of Tourism, Government of India, put me in touch with the appropriate regional authorities. The State Tourism Development Authorities of Madhya Pradesh, Maharashtra and Rajasthan, provided accommodation and logistical support when needed. Without the guidance and hospitality of the Himachal Pradesh Tourism Development Corporation through its able staff members, in particular Renu Sahni Dhar, Secretary Tourism, Gopal Sharma and Neena Sehgal, I could not have explored the most important group of hill resorts in the Himalayas as well as I did.

I would also like to thank others who helped me at various stages of this endeavour, sorting the archival records, checking historical accounts, and visiting resorts and locations. At short notice they arranged visits to buildings which were off limits to the public, helped identify and set up interviews with long-term residents.

To Charlotte and Pravin Mukhia I owe special thanks for their help while I was in the Darjeeling area. Similarly, in almost every resort there were individuals who helped me readily, among them Mr. and Mrs. Medaiah and M.M. Chengappa in Coonoor; Rajindershigh Jandrotia and Jagganath Plaha in Dalhousie; B.D. Katoch in Kajjiar; Sunil Pal and J.Sokhey in Kasauli; Zai Whitaker and Mrs Raju in Kodaikanal; J.R. Verde and Irani in Mahabaleshwar; Mr. and Mrs. Jamshed Lord and Shankarao Mahadev Savent in Matheran; Anand Jauhar, Ruskin Bond and Ganesh Saili in Mussoorie; G.S. Babu and Robert D'Cruz in Ootacamund; Dennis Torry and Bhowmik in Pachmarhi; the Butail family in Palampur; Uday Singh, Dev Nath, B.P. Malhotra, Mrinal Miri and Ratanjit Singh in Simla; Thelma and Victor Tate in Yercaud. Special thanks are also due to Pratima Bhatt and family in Bombay and Bhalla, Hora, Pande and Thukral families in New Delhi who made my stay comfortable and productive.

I would also like to acknowledge the support of the staff of the British Library, India Office Library and Records, London; the staff of the National Archives of India, New Delhi; the staff of the Canadian Centre for Architecture, Montreal, and the staff of the McGill University Library, Montreal. For the historical information and a number of illustrations presented in this book I have used McGill University's Rare Books and Special Collection and Humanities and Social Sciences Libraries and would like to acknowledge their kind support.

Soon after my visit to Simla, Bipin Shah at Mapin Publishing and I discussed the idea of this book, and sooner than we realized, we were both committed to it. His enthusiasm was unwavering, and to him I owe special thanks. David Covo, Norbert Schoenauer and Peter Scriver looked at the draft of the book and made helpful suggestions. François Dufaux and Rick Kerrigan helped with the illustrations. My thanks also to Maureen Anderson for her valuable editorial comments and my editor Shernaz Cama.

My wife Suzie Bogos was by my side all along and helped me with the research. To her I dedicate this book.

Vikram Bhatt, April, 1997, Montreal

Contents

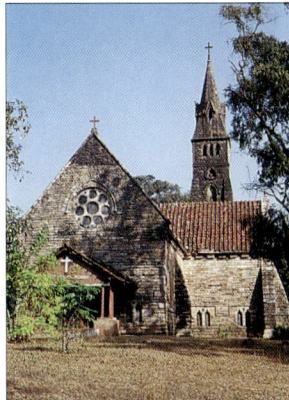

Map of places mentioned in the text

JAMMU & KASHMIR

17
18
2
3 8
1 4
6 5
7

Indus

Jhelum

Chenab

13
9
12
10 15 14
Beas
26 19 22 23
24 20
25 29 11 21
28 27 30
31

PUNJAB

Ravi

Sutlej
16

PAKISTAN

HIMACHAL PRADESH

CHINA

32
33
36 40 39 44
34 38 41 43
35 46 47 42
37 45

Garhwal

Kumaon

HARYANA

New Delhi

UTTAR PRADESH

Himalayas

Brahmaputra

ARUNACHAL PRADESH

NEPAL

SIKKIM
49
48 52
51 50

ASSAM

MEGHALAYA

NAGALAND

53
54 55
56
MANIPUR

TRIPURA

Thar Desert

Indus

Sind

RAJASTHAN

Aravalli Hills
64

Jamuna

Bagmati

Ganges
61

BIHAR

58 60
59
57

BANGLADESH

MIZORAM

GUJARAT

I N D I A

WEST BENGAL
Calcutta

Narmada
62

MADHYA PRADESH
63

ORISSA

MYANMAR (BURMA)

65

66

Godavari

ANDHRA PRADESH

Mumbai (Bombay)

70
69
68
73 67
71
72

MAHARASHTRA

Krishna

74

Arabian Sea

KARNATAKA

Bay of Bengal

Western Ghats

Horsley Hills
75
78

Chennai (Madras)

76

TAMIL NADU

90
91
79
82
81
80 83

Nilgiri Hills

77

Shevaroy Hills

ANDAMAN & NICOBAR ISLANDS
(India)

LAKSHADWEEP
(India)

Palni Hills
86
85 84
87 88
89

KERALA

SRI LANKA

0   100   200   300 miles
0 100 200 300 400 km

Indian Ocean

10

1. Srinagar	31. Mussoorie	61. Benaras	**Notes:**
2. Gulmarg	32. Kedarnath	62. Pachmarhi	
3. Kilinmarg	33. Badrinath	63. Chikalda	1) The Imperial measures have been used in this book because old documents quoted here always used these measure plus the hill resorts were established before the IS system (the International Standard Measures or the Metric system) was introduced to India.
4. Sonamarg	34. Dehra Dun	64. Mount Abu	
5. Pahalgam	35. Hardwar	65. Saputara	
6. Acchabal	36. Lansdowne	66. Khuldabad	
7. Verinag	37. Naini Tal	67. Poona	
8. Yusmarg	38. Ranikhet	68. Khandala	
9. Dalhousie	39. Baijnath	69. Lonavala	
10. Bakioh	40. Kasauni	70. Matheran	
11. Chail	41. Aalmora	71. Purandhar	
12. Dharamsala	42. Bhim Tal	72. Mahabaleshwar	2) The spellings of places in the book are also from the British period i.e. Simla not Shimla or Bombay not Mumbai.
13. Chamba	43. Mukteshwar	73. Panchgani	
14. Kulu	44. Bageshwar	74. Amboli	
15. Kangra	45. Bhowali	75. Madanpalle	
16. Lahore	46. Choubottia	76. Bangalore	
17. Abbotabad	47. Kathgodam	77. Yercaud	
18. Murre	48. Darjeeling	78. Palmaner	3) The East India Company or the Company refers to the British East India Company.
19. Simla	49. Lebong	79. Ootacamund	
20. Mahasu	50. Ghoom	80. Kotagiri	
21. Mashobra	51. Kurseong	81. Coonoor	
22. Narkanda	52. Kalimpong	82. Wellington	
23. Kotgarh	53. Shillong	83. Coimbatore	
24. Sonawar	54. Cherrapunji	84. Kodaikanal	
25. Kapurthala	55. Jowai	85. Munnar	
26. Sabathu	56. Haflong	86. Alwaye	
27. Solon	57. Ranchi	87. Pirmed	
28. Dogshai	58. Hazaribaug	88. Periyar	
29. Kasauli	59. Parasnath	89. Ponmudi	
30. Chakrata	60. Madhupar	90. Coorg	
		91. Mysore	

Great things are done when men and mountains meet.

William Blake

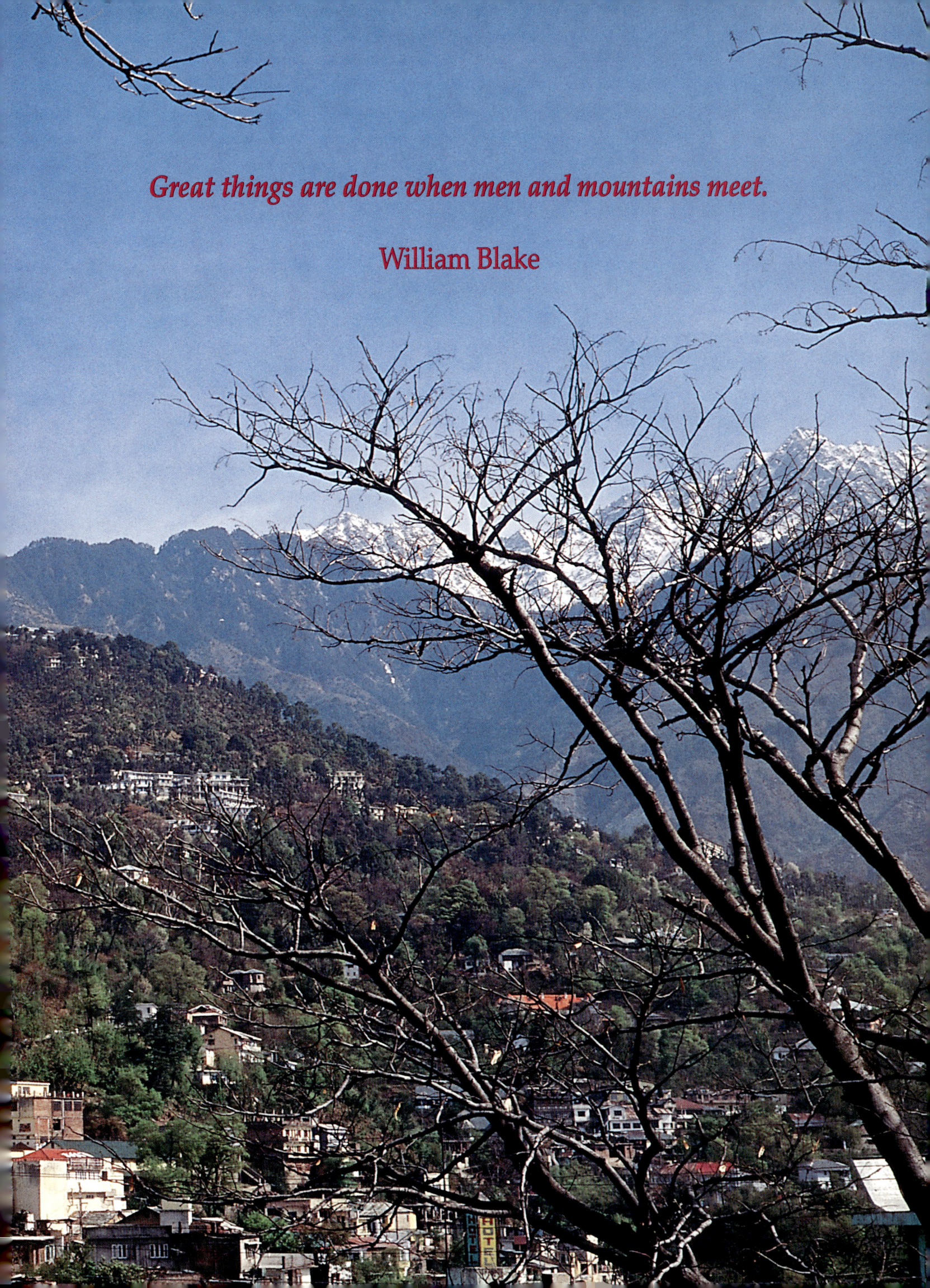

Introduction

A love of mountains is not shared equally in all cultures. To be born in the mountains and to love them is one thing. To be born in the plains and to learn to climb great heights, or to choose to live in the mountains for pleasure, is yet another.

Born and raised in a coastal town in western India, I have no inherent inclination for mountains. But I was taken to mountain resorts as a child and developed a liking for them. I must admit, my fondness for mountains was not immediate; it was acquired – slowly.

I was only five when I visited a hill resort for the first time, but I distinctly remember the winding drive up and down to Nuwara Eliya, Ceylon (Sri Lanka), which made me miserably motion-sick. The year after, we spent the summer in Chail, located just opposite the famous resort of Simla, where my uncle was running a youth camp. My impression of this trip was not much better. Nights were cold, and the bungalow lacked central heating. There was no running hot water. My athletic uncle took his daily bath in cold water. I dared that torture once and pledged never to make that mistake again.

Other activities in Chail, however, made up for the physical discomfort. On clear mornings I admired the snowcapped mountains and played in a beautiful garden in the warm afternoon sun. As a cricket fan, I watched matches played on the world's highest pitch, absorbing the colour contrasts of a velvety green field, cream-colour clad players, light yellow willow bats and the bright red cricket ball. The list of childhood impressions is long.

Subsequent experiences helped me develop a subtle appreciation of life in the hills: trekking in the Himalayas and as a young graduate architect, working in Kodaikanal, in the Palni mountains in South India.

Simla lower bazaar with Christ Church in the background, ca. 1860, soon after the church was consecrated. Victoria and Albert Museum.

Previous pages:
Dharamsala, elevation 5,500 feet, with the majestic snow-clad Himalayas, rising above 16,000 feet, as its backdrop.

It was a recent visit to Simla, however, that got me thinking about this book. Some of my architecture students and I were touring Chandigarh, the model city designed in the 1950s by Le Corbusier, the celebrated Swiss-French architect, when we decided to visit nearby Simla. This hill resort had served as the summer capital of the Indian Empire under British colonial rule.

Compared to Chandigarh, with its wide and empty boulevards, Simla felt crowded, especially the Mall which was teeming with people in the afternoon. In contrast to the important government buildings in Chandigarh, there is nothing heroic or stylistically ground-breaking about the public buildings along the Simla Mall. But where the large public spaces of the capital complex in Chandigarh had left me cold, the scale of Simla – the relation of its streets to the public spaces and buildings – felt comfortable and welcoming. It was ironic that Chandigarh, considered a model of free and democratic India, should feel alienating – forbidding almost – compared to Simla, a product of British colonial rule.

During the Simla visit we also stopped at Christ Church, a modest neo-Gothic edifice that sits conspicuously on the Mall. The church needed repairs. The garden fence around it was broken and most of the plants had withered. Inside, the wooden floors were dry and cracking, the staircase leading up to the choir stall needed fixing, as did the stall, parts of the roof, and the bell tower. The stained glass windows were still intact, and in the well-appointed interior, there were two neatly arranged rows of pews. A layer of dust covered them but they were placed in the right order. Brass plaques designated their former users: row one, His Excellency the Viceroy, and row two, the Commander-in-Chief.

Simla served as the spring and summer capital of British India from 1864 to 1939, and during those 75 years, between March and November, a long line of

Christ Church today still occupies a prominent position on the Simla Mall.

General view of Simla with a distant view of Christ Church, top right.

Beautiful stained glass windows have been preserved, not only in Simla's Christ Church, but in most of the fine churches of the hill resorts, as in St. Stephen's Church, Ootacamund, above.

Passages within and beside Simla Town Hall elegantly link the main bazaar with the Mall on the far side.

Court House, Ootacamund.

officials and other notables of the Raj had come to Christ Church for Sunday prayers. Almost half a century had elapsed since the last Viceroy of India prayed here, yet despite the gradual decay of the Church, nothing seemed to have changed. It was as if the colonial rulers had never left India, but had just gone down to the plains for the winter months and would return for the summer season at any moment.

This aspect of time standing still, of a British presence in wisteria winding over 'Tea-rooms' and in houses called Waverley and Cyclesmere, pervades India's hill resorts. The Simla visit and the incident in Christ Church had captivated and intrigued me. I started looking at such resorts with interest, and I quickly discovered that the most extensive network of settlements built by the British in India, besides the military cantonments, were the hill resorts, a large percentage of which were established and continue to function as cantonments. Beginning with Simla and Mussoorie, in 1819 and 1826 respectively, approximately eighty hill resorts were built in just thirty years, all of them situated at elevations between 1,200 and 8,000 feet (370 and 2,462 metres).[1]

In most hill resorts significant portions of their building stock have endured in the post-Independence era. As in Christ Church in Simla, the ghosts of the past seem close and in some, the lingering charm is exceptional. I was convinced that the resorts of the British

17

Raj are perhaps the most representative legacy of colonial rule in India.

In British India the place of residence of the British administrative or military officers of a given district was called a "station." Likewise, a British officer was not sent or posted, but "stationed" at one place or another. Hence, these resorts are popularly known even today as "hill stations."

In the United Kingdom, heights under 2,000 feet are generally called hills; "mountains" refer to places such as the Lake District, North Wales, and the Scottish Highlands, but there is not a peak higher than Simla, elevation 7,200 feet (2,215 metres). So it is odd that these stations, most with elevations well above 5,000 feet (1,540 metres), are referred to as "hill stations" instead of "mountain stations."[2] In India, ranges of 5,000 and even 10,000 feet (1,540 to 3,080 metres) are commonly called "hills" to contrast them with the Himalaya mountains, many peaks of which rise beyond 20,000 feet (6,160 metres); this is probably why their resorts are referred to as "hill stations."

One reason behind the development and proliferation of hill stations was the intense heat of the Indian plains, which the British loathed. In the plains, the summer temperature often soars above 110 degrees Fahrenheit (43 degrees Celsius) and hovers there for weeks. Flora Annie Steel, author of several influential books, including *The Complete Indian Housekeeper and Cook,* a kind of survival book for British women in India, came to India soon after her marriage. One can imagine the suffering and the shock of this young Victorian bride from the descriptions of her first Indian summer. "It was now May, the heat was terrible, the mosquitoes raised huge blisters all over me, and at Jamalpur on our way by train up country the thermometer stood at 117 degrees at 11 o'clock at night in the railway station. It was here I had my first experience of tea in which had been put milk from goats who fed on castor-oil leaves. It was horrible".[3] It was to escape such insufferable heat, strange habits and foods, and the natives, that beset them in the plains, that the British started to take refuge in the hills. The early 19th century beginnings of the hill resorts were modest. But soon these settlements emerged as the shining emblems of British

Police Station, Mahabaleshwar., ca. 1870. After *Letters from India and Kashmir.*

colonial rule in India atop the ridges of the lower Himalayas, the Nilgiris and other lesser mountain chains. Some stations developed into full-fledged towns, even capitals.

From 1864 onwards, against all administrative logic, the British chose to run the country from two capitals: Calcutta remained the executive seat of the Empire for the fall and winter months, but Simla, in the Himalayas, and almost 1,200 miles (1,700 kilometres) away, was made the spring and summer capital. The governors of various Presidencies noticed the physical benefits of such an arrangement, and soon hill stations like Darjeeling, Mahabaleshwar, and Ootacamund became the summer headquarters of provincial administrations as well.[4]

Health accounted for a major reason in the development of hill resorts. According to Walter Campbell, a young subaltern who kept a careful journal of his experiences, "India was like a land of hopeless banishment – a living grave, a blank in their existence – a land from whence, if they escaped an early death, they were to return with sallow cheeks, peevish tempers, and shattered constitutions."[5] However, the country did offer havens from such ravages. During the cholera epidemic of 1817-19, soldiers living at high elevations remained free of the disease, and the removal of troops from an infested district to an elevated station was followed by a speedy disappearance of the illness from among them.[6] Some early hill stations were therefore established as sanatoria.

To understand the widespread success of hill stations as a place of refuge for the British in India, several other factors must be considered besides climate, health and politics. The social and cultural factors, although less tangible, played a critical role in the success of the hill stations.

Most hill resorts were established during the early Victorian period. Until the beginning of the 18th century, however, Europeans had generally viewed mountains with abhorrence and fear. What cultural changes had taken place in the intervening 100 odd years to transform European thinking about mountains? These changes are to be examined by looking at paintings,

Distant view of Mussoorie, ca. 1870. Much of the dense woods surrounding the station have now disappeared because of intense population pressures. After *Letters from India and Kashmir.*

Distant view of Ootacamund, ca. 1870, from the road to Dodabetta peak. After *Letters from India and Kashmir.*

literature, and other social and cultural aspects of life, for they are fundamental in understanding how Europeans, particularly the British, came to discover and love mountains and made the hill resorts an integral part of their daily life in India.

The life of British soldiers housed in army cantonments, and of *sahibs* living in their bungalows, was different from that of the natives living in traditional Indian cities. As Walter Campbell aptly put it, "(moving to the hills) was like passing through the Valley of Death to Paradise." Consequently, a hill station for the British, "...was not India; it was the little patch of England that each exile discovered it to be. Or, rather, it was an English dream made a shade delirious and out of the true by the thin, high air, combined with all that many a heart loved with passion in India – the outdoor life, the horses, the wild animals, the early walking in the Indian mornings, with their matchless dazzling purity that makes each day seem the first ever created. The lanes, the downs, the tumbling streams were all there, to be tamed and enjoyed as much as possible in the likeness of home."[7] Undoubtedly in the British psyche the hill station was "A Home Away from Home."

General view of Ootacamund, today, from the road to Dodabetta peak.

Lady Wilson had enough opportunities to visit different hill resorts as her husband rose rapidly through the ranks of the Indian Civil Service from the post of a District Collector to that of Secretary to the Government of India. She wrote several books about India, including *Letters from India*, in which she sums up her notions of hill resorts and the feeling of home quite beautifully:

"Blessings on the man who dreamt of Sakesar (a tiny resort in Sind, Pakistan) and made it an

Mount Abu and Nakhi Lake at daybreak.

20

Staff Bungalow, Indian Military Academy, Dehra Dun.

English home. I am delighted with our new quarters. You can't imagine the kind of material pleasure one has in material things that simply look English. The roof of this house enchants me, merely because it slants instead of being flat: the ceilings, because they are very much lower than those at Shahpur and are plastered, so that beams are concealed. The woodwork is actually varnished: the bow-windows are really windows, not doors: the fireplaces are in the right place; and now that our books, pictures, piano and general household goods have arrived, we are cosy as cosy could be, and feel as if we had been established for centuries, instead of five weeks."[8]

In addition to private residences, the social and cultural institutions, such as town halls, court houses, schools, clubs, libraries, churches, band stands, Assembly and Tea-rooms were created in the image of home to make these far-flung outposts successful replicas of picturesque English villages and towns. The daily and seasonal life-cycles of the residents were organised around these institutions which made the hill stations ideal places to raise families. Here wives and children could live safely, and the working husbands could join them for a short while during their summer vacation.

One can also discern the underlying political, urban and architectural order of hill stations from the prominent structures, perched on the highest hills, to the lower town, occupied by the natives.

Simla deserves a detailed analysis. The British made tremendous investment in the actual building of this station, making it "the true imperial city," pre-dating the capital New Delhi. As the place of "the high and the mighty," the story of Simla deals with its political importance and the pomp and the circumstance surrounding it.

Stations such as Kasauli near Simla, Coonoor near Ootacamund, Mount Abu and Dehra Dun started primarily as sanatoria, and for many years kept that basic function. Beautiful bungalows, medical facilities, educational institutions and, occasionally, attached army cantonments, made them ideal health resorts. Compared to the more fashionable hill stations where the powerful and the rich met, these stations are unpretentious yet pleasant due to their substantive character. The significance of these small stations and their institutions continues in post-Independence India.

The coherent physical character of hill stations, which blend beautifully with the surrounding landscape, is rooted in the successful integration of the man-made and natural environments. The conceptual planning and

The Indian Military Academy, Main Building, Dehra Dun. This prestigious Academy was started in 1932 to train officers in India instead of sending them to Woolwich and Sandhurst.

development of hill stations was done with a certain environmental respect. There is a need to explore how the sound physical planning, municipal and administrative organisation of the Raj might serve as a vehicle in efforts to address the environmental crisis faced by people now suffering in the hill regions because of uncontrolled development.

For such a significant facet of British India, hill resorts have received little attention in the wave of new literature on colonial India and its legacies in recent years. Only two books expressly devoted to the topic, Gillian Wright's *Introduction to Hill Stations of India*, primarily a travel guide, and Graeme Westlake's *An Introduction to the Hill Stations of India*, are currently in print. A few other books deal with specific stations. They include: Ruskin Bond and Ganesh Saili's *Mussoorie & Landour, Days of Wine and Roses*, Pamela Kanwar's *Imperial Simla: The Political Culture of the Raj*, Nora Mitchell's *The Indian Hill-Station: Kodaikanal*, and Mollie Panter-Downe's *Ooty Preserved: A Victorian Hill Station in India*. Considerable scholarship in recent years has been focused on colonial planning and architecture activities. Philip Davies' *Splendours of the Raj: British Architecture in India 1660-1947*, Anthony D. King's *Colonial Urban Development: Culture, Social Power and Environment*, or Jan Morris and Simon Winchester's *Stones of Empire, The Buildings of the Raj*, are among more careful studies of British India in this regard. However, none of them devotes more than a chapter to hill resorts. The present book will, I hope, redress the imbalance.

This book considers how a complex web of historical, social, health, cultural, and physical forces acted in concert to create the hill stations of British India. I hope it will also serve as an introduction to the wonderful resorts that these lofty destinations remain today.

Cultural Antecedents

If DOWN here I chance to die,
Solemnly I beg you take
All that is left of "I"
To the Hills for old sake's sake.
...
I could never stand the Plains.
Think of blazing June and May,
Think of those September rains
Yearly till the Judgement Day!
I should never rest in peace,
I should sweat and lie awake.
Rail me then, on my decease,
To the Hills for old sake's sake![1]

From "A Ballad of Burial" by Rudyard Kipling

*I*n the Indian plains, where young Kipling wrote many of his early stories and poems, the mercury starts to climb rapidly from the beginning of March. During the next three months 100 degrees Fahrenheit (38 degrees Celsius) plus temperatures are common. The heat is insufferable, particularly in May, with its dust storms, and in June, when the humidity can reach saturation point without a hint of a breeze in the atmosphere. There is no respite. For the British rulers, living at a time without electricity, it was physically unbearable, leading to filled-up graveyards and empty homes, and a constant longing for the only escape possible. "What *would* we give for a half hour's visit of a Simla zephyr."[2] The only escape from this inferno is to be found on the salubrious slopes of the Himalayas, the Nilgiris, and other mountain chains, where temperatures oscillate between a comfortable 80 degrees Fahrenheit (22 degrees Celsius) during the day and a refreshingly bracing 50 to 60 degrees Fahrenheit (10 to 15 degrees Celsius) at night. Having endured many heartless summers, Kipling always yearned to go to the mountains, if not in this life, at least in the next.

Nowadays with the widespread availability of electric fans and air-conditioners Kipling's verse may sound curious. Still today, the exodus from the Indian plains continues each summer. To fully appreciate his poem, we need to consider the current, but reverse, practice: chasing the sun to flee cold winters, inspite of centrally heated homes, heated automobiles, buses or subway trains. Compare Kipling's desire to escape the tropical heat with our seasonal rush to southern Spain, Florida, or the Caribbean islands.

Kipling's yearning for the mountains, however, would have puzzled 17th and 18th century European thinkers. They did not have to survive tropical summers, as their Victorian descendants did, but they also looked at mountains in a very different light.

Mountain Gloom and Mountain Glory[3]

Indeed, until the 17th century, to European scholars, mountains inspired horror. They were seen as the "chaotic vestige of the disaster, which were pudenda of Nature, ugly, aggressive warts that grew on the surface of the new continents."[4] It was also believed that men would never be able to restore the antediluvian Earth, on whose surface could still be seen the traces of earthly paradise, for the mountains stood out as a constant reminder of heavenly wrath and diluvian destruction. Since mountains were viewed with such fear and repugnance, Europeans hardly ever visited them, or for that matter, climbed them for pleasure – let alone asking to be entombed atop one.

A remarkable change in the perception of the wilderness and mountains took place during the 18th and early 19th century. Fear and abhorrence gave way to love and adoration of nature, particularly among British poets and thinkers, a change which was contemporaneous and parallel with the rise of the hill resorts in India which were established in rapid succession during about 30 years, between the 1820s and 1850s.[5] In all, the British built around 80 resorts throughout the Indian subcontinent. India's landscape varies greatly, so do its

A dust storm on the Punjab plains. After The Illustrated London News.

Previous pages:
The well-preserved Yercaud Club, with a dwindling roster of 17 members, remains a little gem.

hill resorts. The main difference between the northern, or the Himalayan stations, and the ones in the south and centre is of density. There is relatively less space on the lower Himalayan ridges compared to the table lands of Pachmarhi or Mount Abu in the central region or the rolling hilltops of the deep south, i.e. Ootacamund or Kodaikanal. The space limitations are clearly reflected in the way communities are organised and buildings built: The southern stations are spread out like the English rural landscape, as are the central stations. In contrast, the Himalayan stations, especially the central portions of the high elevation ones, are like English villages; the best examples would be Simla, Darjeeling, and Dalhousie. In the Himalayas the buildings generally have two floors; in other stations single storey buildings predominate.

The foundation-stone laying ceremony for the new barracks, Nilgiri hills. After The Illustrated London News.

Widely used in the north, wood is a material which has close affinity with Swiss chalet-style buildings, or Tudor half-timbery structures. In Pachmarhi, and to a lesser degree in Mount Abu, wood is combined with brick and stone. As a result the central station buildings are more a dry climate bungalow type. Buildings in the south use a mix of materials similar to those in the centre. Buildings have greater visual presence in the central region, but as one moves further south, the pastoral English landscape takes over; here buildings and their surroundings blend beautifully.

In all stations, important public buildings are generally built with more permanent materials. Less expensive ones are of brick and covered with stucco. Expensive ones employ dressed stone.

Himalayan glaciers near Sonamarg, Kashmir, photograph by Samuel Bourne. The British Library.

Although the hill resorts were primarily established as escapes, the timing of their establishment and their widespread success in India is further evidence of the changing European attitude towards mountains. This would become evident as we will look at how the early visitors to the hills chose to depict and describe the mountain scenery of India.

The repulsive connotation of mountains was rooted in the belief that the world was in decline. This belief started to change between 1690 and 1730 with the progress of "physico-theology" the spirit of which was edification of nature based on empirical observation. Physico-theologians postulated that the Creator appreciates the devotion of the scholar trying to discern the religious meaning of the working of nature. Quickly, "physico-theology was attuned to the rites of the Church of England... Sanctuaries echoed with the sounds of *Te Deum laudamus* and *Benedicite omnia opera Domini,* which praise the sun and the moon, the mountains and the hills, the dew and the frost."[6] This new stance towards nature, in particular mountains, reached out into other spheres: the fine arts and literature and eventually tourist travel.

Mountain Paintings

John Ruskin, in his mid-19th century work *Modern Painters,* traced this change of attitude in the field of painting. He was surprised to discover the number of landscapes with mountains, and wondered: "There is something strange in the minds of these modern people! Nobody ever cared about blue mountains before,... The Greeks did not."[7] Passing on to medieval art he came to the

This sketch was used by John Ruskin, in *Modern Painters,* to illustrate mountain realism. After John Ruskin, *Modern Painters.*

same conclusion and cleverly noted that landscape had become engrossing to modern 19th century painters, and mountains, ravines, forests, and ruins the subject of reverent contemplation.[8]

Once it became desirable to explore nature with theology's blessing, the rage for mountain scenery took firm possession of the holiday-seeking public in 18th-century England. Visitors started pouring into the Lake District, the Wye Valley, Snowdonia and the Scottish Highlands. More adventurous tourists and explorers went further afield, to Savoy, France or Switzerland. Those who stayed at home, however, could buy prints of mountain scenery which from the middle of the century were produced in increasing numbers.[9]

While Scottish, Welsh and Swiss alpine scenery, captured in lithographs and aquatints, adorned salons of London, and while Wordsworth and other Romantic nature poets captivated the imagination, the lure of an exotic and distant tropical world ferried European explorers and artists to India. Once there, some of these artists sought out the Himalayas, the highest and the most stunning mountains in the world. William Hodges and the uncle-and-nephew team of Thomas and William Daniell charted the monuments of the country and

It was not until the 1814-15 Gurkha War that the British gained control over parts of these mountains. Bringing up supplies – not to mention military equipment – through the lower Himalayas was a herculean task, as shown in this rendering dating back to the 1840s. After The Illustrated London News.

A view between Natan and Taka-ca-munda, by Thomas Daniell; the first ever painting of the Himalayas made by a Britisher. The British Library.

produced large travel books illustrated with their aquatints.[10]

Unlike the previous Mogul rulers who had entered India through the Himalayan passes, the early British artists arrived in India by boat. Hence they first encountered its shores, its peoples, plains, the lush tropical vegetation, the splendour of its sacred places and monuments, and finally, its mountains. They tackled these subjects in almost the same sequence. These artists coming from the temperate region did justice first to the tropical landscape and exotic wonders before dealing with the mountain scenery, however majestic.

In any case, in the 1780s and 90's, when Hodges and the Daniell pair worked in India, the mountainous region of the Himalayas was not controlled by the British East India Company. Similarly, the southern territories, including the Nilgiris, were slowly being wrested from Tipu Sultan, the ruler of Mysore, and not yet explored or settled by the British. Nevertheless, the enterprising team of Thomas and William Daniell ventured into the Himalayas, and they were the first Western artists ever to visit and record them, in particular, the Garhwal region, where the *Vedas,* the most ancient Hindu texts, were supposed to have been composed. "The *Vedas* refer to the land of the Saptasindhu – seven rivers – as the home of the Vedic *people,* the Aryans. These seven rivers are the seven streams of the Ganges which flow through Garhwal."[11]

The account of the Daniell team's journey into the Himalayas is as exciting as their work. After spending the first two years of their stay in Calcutta, armed with a camera obscura – a device which they used extensively in their work to set up compositions quickly – a load of drawing supplies and letters of introduction, the team sailed up the Ganges in August 1788.[12]

After recording parts of northern India, including Agra, Delhi and Haridwar, they entered the Garhwal mountains, accompanied by fifty guards. Near the village of Natan, Thomas made a sketch, described as a *View between Natan and Taka-ca-munda,* included in their portfolio of Oriental Scenery, IV. Thus the Daniells were the first European artists to have gazed on the majesty of the snow-clad mountains.

From Natan they reached Serinagur,[13] where the Rajah and his brother came to meet them outside the town. "Soon after breakfast the next day, messengers from the Rajah brought disturbing news... the Rajah was concerned for their safety, as his troops had just been defeated in a battle, and the victors were pursuing them in the direction of the town, where they were expected in a couple of hours."[14]

Instead of crossing to the safe side of the Alaknanda River (also known as the Vishnu Ganga) Daniells chose to stay on the other shore, and made sketches of the rope bridge, an ingenious but simple contrivance that could be quickly erected and removed.[15] The Rajah asked Daniells and Captain Guthrie, who with his men was chaperoning the artists, to help fight the advancing Gorkhas. The request was declined by the Britishers who chose to withdraw. Even in flight, however, the Daniell team made sketches of mountains and Serinagur from a distance. Although their expedition to the Himalayas had ended more quickly than they had envisioned, the team had not only brought back drawings of places only vaguely heard of, but were later able to assist the map makers in their survey of a little-known district.

Soon after their return to Calcutta, in January 1792, the Daniells announced a "Lottery of pictures painted during the extended tour." Unfortunately, no catalogue of this show can be traced, so it is difficult to know how many views of the Himalayas were included in this exhibition. Nevertheless, out of one hundred and fifty pictures exhibited in the Lottery only a few remained

The Rope Bridge of Serinagur in the Sevalik Mountains. This 240-foot bridge, an ingenious yet simple contrivance that could be erected and rapidly removed, so fascinated Thomas and William Daniell that, despite an advancing hostile army, they chose to stay on the wrong side of the river to make this painting, rather than cross over to the safe side. The British Library.

unsold, a remarkable fact since "the whole European population of Calcutta at this period hardly amounted to 300 souls (excluding the rank and file of the Company's European Regiment, who were hardly likely to be purchasers of expensive prints)."[16] The beauty of the mountainous region captured in Daniells' sketches was instrumental in spurring British interest in the Himalayas; there are altogether nine versions of the Rope Bridge, including a well-known engraving by J.H. Kernot from a drawing made by William Daniell and reproduced in the *Oriental Annual* (1828).[17]

The European painters who followed the Daniells always recorded the mountain landscape of India, especially after the 1815 Gurkha War which gave the British control of the parts of the Himalayas. This fascination with the indigenous and ingenious methods

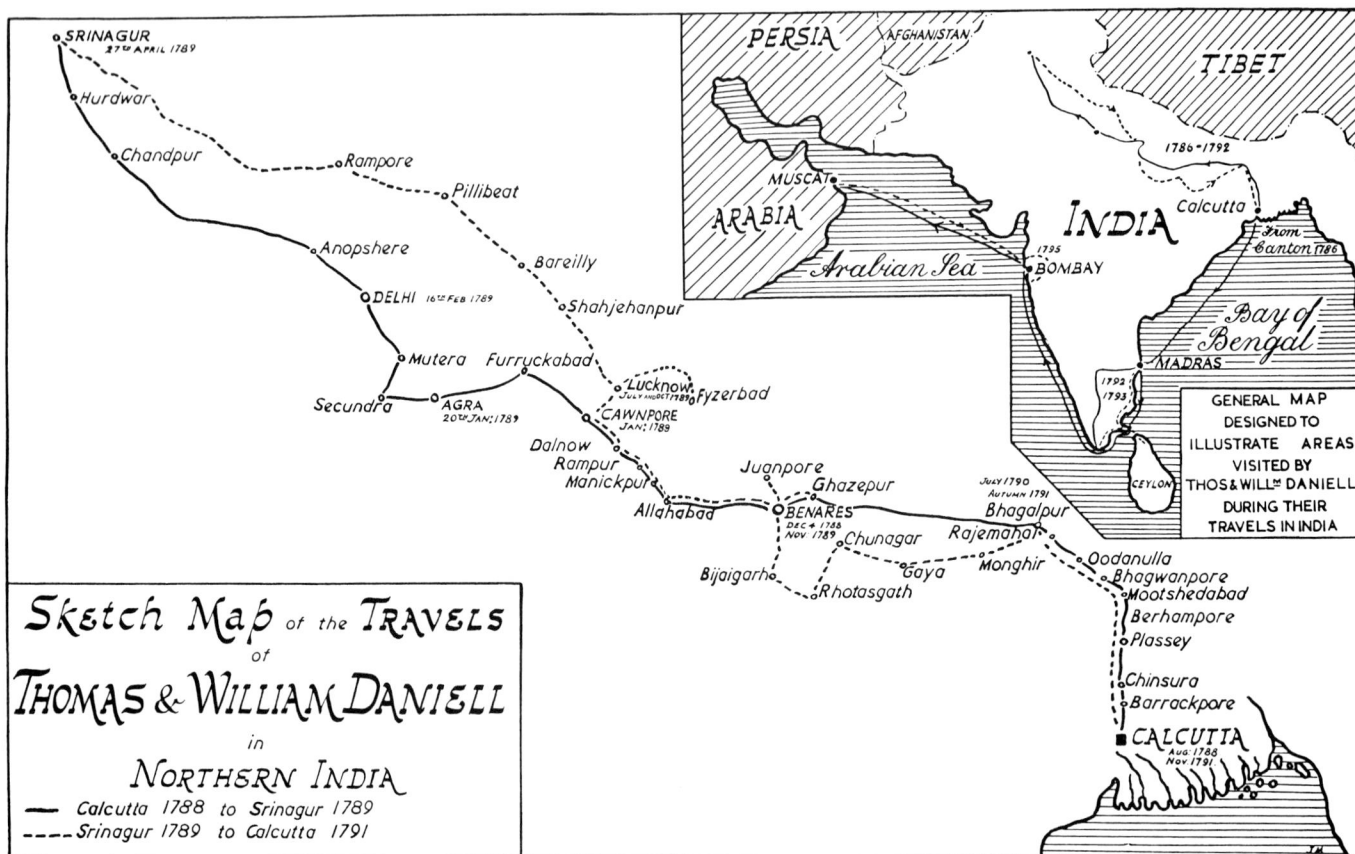

Map of the travels of Thomas and William Daniell in northern India, 1788-91. After Thomas Sutton, *The Daniells.*

To ferry people across rivers, in remote regions of the Himalayas, inflated animal hides were used. A passenger would sit on – cling on to – an inflated hide in a riding fashion. The ferryman, with his body submerged in water but still holding on to the hide, using his two feet as a rudder, would carry the passenger to the shore across. To transport large parties rafts using several inflated hides were employed.

"The Viceregal Progress in the Himalayas." Lord Elgin, on a raft made of inflated buffalo skins, crossing the Beas River beyond Simla on his way to Kulu at Rohtang Pass. After The Illustrated London News.

of river crossing continued to intrigue foreign visitors well into the photographic era. Samuel Bourne, a great name in British Indian photography, took several inspiring photographs of bridges in the Himalayas, and the Sutlej and other river crossings where air-inflated animal hides were employed as rafts. In this century, Spike Milligan gave it due coverage in his hilarious history of transport. This crude method of river crossing could be compared to our contemporary white-water rafting; the technique then was used out of necessity, it is now a source of excitement and adventure.

To all foreigners, the first glimpse of the Himalayas was special; Robert Minturn, an American visiting India just prior to the 1857 Mutiny, describes the view. "After passing the forest, we arrived, about ten o'clock, in a valley from which I had my first view of the Himalayas – a range of mountain monarchs, sitting in state, looking over the broad plains of Hindoostan; covered, as to their heads, with turbans of clouds, as becomes sovereigns of the Orient."[18]

The first book to deal exclusively with the splendour of the mountain scenery of India is George Francis White's *Simla and Mussooree (Mussoorie), Himalayan Mountains,* which first appeared in print in 1836. During his stay of several years in India, White, a Lieutenant in the British Army, produced many sketches including those of the lofty Himalayan peaks. On army duty, White undertook the arduous journey to record the progress of the rivers Ganges and Jamuna through the lower Himalayas to their sources. White also made a series of sketches of the emerging hill resorts of Simla, Mussoorie and Dehra Dun. White did not keep a travel journal, nor intended to have his sketches published. The observational notes which accompany the plates, however, contain a thorough description of the alpine regions of the East, and are a delight to read. Describing his approach to Gungotree, source of the Ganges, White wrote:

> "...the scene became wilder and wilder at every march, the valley narrowing as we advanced, and the rocks on either side rising with great abruptness: the stream which flowed along our path, sometimes boiling over rocks, making a sea of foam, at others diving into darkness, and gurgling beneath impenetrable brushwood. Occasionally, the savage landscape was relieved by spots of a calmer and quieter nature,... with the greensward beneath sloping downwards to the water, embellished with scattered trees, and approached over a carpet of sage and thyme, intermixed with flowers of every hue."[19]

Besides, the Publishers "spared neither pains nor cost in the Engravings,... got up at a vast expense (£2,400),"[20] in producing *Simla and Mussooree (Mussoorie), Himalayan Mountains.*

The pair of suspension bridges, Chamba. The bridge in the foreground dates from the British era.

In the 1840s, soon after White's book appeared in print, folios of George Powell Thomas's *Views of Simla* and Alicia Eliza Scott's *Simla Scenes Drawn From Nature,* were published by Dickinson & Son. Thomas and Scott's sketches captured the scenic beauty of the Himalayas, as well as the high social life of Simla, depicting events such as, the Fête held in honour of Prince Waldemar of Prussia and the Fancy Fare, the annual charity ball held at the Annandale race-course, a location often used for Viceregal staff picnics and other social events.[21]

Important members of British society, such as the wife of Governor General Amherst and Emily and Frances Eden, sisters of Governor General Lord Auckland, also sketched the Himalayas extensively. They helped popularise Simla among the European elite, even if their works are of lesser artistic merit.

A mention should be made of Godfrey Charles Mundy's *Journal of a Tour in India, Pen and Pencil Sketches in India,* which was first published by John Murray in 1838. The book promised, "if not 'Good Entertainment,' at

A series of sketches made by George Francis White of a) entrance to Keeree Pass near Dehra Dun b) Mussoorie from Landour with the Gangetic plains in the distance c) The source of the river Jamuna and d) Gangotri, the source of the river Ganges. After: George Francis White, *Simla and Mussooree, Himalayan Mountains.*

Fancy Fair at Annandale in 1839. The Annandale race-course and picnic grounds were the site of many social events. The British Library.

least 'Expeditious Travelling',"[22] and became a sort of best seller; three editions appeared in less than twenty years. Mundy's book contains only a few average sketches of mountains, but his vivid descriptions of life in Simla, and clear narrations of the Himalayas which evoked images of the European mountain scenery and vegetation at home must have attracted a few tourists to the hills. According to Mundy, their route from Haridwar to Dehra Dun was most beautiful and reminded him of "much of the milder and least wild regions of the Alps."[23] Describing his trip from Landour to Mussoorie, he wrote:

> "I was delighted to recognise many old English friends. The oak and the rhododendron are the largest timber trees; and from the latter, which in Europe and America is a mere shrub, the beams of Llandowr (Landour) houses are formed. At this period they are covered with a luxuriant crimson flower, and their stems, as well as those of the oak, are thickly clothed with long and hoary moss... I also discovered the cherry, pear, barberry, and raspberry, which are unknown in the plains."

Memories of England and childhood are revived:

> "...The glimpse that I caught of its silver bark (birch trees) and graceful pensile branches transported me, in spite of the petty obstacles of time and space to those distant spires and antique towers under whose classic shadow I ought (according to the self-deceiving theory of some of Mater Etona's stepsons) to have passed the happiest days of my life."[24]

Artists explored other mountains. For example, Captain Richard Barron made remarkable sketches of Ootacamund, which were published in a portfolio of aquatints titled *Views in India, Chiefly Among the Neelgherry (Nilgiri) Hills* in 1837, and Major McCurdy's *Panoramas of Ootacamund* dating back to 1842 are quite beautiful.

If ever there was a patch of antediluvian Eden, the British created one in Ootacamund, or "Ooty," as it is popularly known, nestled on the Nilgiri downs at an elevation of 7,000 feet. Another of Barron's early paintings, "Ootacamund from our verandah, 1851," showing the hills, the native village, and important European buildings including Saint Stephen's Church, unfolds like an Indian miniature.

As for other southern hills, Douglas Hamilton made *Sketches of Shevaroy Hills*, published in 1865. Hamilton, who was educated at Harrow and Addiscombe, joined the Madras Native Infantry in 1837, and maintained a journal from the day he "embarked for Madras in 1837 to the day of his death in 1892."[25] The portfolio of Hamilton's sketches, essentially a topographical survey carried out for and published by the Government Military Department, remains the best artistic record of the Shevaroy and Palni mountains. For the author of *Overland, Inland and Upland*, "A.U", the Shevaroy hills were reminders of Wales, but, "on a grander scale;... Any one who knows the finest Welsh passes can fancy the scenery by magnifying what he recollects."[26]

Today one can still visit Ootacamund, Kodaikanal and Yercaud and admire both the present and the past recorded in these pictures. A couple of Barron's aquatints hang in the reading room of the Nilgiri Library in Ootacamund. Several of Hamilton's beautiful lithographs of the Palni Mountains can be seen in the home of the younger brother of the Maharajah of Puducottai in Kodaikanal. Hamilton's sketches of the Shevaroy Mountains and Yercaud grace the main room of the Yercaud Club. The Club itself, with a dwindling count of 17 members,[27] is a little gem of a structure.

Above and opposite page: A panorama of Ootacamund, by McCurdy ca. 1830. The British Library.

It is difficult to trace to what degree the work of contemporaries such as J.M.W. Turner, who worked primarily in England and on the Continent, inspired British artists in their renderings of Indian mountains. Turner's works such as *Snowstorm, Hannibal and his army crossing the Alps,* (1812), or his drawing, *The Alps at Daybreak,* showing the rising sun and bright snow-clad mountains in the distance set-off by the dark foreground, with hunters and wild-life aptly incorporated within, were well known. Turner's *Daybreak* was engraved by Edward Goodall for Samuel Roger's *Poems* (1834).[28] Ruskin's *Modern Painters: I* (1843), written as if defending the work of Turner, whom he passionately admired,[29] had also helped popularise the artist's work. It is not surprising, therefore, that certain works of Captain G.P. Thomas, Captain Walter S. Sherwill, and Douglas Hamilton (Views of the Palni mountains, 1865) remind one of typical picturesque – even Turner's – compositions.

Edward Lear, who worked in India from 1873 to 1875, also painted its mountain scenery, including his famous painting of *Kanchenjunga from Darjeeling* (1877). In Lear's work, however, where a V-shaped composition emphasises the grandeur of the Himalayas, "one can see in the distance snow-capped ranges reminiscent of his view of Mont Blanc in Switzerland, and a foreground similar in treatment to that of his rendering of Mount Tomohrit in Albania."[30] Lear's works have all the roughness, irregularity, and the set arrangement of the elements of landscape found in "picturesque" compositions. Lear is the last major British artist to have painted Indian mountain scenery before the arrival of popular photography.

It is quite remarkable that, beginning with Daniells and ending with Lear, all the British painters who recorded Indian mountain scenery rendered it as if they were working at home. By doing so, they managed to familiarise the unfamiliar for their viewers at home and in the colonies. By the time Lear arrived in India, the mountains had become a familiar part of the colonial existence and the picturesque setting of homes among them, an integral part of it.

Venerating Mountains

As was the case with the visual arts, for the first 17 centuries of the Christian era neither poets nor writers dealt with mountain scenery. However, in the literary works of Byron, Shelley, and Wordsworth – a generation before Ruskin – a marked shift in the treatment of nature, and in particular of mountains, becomes evident. The 19th century celebration of mountains, as Marjorie Hope Nicolson has observed, "was a result of one of the most profound revolutions in thought that has ever occurred."[31]

Benjamin Stillingfleet and William Windham accompanied an English expedition from Geneva to survey the Mer de Glace in 1741, and the journey was described in Windham's *An Account of the Glaciers or Ice Alps in Savoy.* In that mid-18th century account, "only by indirection could Windham communicate his impressions of the wild, astonishing scene: the glacier comparable with nothing in the world, save possibly the 'Seas of Greenland'... the pinnacles that, being naked and craggy Rocks, shoot up immensely high, something resembling old Gothic building ruins."[32] In 1760 Saussure visited Chamonix for the first time and in 1761 offered a reward for the discovery of a route to the summit of Mont Blanc. "The quarter of a century which elapsed between that time and the final accomplishment of his wishes may be regarded as the period of the first great invasion of sightseers (to the Alps)."[33] By the beginning of the 19th century all the great English poets – Scott, Wordsworth, Shelley, and Byron – "loved the mountains and

Kanchenjunga from Darjeeling, painting by E. Lear. After V. Dehejia, *Impossible Picturesqueness.*

expounded their teaching with a power which has met with no rivalry."[34]

William Wordsworth, who called himself "an Islander by birth, a Mountaineer by habit"[35] discussed this change of attitude. It was in the form of a letter written to the editor of the *Morning Post* in 1844. The primary reason for Wordsworth's letter to the *Morning Post,* however, was to prevent the introduction of the Windermere Railway which would have cut through the Lake District. With his letter, Wordsworth had also written a sonnet opposing this move:

"Is there no nook of English Ground *secure*
From Rash assault?...
Plead for thy peace, thou beautiful romance
Of nature; and, if human hearts be dead,
Speak, passing winds; ye torrents, with your strong
And constant voice, protest against the wrong."[36]

Exactly a generation after the appearance in the *Morning Post* of Wordsworth's famous letter accompanying sonnet which were instrumental in preventing the entry of the railroad in the Lake District, Emily Eden expressed similar feelings about the coming of railroads in India. In the introduction to *Up the Country* (1866), a compilation of diaries and letters written to her sister during her stay in India, Eden wrote (as if echoing Wordsworth), "Now that India has fallen under the curse of railroads, and the life and property will soon become

as *insecure* there, as they are here, the splendour of a Governor-General's progress is at an end."[37]

In the first half of the 19th century, the era of the great nature-loving English poets, India was still a rough and remote mercantile entity. Painters had regularly accompanied explorers to record the exotic flora and fauna of far away foreign lands, as William Hodges had done on Captain Cook's voyage to the Pacific Islands, before his visit to India, but not poets. The acclaimed poets were exploring Europe and enjoying the Alps. Wordsworth went on his walking tour of France, the Alps, and Italy in 1790; Byron's first prolonged travel abroad, to Portugal, Spain, Malta, and Greece was between 1809 and 1811; and Tennyson's and Ruskin's first visits to the Continent were in 1832 and 1833 respectively.[38] However, India was too different culturally for the British poets and authors to feel at home. The Continent was as far as they could venture without feeling uprooted from the society to which they truly belonged.

Only a few Europeans, such as G.T. Vigne, author of travel books including *Travels in Kashmir* (1842), were private visitors. He was spellbound by the beauty of Kashmir. Vigne "envisioned a little England being established there, where the climate would permit the introduction of the British way of life, British customs, sports, and manufactures... And this magnificent valley, hitherto the theatre of a hundred faiths, will become the

Alma Mater of our Eastern conquests, and the great and central temple of a religion as pure as the eternal snows around it."[39]

As a result, in the field of literature, the accounts of India are only in the form of journals, travel books, or private correspondence and diaries. "Most of the authors of travel books were officials, soldiers, and their wives, and their reactions were invariably related to their interests, aspirations, and personal comforts."[40] For example, consider Lady Wilson's account of her visit to Sakesar. "I was quite naturally and hurriedly dropped (from her *doolie*) when a snake wriggled over the foot of one of the coolies... The journey uphill was, in short, 'a merry time of desolation'; but here we are at last in our garden of Eden,... We spend most of our day in the garden, which is shaded by willows and apricot trees, laden with fruits, while the air is heavy with scent of roses, verbena, mignonette and sweet peas, displaying a mass of colour to which the glow of oleanders is added, and the dropping heads of poppies and passion-flowers."[41] When it was time to describe the Indian mountain scenery, however, the nature-loving poets from home were invoked regularly.

For example, after scaling the highest peak of the Parasnath Hill, which was also referred to as the Switzerland of Bengal, but never became a full fledged British resort, A.U. wrote, "The top once gained, the prospect was magnificent indeed, bringing to mind the words of Heber:

"O God! O God beyond compare!
If thus Thy glories meaner works are fair,
If thus Thy glories gild the span
Of ruined earth and sinful man,
How glorious must the mansions be
Where Thy redeemed shall dwell with Thee!"[42]

Similarly, the author of *Simla: Past and Present*, Edward J. Buck, who once ended up spending a winter at Simla, went as far as saying, "How Shelley could have enriched his wonderful poem on 'The Cloud' if he had written from the summit of Jakho Hill (the highest peak overlooking Simla)! And yet there is a couplet in it which is sufficiently applicable to one of the vertical landscapes of Simla's cloud land:

"From cape to cape, with bridge-like shape,
Over a torrent sea,
Sunbeam proof, I hang like a roof,
The mountains its columns be."[43]

As Sir Frederick Price in his definitive history of Ootacamund determined, the notes and observations of the officers who surveyed the hills were "thickly sprinkled with quotations from English poets."[44] While representing the green rolling hills of South India, the Wordsworthian rural romantic vision was used, while dealing with the more rugged and awe-inspiring Himalayan landscape the relationship was linked to Shelley's feeling of the sublime.

Catholic Church, Pachmarhi.

Although the early travel literature related to India is extensive, the leading nature-loving British authors never visited India and few wrote about it.[45] Therefore, it is not easy to measure the influence of important works printed in England on the British demeanour in India. One indirect approach on this matter is to look at the libraries in the hill resorts. Of all the social institutions in the hills – including the church, the club, the town hall, the theatre – it was the Reading Room or library of the station that allowed the European population to maintain the most tangible links with home. Current European events and thinking, new ideas and attitudes, the latest fashion, travelled through the printed format and popular literature. Consequently, almost every hill resort in India had its own library.

In fact, the institution that has suffered the most in post-Independence India, particularly in the hill resorts, is not the church, or the town hall, or the club, but the library system. Following the departure of the British, the libraries lost not only their traditional membership and economic support, but also their cultural *raison d'être*. In present-day India, the hill station libraries have continued to decline.

Fortunately, one collection remains almost intact: the Nilgiri Library in Ootacamund.[46] This collection is a reliable index to the interests of its former patrons. The Library includes books by most of the nature-loving English authors of the 19th century. It has a good collection of Ruskin's writings – not all, but it can boast several first editions, including works such as, *The Poetry of Architecture, Stones of Venice, Lectures on Architecture and Painting,* and *The Seven Lamps.* Ruskin, the interpreter and writer, who influenced public taste during the Victorian era and popularised mountains in Britain, held a special place among the well-heeled Britishers living halfway around the globe.

What is most impressive and interesting about the Nilgiri Library, however, is its selection on travel books, which represents the largest part of the collection. It is divided into many sub-sections including most countries of Asia and Europe, and remote regions such as the Pacific and the Antarctic.

Embarkation of troops for India, ca. 1840s. After The Illustrated London News.

For 19th century British subjects, discovering the world meant that it had to be conquered, controlled and cultivated. Hence, large sections of the collection deal with military affairs, military biographies, and language dictionaries. The sections on the natural history of the Nilgiri region, agriculture, horticulture, horses, hunting and fishing reflect the eclectic preoccupations of readers.

One can infer only so much into such a collection; attempting to link it to the avocations of its European users could be misleading. How does one judge the tangible influence of Scott, Wordsworth, or Ruskin's writings on the lifestyle of Ootacamund residents, not knowing how extensively they were actually read? Similarly, looking at such a large collection on travel one may conclude that international travel during the 19th century was easy and comfortable, but the reality was quite the opposite.

Faring the Seas

While books on travel were popular in libraries and romanticised adventures eagerly read, the reality was rather different and the harsh trials of long trans-oceanic voyages lasted well into the late 19th century. In 1837, the year young Queen Victoria was crowned, "it still took three days to travel from London to the very nearest of the overseas territories, Ireland (Holyhead)... at least a month to get to Halifax, six months to Bombay, eight months to Sydney."[47] From the time of the first 17th century British overseas settlement until Victoria ascended the throne, nothing had greatly changed in the way people travelled about the Empire. As a result, a very small number of Europeans, most of them men, lived in the colonies.

In the early 1800s international travel was unsafe, difficult and very expensive. "The captains of East Indiamen sailing between the Thames and Madras or Calcutta probably charged their richer clients what they pleased or what they knew they could pay. It was their perquisite, the owners 'never interfering about passengers'."[48] The clippers which sailed between Europe and the Orient did not have furnished cabins. Not only were the passengers, who had made their fortunes in India, expected to pay a high price for their passage but they also ended up paying for furnishing their cabins. When he was going out to India in 1777, William Hickey was charged an extra hundred guineas just for a seat at the captain's table, and had to share his cabin on the *Seahorse* with three other men. Hickey made his final return trip to England in 1808, after he had made his fortune in India. He spent a considerable sum of money making sure that he was comfortable on this return voyage. He paid a total of 29,300 rupees, about £3,660, of which only 8,000 rupees were for cabin and passage, plus 500 rupees for the sloop to convey him down the river to the ship. However the rest, 20,800, rupees were for clothes, furniture for his cabin, and so on. The passage fee did not include wine, for which Hickey paid an extra 1,235 rupees.[49]

Steam changed all this, radically altering the relationship between Britain and her colonies. "By 1840 the Cunard steamer *Unicorn* was sailing to Halifax in 16 days from Liverpool, by 1843 Miss Eden (in India) was receiving her instalments of *Pickwick* in six weeks from London, by 1850 passengers were travelling from London to Holyhead in a day and a night."[50] Army officers and personnel in the employ of the East India Company who might have gone back to England once or twice in their

Arrival of the overland mail from India and Australia at Alexandria, Egypt, ca. 1840s. After The Illustrated London News.

entire career could take several home leaves. "In India a pressure group called the New Bengal Steamer Fund pressed for better steamship services with a poignant list of advantages: 'The shortening by one half the lengthened and heart-rending distance which separates the Husband, the Wife, the Parent and the Child, thus maintaining in continually renewed vigour the best affection of Heart, in affording the means for a more rapid inter-change of commercial communications by which the interests of both countries cannot but be greatly promoted, and last things though not least in opening wide the door for the introduction of European Science, Morality and Religion into the heart of India'."[51] The introduction of steam travel reduced the cost of passage from England to India to between £120 and £150. "Also fixed rates were instituted in India for those compelled to go home on a 'sick certificate', ranging from £200 for a general to £70 for a subaltern or a writer."[52]

After 1830 the round-the-Cape route was slowly replaced by the overland route. Only a very short portion of the so called "overland route" was really on land; most of the journey still comprised three voyages on different boats. Passengers on this route would depart from a suitable European port in a vessel going to Alexandria, Egypt, and from there, in small boats ferrying passengers on the Nile, to Cairo. From Cairo it was over land, through the desert in camel caravans, later by trains, to Suez, on the Red Sea, where passengers would board another vessel going to Bombay via Aden.

The overland route was definitely more interesting than the Cape route even if it did not improve travel conditions much. According to Isabel Burton, wife of Sir Richard Burton the Orientalist, an avid traveller and adventurer in her own right, who arrived in Bombay as late as 1876 from Jeddah on the *Calypso,* a pilgrim ship which had 800 Muslims on board, dying at the rate of two a day in nightmarish conditions, "They covered,... 'every square inch of the deck... men, women, and babies reeking of coconut oil. It was a voyage of horror. I shall never forget their unwashed bodies, their sickness, their sores, the dead and the dying, their rags and, last but not least, their cooking. Except to cook or fetch water or kneel in prayer, none of them moved out of the small space or position which they assumed at the beginning of the voyage. Those who died did not die of disease as much as of privation, and fatigue, hunger, thirst and opium'."[53]

The overland route shortened the travel time almost by half and speeded up the mail delivery. The significance of this was clear for the popular news media which was starting to grow in England. In 1842 'The Illustrated London News' ran a multi-issue feature article describing "the overland route," and soon after, introduced a regular news column entitled "The Overland Mail" which carried the latest news about China and India from their correspondents based in Asia. "The Overland Mail" was such an indispensable part of colonial existence that more than two generations after the column first appeared in 'The Illustrated London

News', using the same title, Rudyard Kipling wrote a poem about the mail foot-service to the hills:

"The Overland Mail"

"IN THE Name of the Empress of India, make way,
O Lords of the Jungle, wherever you roam,
The woods are astir at the close of the day –
We exiles are waiting for letters from Home.
Let the robber retreat – let the tiger turn tail –
In the Name of the Empress, the Overland Mail!
. . .
From aloe to rose-oak, from rose-oak to fir,
From level to upland, from upland to crest,
From rice-field to rock-ridge, from rock-ridge to spur,
Fly the soft-sandalled feet, strains the brawny, brown chest.
From rail to ravine – to the peak from the vale –
Up, up through the night goes the Overland Mail."[54]

The mail service was indeed like the arterial network of the Empire; keeping alive hopes and interests of the British subjects stationed in remote hills of India. "Grass widows in the hills are always writing to their husbands, when you drop in on them, and your presence is not actually delighted in."[55] Writing and receiving letters allowed the expression of feelings and emotions,

Royal Mail boxes wearing fancy caps and crowns can be found in several hill resorts.

40

Dakwalas (postmen) of Bengal, ca. 1850s. The mail in India was carried by people who ran from station to station. Each postman would pick up a packet of mail at one station and deliver it to the next, a distance of about ten miles, where another postman would take that packet to the following station, and so on. The timing of the mail moving in the opposite direction was staggered to allow mailmen to rest for about two hours before running back with the return mail, and to reach their home base before the sunset. After The Illustrated London News.

the sharing of news and accounts of cultural events, for the mail service meant contact with the family, loved ones – home. The perils of the weather often played havoc with the mail service. People would wonder if and when their letters reached their distant destination. As Emily Eden noted in her journal, "I sent off another lump of journal last Saturday, but somehow I feel none of those letters are sure of reaching you. They will be drowned going overland, after the contrarious way of the world. We might have had your April packet by this time, but the Bombay *dak* has not been heard of at all for five days, and it is supposed the rivers have overflowed and that all your dear little letters are swimming for their lives."[56]

Those who travelled to India during the first half of the 19th century did so out of necessity, aware that they might never return to their homeland again. Nevertheless, the arrival of steam travel brought, in ever increasing numbers, wives and children to the colonies. The union of the field officers and their families rapidly transformed the entire structure of daily colonial life in India, for two distinct cultures met in a way that they had never done before.

Domesticating the Mountains

The arrival of women and families had a domesticating effect on the European establishments in colonies. The best example of what a woman could do to transform the domestic space, even in remote hills – especially in the hills – is the decorating of Auckland House, the official residence of the Governor-General Lord Auckland in Simla, which his sister Emily Eden undertook:

"It has been immense labour to finish properly. We did not bring half chintz enough from Calcutta, and Simla grows rhododendrons, and pines, and violets, but nothing else – no damask, no glazed cotton for lining, nothing. There is a sort of country cloth made here – wretched stuff, in fact, though the colours are beautiful – but I ingeniously devised tearing up whole pieces of red and white into narrow strips, and sewing them together, and the effect for the dining-room is lovely,... and now everybody is adopting the fashion."[57] She also cut patterns in paper and managed to get a native painter to paint "borders

CANTONMENT
OF
SOLON.
1880-81.

Scale 24 Inches = 1 Mile.

NOTE

The Heights above Sea Level are based on that of
Kasauli H.S. of the "N.W.Himalaya Series,"
Trigonometrical Branch,
Survey of India, taken at 6322 feet.
The Triangulation is also based on the same series.
Trigonometrical Heights of Stations of Observations
are shown thus..................................4136
Trigonometrical Heights of Intersected points...........3740
Heights of Bench Marks and Road Levels
(reduced in terms of Trigonometrical data)
are shown thus...................................3800
Heights of Buildings refer to doors of verandahs
or plinths of walls.
The Cantonment Pillar Numbers given on this Map
are those which were found inscribed on the Pillars.
The measured or instrumental contour lines
(50 feet Levels) are shown in strong dotted lines, thus.

Note.   This extension so as to show the Reserved Spring should be
applied in its proper position on the south east of this sheet.

REFERENCES

Cart Roads are shown thus.
Made Roads (not Cart Roads) thus.
Foot-paths.
Springs.

Scale of 50   100 200 300 400 500 600 700 800 900 Feet

24 Inches = 1 Mile.

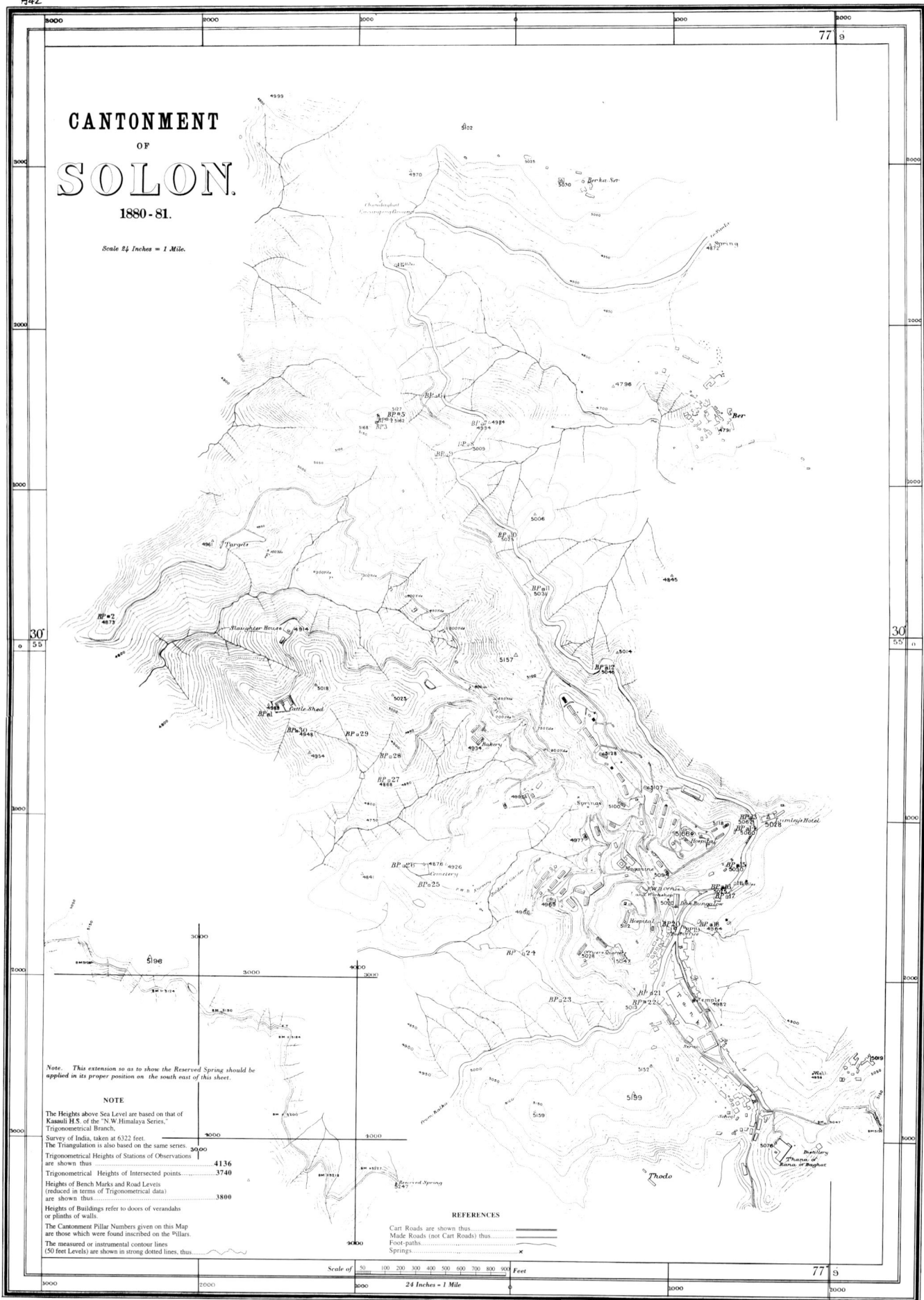

Plan of Solan, near Simla. Notice how the native and the European parts of the town were separated and how their settlement patterns were very distinct from one another! The British Library.

all round the doors and windows,... for the want of cornices."[58]

For those of less exalted stature there were other priorities, "We carry with us our own groceries, which come from England, or rather, as far as we are concerned from the Army and Navy Stores in Bombay – packed in 'tins'. We have also our filter and our supply of soda-water and wine with us. We kill our own sheep and chicken, have our own cows, and make our own bread and butter. We get our vegetables, cabbages, cauliflowers, turnips and peas, from the public garden... and that is where the sweet-peas and roses come from also."[59]

The arrival of women altered the relationship between the European and the native populations. Until the arrival, in increased numbers, of women, relations between the colonial rulers and the native population were rather relaxed. Women who braved the journey to India, leaving behind the familiarity of their home to be with their men had little interest, and few opportunities, to mingle with the native population. If anything, they looked on the natives, especially the local women whom many European men had married, with a certain disregard, if not disdain. Women who came to India "were important not merely as wives for officials, and so opposed to *bibis* as rivals, but also as the nuclei of inward-looking European social groups in every city and town, as well as in smaller 'stations'."[60] Gradually, as the 19th century progressed and the number of European women in India increased, a strict social hierarchy and behavioural code of conduct emerged.

The relationship had started to change from the 1830s onwards with the annexation of considerable territories, the subsequent growth of European regiments and the establishment of British cantonments. The cantonments, in a way analogous to the garden suburbs of London, with spacious new streets lined with trees and orderly compounds of officers' bungalows, staff barracks, clubs and other facilities enforced a sense of social separation between the European and native communities. At this moment, a radical alteration in the spatial as well as the colonial social structure of urban India took place.

In the public realm, European military officers and government servants had to associate with the Indian masses to collect the revenues. On the other hand, European women lived and operated in their own private world. Thus, hill stations became an ideal ground for the expression of their private concerns.

Anthony King, Philip Davies, James Morris and others have suggested that the cultural differences and the power-play between the rulers and the ruled gave a unique imprint to the British settlements in India, in both the cantonments and the hill resorts.[61] Particularly in the building of the hill resorts, on the lower Himalayan and upper Nilgiri crests, the Britishness of Empire found its most intense expression. "At Simla, Darjeeling or Mussoorie the gentlefolk of the Raj, celestially withdrawn from the Indian millions on the plains below, lived for a few months in a year entirely for themselves... and the emotions of the British, all too often inhibited in the stifling heat of the lowlands, vividly flowered in the mountain brilliance above."[62] For the women it was the Indian climate which was most destructive; only the hills offered a respite. Throughout Raj literature this is the one common complaint. To survive India meant readjusting even one's bio-rhythms: "In hot weather – and nine months of the twelve are hot – the Anglo-Bangalee is roused by the punctual warning of his bearer, "Sahib! Sahib! It has struck four; ...and by half-past four taking his constitutional canter round the dew freshened race course... At six..., the arch-enemy of European constitutions, the sun, begins to dart."[63]

After sunrise in the plains, by early March "A.U", wrote how even "in the lightest attire and in lofty shaded rooms one might sit at ten in the morning with beads of moisture standing on every pore... the air strikes in like the hot breath from an oven, and clothes fresh out of the wardrobe feel as if they had been taken from before a fire. Kid boots crack, leather covers of books curl... wooden boxes go off with a loud report... for scarcely any glue will stand this climate... A new nuisance sets in, in the form of prickly heat... causing a maddening irritation. I have seen English children, who arrived a few months before, models of health and beauty, transfigured by these unpleasant complaints till they were equally uninviting to sight and touch" A.U's complaining tone changes once she reaches the hills. One can sense the relief at the small "home-like" delights:

"It was a delightful home-like change after the restraint imposed by the deadly heat of Calcutta, to stroll out after breakfast and dinner into the little poultry yard, and feed the chickens and ducklings, while the beautiful petted pigeons... fed eagerly from our outstretched hands. Even the English pigs were honoured with occasional visits; as indeed they might well be, for surely never did members of the porcine race make a more distinguished entry... On their arrival... they had to be carried up the *ghaut* in large boxes, and appeared at their new residence in state, attended by twelve bearers!"[64]

So once in the hills, the daily routine changed to an English life-pattern. Instead of waking up early as they used to in the plains to avoid the noon sun, in the hills they could wake up late. Day started at mid-morning and lasted till late evening. Free of work duties, the daylight hours were filled with outdoor activities,

Following pages:
Saint Joseph's College quadrangle, Darjeeling.

Lawrence Asylum, Sanawar. The complex, with an arcaded passage connecting all the key buildings, functions like a small English village.

Lawrence Asylum, Lovedale near Ootacamund, still serves as a private school. The imposing Italianate building which sits atop a hill has also served as a set for several Indian films.

Lawrence Asylum, Murree, ca. 1860. After The Illustrated London News.

such as teas, croquet games, horse races, and picnics, whereas parties and balls enlivened evenings. Important stations had their own theatres and musical groups. Even the smallest stations developed their social groups, clubs and watering places.

The hill resorts themselves developed their own pecking order. The important hill resorts were used for political reasons; next in line were military places. Simla and other Presidency summer seats such as Mahabaleshwar, Naini Tal, and Ootacamund remained integral to the administrative framework of the Empire, because the rulers could not only take refuge from the heat of the lowlands but also conduct the affairs of government from there. Resorts such as Darjeeling and Mount Abu at opposite ends of India, were used as administrative seats as well as sanatoria for the European population and the military. Besides these main resorts, the British also built, and patronised, a whole string of smaller hill resorts.[65] The widespread success of such second string hill resorts as Kalimpong, Matheran and Sanawar as places of refuge is based on several factors.

In addition to political, military, health and climatic considerations, the transfer of prevailing social and cultural conventions, particularly the deportment of the British living at home in England, was important in the success of the hill resorts. Some of these factors are obviously less tangible, but they nevertheless played a critical role.

In England at the beginning of the 19th century, holiday resorts were becoming popular. Getting away from the crowded city and out into the country was a fashionable part of urban development. In India it was a necessity. To rejuvenate their spirit and bodies, the British working in the plains had to get away from the Indian masses, and into the tranquillity of the hills. There small picturesque cottages were built, set in an arcadian landscape and based on the romantic nostalgia for rural life. Some of these ideals, the notion of "Arcadia," "wholesome and rustic living," "love of the outdoors" and "return to nature," played a subtle and suggestive role in making hill stations significant in the daily life of the European populations residing in the Indian subcontinent.

Government officials took their yearly vacations in the hills during the hot months. These holidays generally lasted two weeks to a month in duration. Women and families, however, could spend longer periods in the hills, often the entire season, from March to August. The growing presence of European children in the subcontinent meant that new schools had to be established to educate them.

In the 1840s and 50's there was a great increase in public schools in England. Marlborough, Cheltenham, Radley, Lancing, and Rossall were founded in the 40's, Wellington and Bradfield in the 50's.[66] Following the example from "home", many new schools were established throughout India. In 1846, after the terrible

Savoy Hotel, Mussoorie, from its Narang Wing.

battle of the Sutlej, Colonel Henry Lawrence decided to start a school for soldiers' children rendered orphans in the recent warfare. With his own founding contribution of 10,000 rupees and other public subscriptions, a school was established at Sanawar. The objective of the

Lawrence Asylum, as the school was originally called, was to provide for the orphan and other children of soldiers, "First for children of pure European parentage, (and this demand being satisfied); secondly, for children of European fathers by native or Eurasian mothers – an

useful, and, above all, religious education, adapted to their future prospects in life, and calculated by the Divine blessing to make them good Christians and intelligent and useful members of society."[67]

The hills made a perfect setting for schools. In addition, the Western-style education meant that the colonial values would be transmitted to the children who in turn could rule and maintain the Empire. No doubt, the presence of families reinforced the schooling system and made life in the hill stations more normal than in the plains.

In all, four Lawrence schools were established in the Indian subcontinent: at Sanawar near Simla, Murree near Lahore (now in Pakistan), Mount Abu in Rajputana in western India, and Lovedale near Ootacamund. The Lawrence School at Mount Abu closed down soon after India's Independence and its premises are currently used as a Police Academy, but the other three are still in operation as private schools.

Other enterprising individuals, missionaries and religious groups chose different hill stations to start their own schools. The "Home" was established in Kalimpong, the "Woodstock School" in Mussoorie, the "Bishop Cotton School" in Simla, "Saint Paul's School" in Darjeeling, to name just a few.[68] The seasonal and daily cycles of the residents were organised around these institutions. Indian families eventually joined this practice.

In the 20th century, when the native populations were allowed to move relatively freely into previously restricted areas, wealthy Indian families took up residence in hill resorts, especially to educate their children. For instance, an entire section of the Savoy Hotel in Mussoorie is called "the Narang Wing," named after the family who rented it for several years while their children were being educated in a mission-run school.

A complex web of historical, social and cultural factors thus explains the importance and popularity of hill stations among colonial subjects. As Walter Campbell wrote in his diary, moving from the plains to the hill resorts, with their mild climate and women and children around, "was like passing through the Valley of Death to Paradise"[69] both physically and spiritually.

asylum, where they may be rescued from the debilitating effects of the climate of the plains, and from the demoralising influence of barrack life; and where, in connection with the advantages of a bracing climate and healthy moral atmosphere, they may receive a plain but

A
Home
Away from
Home

With every shift of every wind
The homesick memories come,
From every quarter of mankind
Where I have made me a home.[1]

From "The Fires" by Rudyard Kipling

*O*f all European peoples, the British may be considered the most restless, and this was particularly true in the 19th century. The greatest flow of European emigrants, during that century, was from Great Britain, with Italy second and Spain a distant third. Between 1840 and 1872, about six and a half million people left the British Isles and in the following decades an average of 200,000 migrated each year, making strange and distant locations their homes.[2] At the peak of colonisation, one could find British ships in the most remote parts of the globe, and could bank on the services of private English clubs, evangelical churches, and YMCAs.[3] In the last century, for the Britons who roamed the globe, theirs was truly the Empire on which the sun never set.

Most British emigrants flowed to the New World and the new colonies of the British Empire. The Irish chose the United States, while the rest went to Australia, Canada, New Zealand and the temperate regions of southern and eastern Africa. There was ample land in these new colonies, and mild climates, so most of the migrants were content to make these places their final destinations. Long coveted as the jewel of the British imperial crown for its commercial riches, India never inspired significant British immigration. It was too crowded and hot to sustain any large European population. India was so densely populated that, as far

back as early 1800, Lord Amherst had said: "The Emperor of China and I govern half the human race and yet we find time to breakfast."[4]

The British focused on trade with India for their own commercial development. India was a reliable source of spices and silk, an ideal place to obtain the opium sold to the Chinese, a suitable place to grow coffee and tea for the East India Company's global monopoly. Although over crowded its large native population was a source of cheap labour within India and in other colonies where they were taken as indentured workers.[5] Thus, it was imperative to maintain a firm control over this most precious possession. And to do so, the Company maintained a well organised administrative and military structure in India.

From the beginning of the 19th century, the East India Company emerged as the predominant power in India. Lord Wellesley, then the Governor-General, considered servants of the Company in India to be no mere commercial agents, but full-fledged governors. To assume that mandate and run the affairs of the Company efficiently, however, Wellesley believed that his agents required a superior education. Accordingly, in 1800 he established the College at Fort William in Calcutta, a precursor to the East India Company's Training College at Haileybury.[6]

The Ootacamund Club was built in 1831-32 as a private residence by Sir. William Rumbold. In 1834, it was rented by Lord William Bentinck then Governor-General, as a temporary residence for Thomas Babington Macaulay. The building was later converted into a hotel after which it reached its present status as the Ootacamund Club.

Previous pages: Christ Church, Pachmarhi.

United Services Club, Simla. The rambling club complex has been taken over by the Government, the main building used as the local Planning Authority office and outbuildings, such as this one, for government staff residences.

The transformation of Company officers from managers of a mercantile entity to rulers of India was a gradual process. For Lord Wellesley, who personified the new attitude among the ruling British elite, this change was quite natural. With the help of his brother Arthur, a brilliant military advisor, Wellesley was responsible for a major military and territorial expansion of the Company's possessions. In the far south, Tipu Sultan was defeated, and in the Deccan, the Marathas, the last major power big enough to hamper the British hegemony in India, were brought under the Company's control.[7] From this point on, the East India Company's authority in the subcontinent was absolute.

Lord Wellesley's outlook is best seen in the new Government House which he had constructed at Calcutta as the supreme seat of British power in India. The Company's Board of Directors in London bickered about cost overruns, but Wellesley was unperturbed by this reproach, "India is a country of splendour, of extravagance and outward appearance; the Head of a mighty empire ought to conform himself to prejudices of the country he rules over... In short, I wish India to be ruled from a palace, not from a country house, with ideas of a Prince, not with those of a retail-dealer in muslins and indigo."[8] The new Government House was completed in 1803 at a cost of £63,291.[9] The Directors may have regarded this sum as excessive, but it was

Tea plantation Palampur, Kangra Valley. Kangra Valley plantations are the oldest in India. It was here that the British carried out their initial experiment in tea growing, before moving to Assam, Darjeeling and the Nilgiris.

Government House or Palace of the Governor-General, Calcutta, ca. 1840. Until it was upstaged by the Viceroy's House, New Delhi, inaugurated in 1931, this building was the finest governor's palace in the world. After The Illustrated London News.

remarkably little for a symbol of the growth of British power in India. Until upstaged by the Viceroy's House, a monumental palace conceived by Sir Edwin Lutyens as the centrepiece of the new capital of New Delhi and inaugurated in 1931, the new Government House in Calcutta was the finest governor's palace in the world.[10]

Even with such grand designs for the Empire, the total number of Europeans living in India was never very large. In 1837, when the native population of India was around 150,000,000 there were only about 41,000 Europeans living in that country, "37,000 of these were soldiers... The civil service accounted for 1,000, of the remaining Europeans, and, of those not in service, there were about 2,000 in Bengal and 500 each in the Bombay and Madras"[11] provinces, or Presidencies as they were known. Thus, men who looked after the Company's Indian empire were few and more than 90 percent were military personnel. Combined with the native troops, who were under direct European command, the East India Company had 200,000 armed men in India;[12] a mighty military machine by any standard.

In the Service of the Company and the Crown

As early as 1793, a regular system for the distribution of appointments to the East India Company's service had been established among the members of the Court (Board) of Directors.[13] To seek out the best nominees, during the first half of the 19th century, the Company ran two institutions in England: the Haileybury College for civil administration, and the Addiscombe Military Training College. A candidate seeking a place in either of these colleges had to pass a stiff entrance examination. A competent recruit could follow the "civilian" route, but the less talented was directed to the "military service." After successful

completion of a rigorous course of studies, based on their performance in the final college examination, graduates were sent out to their respective postings.

The Haileybury graduates were sent to various civilian locations; Addiscombers, in a descending order of merit, entered the engineers, the artillery, or the infantry.[14] Until the establishment of the Public Works Department in 1854, the army remained in charge of all civil construction, including the state buildings, civil and military, also all engineering and communication works such as roads, irrigation canals, and eventually railways.[15] Among the military cadres of the combined administration, the Engineers were therefore regarded more highly than others. Entry into the Company's cavalry required no training or examination at all. Directors of the Company had the right of nomination, and a *protegé* too dull for the civil service might easily find himself with a cavalry commission instead.[16] The number of aspiring candidates far exceeded the demand since the rewards of service in India were handsome.

According to Mervyn Davies, officers of the East India Company, namely Clive, Barwell, Francis, Hastings and Macaulay, took home nearly £2 million between them; Macaulay, in his short Indian service must have saved money at the rate of nearly £8,000 a year.[17] The entire staff in the Company's service, especially the enterprising types, also had opportunities to squirrel away significant savings. "Bob Pott, when Resident to the Nawab of Bengal, had the whole of the Nawab's stipend (pass) through his hands 'in which channel a considerable portion of it always stuck to his fingers,'... Even chaplains sometimes took on the sordid office of undertaker to the European community because there was money in it with such an assured death rate. The Reverend Mr. Blanchard of Calcutta who 'accumulated a large fortune' alluded to

Today, the Anglican Cemetery behind Saint Stephen's Church, Ootacamund, is surrounded by giant eucalyptus trees which were brought from Australia in 1849-50.

the cold weather in Calcutta as 'our profitable season... the period of our harvest'."[18]

Among Company employees civilians had the best terms of employment. An average civil recruit would start as an assistant to the Commissioners of Revenue or Circuit, or both, if stationed in a remote area. He could hope to become a district Collector or even a Commissioner after eighteen or twenty years of service. A close look at the terms of employment of a superior civil officer, such as a district Collector, shows that he would have earned 3,000 Rupees per month, about £375 per month or £4,500 per annum.[19] As a senior civil officer, he would have managed the public administration of an entire district, and wielded enormous administrative powers. Notwithstanding the position of prominence and power, he would have had to live for ten years in India before home leave was granted.[20]

The primary reason for such long terms of duty in the field was that it took sailing ships from four to six months to reach Bombay from Britain, via the Cape of Good Hope. It took longer still to reach Madras or Calcutta, the ultimate destinations for most travellers, because of their commercial and administrative importance in those days. In any event, a minimum ten-year term of duty in the field meant that the European staff going to India had to leave behind the physical and psychological comforts of home. Anyone who went to India to serve the Company or the Crown was bound to exile.

A 20-year-old officer would leave for India, return home ten years after, with a weakened constitution

The Anglican Cemetery behind Saint Stephen's Church, Ootacamund, ca. 1860, before the widespread introduction of eucalyptus trees. The British Library.

and receding hairline, looking prematurely old. One might well wonder why, at this stage, an officer returning to Britain after ten years of de facto banishment would choose to go back to India? The answer may be found in the nature of service in India.

European officers, whose colonial existence revolved around service, associated mainly with colleagues, many of whom they knew from their college days in England. As a result, the "British officials in India formed a most unusual kind of society with a fossil culture cut off from contact with home,"[21] not very different from those observed among close-knit immigrant groups in America or Europe. So after spending ten or 12 formative years in India, only a few of the returning officers, mostly the landed, the rich and the well-connected, felt at ease, and chose to remain in Britain. For the others, India prevailed: India would remain their sentence and also their salvation.

After a quick marriage, the officer would return to India with his bride. The new family lived abroad until retirement managing one or at the most two home visits during their entire Indian service. Many officers with limited means did not bother going back home, but opted for mail-order brides instead. Usually children grew up without any real contact with their parents' homeland – England. This situation gave rise to another particular practice. Every winter groups of young women, popularly known as the "Fishing Fleet," would come to India; the practice remained prevalent well into this century. "The Fishing Fleet was by long-established custom made up of the 'highly eligible' beautiful daughters of wealthy people living in India. This was the only way in which they could meet eligible young men and marry.' Those who failed returned to England in the spring and were known as the Returned Empties."[22]

Without any immediate family ties with Britain, most young men of the subsequent generations chose service in India. "Few who went into one or the other of the Indian services could fail to claim an 'Anglo-Indian' ancestor. It was a fact of Empire: 'One's brothers, one's friends' brothers and so on were all either in the civil service in some part of India, or in the forces or the police or in something else. The men of the family served the Empire as a matter of course'."[23]

Semblance of a Home

For 19th century Europeans, life in India was a leap into a land of unknown malady and a race against death. For the lucky ones who survived the trials of the tropical climate and its endemic diseases, India posed the additional challenge of an alien oriental culture. India was – and remains – a place of extremes, beauty and decay, wealth and poverty and an enduring civilisation. For the beef-eating Britons it was a country like no other they had seen before.

Different races, polytheism, strange religious practices, such as idol worship and *suttee,* curious dietary habits, and vegetarianism confronted the British cultural prejudice with still greater challenges. Many Indian men and most women wrapped themselves in six-yard long pieces of cloth and still looked half naked. They squatted on floors and had little or no use for Western-style furniture, and a large percentage of the population went barefoot. Such differences in the respective Indian and British notions of "civilised" norms of comfort and dress were to be highly consequential in the complex semiotics of colonial rule. For example, prejudices concerning the wearing or not wearing of footwear caused a major controversy for official etiquette. In metonymical logic, "the wearing of shoes by Indians in the presence of the British was seen as an effort to establish relationships of equality between the ruled and their rulers. Hence, Indians were always forced to remove their shoes or sandals when entering what the British defined as their space... On the other hand, the British always insisted on wearing shoes when entering Indian spaces, including mosques and temples."[24] Indians consider these places and their homes sacred and remove their shoes before entering them.

One possible way for the young enlisted man to survive in this alien environment was by "going native" as many Europeans had done previously. But this option was ruled out, steadily, with the gradual and complete conquest of India. By the 1830s, when the hill resorts were emerging throughout the Indian subcontinent, "self-confident and assertive, their views shaped by the powerful currents of evangelicalism and utilitarianism, the British had regarded all "Eastern" societies as hopelessly inferior to their own."[25] James Mill, a powerful functionary in the East India Company's London headquarters and a committed utilitarian, published his *History of British India* in 1818. This opinionated work, considered mandatory reading for all officers going to India, continued to be the most widely-read and influential work on India's history until the 1857 mutiny. According to Mill, "India had remained always a civilisation bound down at once to despotism" and, in Hinduism, to "the most enormous and tormenting superstition that ever harassed and degraded any portion of mankind." This "hideous state of society" had to be entirely rooted out and replaced by a new system of laws and government that would properly secure the happiness of India's people... this reformation was Britain's mission in that blighted land."[26] Going native in such an intellectual, social and political climate was out of the question. On the contrary, this nation had to learn and evolve according to the European "laws." Prinsep, an artist commissioned to paint for the Indian Government emphasised in his *Imperial India,* that it was the differences that enabled the English to "have acquired this vast Empire. The secret lies in the contrast we present in our characters... we owe our success to the squareness and solidity of our character, in every way the reverse of the fickle and treacherous nature of the native. Our thoroughness inspires his respect. He believes in our honesty – he has every reason to trust our courage. We give him peace such as he never enjoyed before. There is no power that can take our place in the country."[27]

Norms of comfort and dress were complex in the semiotics of colonial rule. Notice that all pullers of the Viceroy's rickshaw are barefoot except for their bearded supervisor on the extreme left. The British Library.

Hence, along with their moral burden and their missionary zeal, by choice or necessity, Englishmen brought their European lifestyle to the colony, and to preserve it they would distance themselves by going to the hills. Although travelling to India was not easy, a system had evolved over the years, allowing the Company men to transport part of their "home" to the far away colony.

As mentioned in the previous chapter, passengers going to India on the tall ships generally purchased an empty cabin on the vessel which was outfitted with a wide range of furnishings and furniture. If the passenger was sensible, "he bought the cabin furniture which was so designed that it could be converted for use when he arrived in India. But whatever the traveller's taste and financial resources, the absolute necessities included a sofa with mattress, pillow, and a chintz covering for the day-time; a wash-hand stand; a hanging lamp; a looking glass with a sliding cover; a chest of drawers in two pieces, the upper part having a ledge around the top for the purpose of holding a small collection of books, or for preventing articles from falling off; a foulcloth bag and an oil cloth or carpet... merely for the sake of appearance."[28] For senior officers, it habitually included other pieces of bedroom and dining room sets, boxes loaded with household items, and of course, complete sets of china and silver.

In Victorian England, the display of extravagance, "was at its heaviest on the dinner-table,

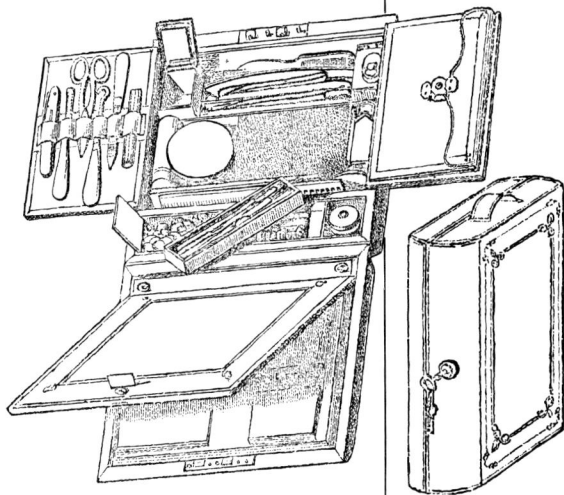

Bellamy Savoy's "Tourist Companion," Officers going to India were advised to carry items like these. Similar items are included in a partial list from the Henry King & Co. catalogue. After The Illustrated London News.

57

because the dinner was the great occasion for the display of wealth and dignity. The plate matched the fare and both had to be on the baronial scale."[29] In colonies, this opulent display was an essential part of decorum, especially among low-ranking officers wanting to create an impression of higher social status.

This bourgeois concern about creating the right public impression is also evident in the personal items that a young officer took to India "thirty-four different items, ranging from 'ten dozen shirts; a blue camlet jacket; two pairs of merino, camlet or gombroon trousers;' to a 'dressing-case and Russian writing-case, suitably filled'."[30]

Steam travel and the opening of the over-land route which became increasingly popular after 1837 raised the frequency of travellers going to India. Though still harsh, regular and reliable modes of travel eased the entry of women to the Indian subcontinent. They were wives and daughters of the Company officers as also venturesome young ladies headed for the marriage market.

These women often carried numerous accessories including provisions such as "'hair powder; a good supply of papillote paper; pomatum, smelling-bottle, hartshorn, aromatic vinegar, aperients, and a case of cologne-water'. "[31] "They visited specialised tailors on Saville Row, Conduit Street or Bond Street for valuable advice, and a description of a corset of inestimable utility in a relaxing climate'."[32]

In India, that relaxing climate – both physically and culturally – was found only in the highlands where their precious attire could be worn and appreciated. The memsahibs proudly donned English garments, such as gloves and bonnets and woollens on their promenades.

Items of home decoration and musical instruments were considered essential for the tropics. Travellers were advised that "if there was a piano on board, there might be music. But the female passenger was warned not to unpack her own, if she had one, as 'the damp sea air and the motion of the vessel are calculated to seriously damage the delicate machinery of a Broadwood... even though it be clamped and fastened and *clothed*, to suite the climate of the tropics'."[33]

Well into this century, "for both sexes there was also the ritual of topee-buying at Simon Artz, since 'when one arrived at Port Said it was the accepted thing for every newcomer to buy a topee.' As Percival Griffiths recalls, 'No young civilian ever got out to India by sea without falling into the clutches of Simon Artz, where you were always inveigled into buying a Curzon topee which you probably never wore the rest of your life, because what you did wear was an old pig-sticking topee that you probably bought in Calcutta or when you first got to your station'."[34]

To survive the tropical sun a topee was a must, and a wide variety was sold by the Army and Navy Stores and other outfitters. After The Army and Navy Stores Catalogue.

Outfitters took care of everything; one establishment which stands out was the Army & Navy Co-operative Society's Stores, founded in 1871. The Society's Stores clothed and equipped almost all the important individuals who were going on duty to India until the end of the Second World War. The beginning of the Army & Navy Stores is amusing. A group of army and naval officers who felt that wine was too expensive decided to reduce the cost by ordering it at wholesale prices by the case. Six years earlier, a group of clerks working in the General Post Office had come together to buy a chest of tea. "How appropriate that the Civil Service Stores should have started with a chest of tea, and the Army & Navy Stores with a case of wine."[35]

In 1901, the Army & Navy Stores opened branches in Bombay, Delhi, Calcutta and Karachi. Bound in calf hide for Royalty and Embassies, the price list grew fatter and heavier.[36] When far from England, the expatriate could keep in touch with home – indeed the great cloth-bound catalogue was a tangible part of "home."

The outfitters carried a wide range of contraptions. Items such as the Canvas Bath, round in green case, diameter 24 inches. Note: Canvas Baths are

MOSQUITO NETS, ROOMS, AND FRAMES.

Left catalogue page showing Mosquito Nets, Mosquito Frame House, the "Bellamy" West African Carrier, Portable Mirrors, and Bedding for Barrack Beds.

"PUKKA" LUGGAGE.

The absolute reliability of which is guaranteed to each purchaser by a bond supplied with every article, undertaking to keep same in repair free of charge for 5 years, and replace gratis if beyond repair. No complicated conditions, but a simple, straightforward guarantee

Right catalogue page showing "Pukka" Suit Case, Hat-Box, Imperial, Cabin, and Wardrobe Trunks.

ALL PRICES ARE SUBJECT TO MARKET FLUCTUATIONS.

British officers carried a broad array of items such as a canvas bath, colonial chairs, mosquito-nets, X-latrine, and so on for their personal comfort. After The Illustrated London News.

for outdoor use only; a slight leakage is inevitable; the "X" Latrine, made from hardwood with polished seat, folds flat in bag, weight, 8 lb; combination Knife, Fork, and Spoon; variety of Colonial Chairs; Zinc-lined Chests (Recommended for Officer's use in India); Mosquito Nets, Rooms, and Frames; Mosquito Head Guard; and objects mentioned earlier i.e. the Portable Mirror, and the Rigid Washstand – quintessential Victorian item of personal hygiene. To transport these valuable belongings, into the rugged and distant interiors of India, the Army & Navy Stores also sold the "Pucca" (pukka) Luggage Set, comprising Suite Case, Hat-box, Imperial, Cabin and Wardrobe Trunks.

The best way to sum up the range of items which an English family, consisting a lady, three or four children, and an English Nurse, needed to maintain its European lifestyle in India is to look at the packing list of household items which Flora Annie Steel gave in her classic *The Complete Indian Housekeeper and Cook*:

"1st camel load: Two large trunks and two smaller ones with clothing.

2nd camel load: One large trunk containing children's clothing, plate chest, three bags, and bonnet-box.

3rd camel load: Three boxes of books, one box containing folding chairs, light tin box with clothing.

4th camel load: Four cases of stores, four cane chairs, saddle stand, mackintosh sheets.

5th camel load: One chest of drawers, two iron cots, tea table, pans for washing up.

6th camel load: Second chest of drawers, screen, lamps, lanterns, hanging wardrobes.

7th camel load: Two boxes containing house linen, two casks containing ornaments, ice-pails, door mats.

8th camel load: Three casks of crockery, another cask containing ornaments, filter, pardah (purdah) bamboos, tennis poles.

9th camel load: Hot case, milk safe, baby's tub and stand, sewing-machine, fender and irons, water cans, pitchers.

10th camel load: Three boxes containing saddlery, kitchen utensils, carpets.

11th camel load: Two boxes containing drawing room sundries, servant's cots, iron bath, cheval glass, plate basket.

Or the above articles could be loaded on four country carts, each with three or four bullocks for the uphill journey... A piano, where carts can be used, requires a cart to itself, and should be swung to avoid being injured by jolting. If the road is only a camel road, the piano should be carried by coolies, of whom fourteen or sixteen will be needed."[37]

As the century progressed, increased trade and travel between Britain and India gave rise to luxury liners. The famous Oriental and Peninsular Steam Navigation Company was founded in 1837. The title was later reversed and the Company became popularly known by its acronym the P&O. The P&O was the largest and the most popular shipping company for those going out East, and ran "travelling hotels" from Southampton to Bombay. The coming of large and homelike steam liners, however, did not reduce what the European travellers carried on board; it simply expanded the volume of passengers and their baggage.

Like contemporary business-class frequent flyers with pre-selected seats, "Seasoned travellers had their passages booked on the port side of the ship going out and starboard home, travelling POSH and so avoiding the worst of the sun."[38] The increased paraphernalia and the improvement in travel yet could not alleviate the living conditions of British officers and their families in India.

Taking along personal items is one matter; the adjustment to its tropical climate, is yet another. The harder one tries to fight the heat – not to mention the dust – of the tropics, the more unbearable it becomes. Soon, however, one succumbs to exhaustion from the heat, to sunburn, or worse still, heat stroke. Enduring the heat, season after season, and for years on end, simply wears one down.

Lifestyle and clothing can either ease or aggravate these conditions. "Indians had of course over centuries developed ways to accommodate the country's severe climate in their building. Among these were the enclosed courtyard, small shuttered windows, and arrangement of rooms which provided a cool basement (*tykhana*) and open sleeping roof."[39] British decisions about their dress code and where and how they resided in the plains did not in any way mitigate their physical discomfort.

The Planning Plights

The 17th and 18th century British traders had built European style, mostly classical, closely packed buildings in Madras, Calcutta, and Bombay. All three cities were trading settlements surrounded by defensive fortifications, and

hence, had rather restricted space. From the late eighteenth century onwards the East India Company's empire started to grow and included large areas in the hinterland. The old fort structures could no longer guard the large areas which came under British control.

Indeed, it was an unauthorised British extension of Fort William in Calcutta that precipitated the Nawab Suraj-ud-daula's 1756 attack that led in turn to the encounter at Plassey the following year. There Robert Clive defeated the forces of the nawab and so laid the foundations of the British rule in India. Following the conquest of Bengal, political changes required a new type of strategy demanding rapid troop movement and open deployment of the British forces. It was necessary to move them out of fortifications and into its periphery, where the soldiers were housed in cantonments, with their extremely scattered buildings, which developed as the most spacious of all urban patterns.[40]

The loose suburban pattern of the cantonments could be easily replicated wherever military control was deemed crucial. Sten Nilsson has compared cantonments with army camps of military states such as Rome or Vijaynagar in India, and their origins to a strictly arranged camp, or "moving city," suited to a hot climate.[41] The camp structure had to be light in weight – they were made from canvas-type materials – for comfort in the hot climate, and to remain mobile to ensure their relocation in cool places during hot summers.

The imperial Moguls, who ruled India before the British, had maintained this pattern closely. In hot summers, their military establishments, also their entire harems, would move up to relatively cooler locations. Penjor Garden, near the present-day Chandigarh, or the famous Shalimar Garden in the valley of Kashmir were used as summer pleasure grounds. The British cantonments on the other hand did not adhere to this model, nor did their camps remain light for very long.

Soon after they were established, most cantonments became permanent, and the light tent structures were replaced by heavy brick and mortar ones. "In 1801 an observer described the English as living in 'what are really stationary tents which have run aground on low brick platforms.

British officers at breakfast, ca. 1860. Note the folding chair, box containing flatware on the stool, china set on the table, and the solar topee on the floor. After The Illustrated London News.

Loodianah (Ludhiana) cantonment, ca. 1840, in the early stages of its development. The rows of tents were well disposed for army manoeuvres but not from the point of view of protection from the tropical climate. After The Illustrated London News.

They are 'Bungalows', a word I not know how to render unless by a Cottage."[42] A typical bungalow is a modest one storey rural structure, thatched or tiled, surrounded by a veranda. Although native to India a bungalow offers very limited protection from the heat compared to the inward-looking courtyard housing, also indigenous to India.

Consequently, the designs of loosely packed cantonments, with wide boulevards, barracks and bungalows placed in large compounds, offered little or no protection from the tropical elements. Cantonments were also inspired by the garden suburbs that were becoming popular in early 19th century England, which used extensive planting. Devices incorporated in the designs of the classic bungalows, such as deep verandas, high ceilings and clear-storey windows, somehow helped reduce the effect of the heat. Planting, in the form of tree-lined avenues and shade-giving trees around buildings were also used to reduce the impact of the sun.

In the hot summers of India these design features are however inadequate. It was necessary to attach *khas tattis*, woven panels of fragrant vegetal matter, which were tied between the veranda columns and kept wet to humidify and cool the passing air. A *punkah*, or a fan, served to induce a gentle breeze in living areas and bedrooms. Without electricity, the fan comprised a piece of canvas stretched over a rectangular frame which was rigged from the ceiling and pulled from the veranda with the help of a cord by a *punkah-wallah*, a fan-attendant. Eventually all British officers followed the good example

of Lady Canning, who had "hardened her heart towards the *punkah-wallahs* as the weather grew hotter, having at first felt guilty that they should have had to pull at their ropes day and night to keep her cool."[43]

All buildings, houses, barracks, cutcherries, churches, were equipped with punkahs. Norman Macleod, one of her Majesty's Chaplains for Scotland journeyed to India to report to the Church of Scotland about her missions. He had to preach in Madras with "punkahs cooling the church. The effect was most distracting," he wrote, "for the swinging of the huge fan alternately revealed and concealed my hearers. I no sooner caught the look of an individual, or number of individuals, which so much guides a speaker, than instantly lost them again. But though this is a trial of patience as regards the preacher, yet were the punkahs dispensed with there would be a worse infliction on every one of the hearers."[44]

When the *punkah-wallah* got tired, which was usual in the hot weather, he would tie the cord around his big toe and pull on it by swinging his leg from the knee. A *punkah-wallah*, spread out cross-legged on a cool veranda floor, his leg, no longer moving since he has fallen asleep, and the *sahib*, with sweat dripping down his temples, shouting from his bedchambers to wake him up, was a common scene, and the subject of more than one satirical cartoon.

Humour could momentarily lighten the discomfort of the tropical climate, but it could not be eliminated. So instead of adjustment, escape was the only remaining solution. Lord Wellesley arrived at the sensible conclusion: move to a cooler place. To find relief from the oppressive heat of Calcutta, he decided to build a summer palace at Barrackpore, about 15 miles outside the capital on the bank of the river Hooghly.

Lord Wellesley took over the Commander-in-Chief's bungalow at Barrackpore, which had been used as a cantonment since 1775, and appointed Captain Charles Wyatt to look after the repairs and renovations of the building. However, the summer palace was never completed in time for Lord Wellesley to enjoy it, as he was summoned back to England by the board of directors for his self-serving ways and for squandering the Company's fortunes on his personal official residence – the Government House in Calcutta.

Subsequent residents, Lord Hastings and the Cannings, made a considerable effort to develop the surrounding gardens, introducing marble basins and fountains, and a series of walks designed on English lines with exotic planting. Harriet Tytler, born in India, and famous because she gave birth to her son during the 1857 siege of Delhi and survived, visited these Barrackpore gardens as a child. Wild strawberries are native to the hills of India but in her childhood memories of the plain she recalls: "The first strawberry plants that ever grew in India were grown in the Barrackpore gardens. This must have been in 1836. My father and mother, with some friends, went to see these wonders, and I was allowed to accompany them. Two of the plants had one ripe berry each. Of course everyone was delighted at the novel sight. No one touched them, but all expressed the desire to be Lord

Auckland to have the pleasure of eating the first Indian strawberries... No sooner had my father and his friends gone on, chatting away, than I thought I really must taste the strawberries. Accordingly, I picked and ate them both."[45]

Thus "Wellesley's pursuit of the Picturesque in the form of an English country retreat on the banks of the Hooghly was fulfilled by his successors."[46] Barrackpore remained popular with the subsequent Governors-General and Viceroys, and served well as a weekend retreat, but still was not a perfect solution as a summer residence during the full heat of the season. Similar attempts to locate cantonments along the seashores of India in places like Ghizree near Karachi and on the coast of "Kattiwar" (Kathiawad) which is a part of modern Gujarat state, were attempted at the recommendation of the military sanitary commission,[47] but also proved unsatisfactory.

True relief from the heat and dust of the plains could only be found on the shady slopes of the mountains. The British had striven hard to gain and maintain control over the plains of India; they had succeeded over everything but the climate. The British had created settlements which, at their best, had a superficial semblance of home, but unfortunately offered no relief from the local elements. When relatively later in the game, the British gained control of the mountainous regions of India, they considered those cooler, more salubrious heights as a particularly important prize. Plus, having discovered climate and landscape similar to their own homeland, the establishment of the hill resorts was, of course, like creating a home away from home.

Church, Mount Abu, soon after its completion, ca. 1850. After The Illustrated London News.

Church erected for the sanatorium at Nuwara Eliya, Ceylon (Sri Lanka) ca. 1850. After The Illustrated London News..

A Home Away from Home

The East India Company controlled large parts of India indirectly by assuming the role of protector and supervisor of native territories, while respecting the rights of the local rulers as sovereigns. From very early on, however, the hill resorts were perceived as private and exclusive retreats for European populations living in India. To ensure that these resorts would have a distinct European flavour within the Company protectorates, the Company either leased, or acquired, lands from the native rulers.[48] In the early 1830s for example, once Simla had started to grow, the Company acquired the resort and its surrounding hills from several native kings. Similarly, a year later, the Company obtained a tract of land for the Darjeeling sanatorium from the Rajah of Sikkim.[49]

This uncommon arrangement meant that the hill resorts, even those located within various protectorates, were managed by British officers, and that they developed as European enclaves within feudal India. This ensured that most hill resorts evolved not only as a unique administrative entity, but also as physical, social and cultural outposts with English qualities.

When the land for the Darjeeling sanatorium was obtained, the Rajah of Sikkim had offered to build the necessary structures for the European community as a goodwill gesture to the Company. The reaction of the Governor-General Lord William Bentinck. to this offer is very telling with regard as to how the British viewed the development of these resorts. The Darjeeling sanatorium was to house mostly Europeans, therefore it was necessary to develop an oasis of European civilisation nestled in the Himalayas. The Rajah of Sikkim was ignorant of a Western lifestyle, notions of comfort, and building practices, particularly elements such as fireplaces and chimneys. If allowed to go ahead, it was felt that the Rajah would build something completely foreign to the English, and under the circumstances, it was thought best to politely turn down his offer.[50]

For the first two centuries of their rule the British had built mostly neoclassical buildings in the plains. From the second half of the 19th and the first half of the 20th century, however, concerted efforts were made to develop a hybrid between European and Indian styles of architecture for the plains. It was the British "conviction that there is no style of Architecture suited in its entirety to the requirements of Europeans in the plains of India."[51] It was essential, therefore, to develop a new style. The expectation was that this style of architecture would symbolise the greatness of the British Empire, just as the buildings of the Moguls had symbolised their reign. No stylistic debate ever took place, however, about buildings built in the hills of India. The hill stations were located in the temperate reaches of India where a European style of architecture was adequate. The British knew how to live comfortably in such climes, but typical colonial servants working in India, far from being expert builders, often lacked even the rudiments of training in construction. For such staff, architects' and builders' pattern books proved to be a handy and effective tool. There are however no guidebooks or pattern books on architecture written specially for the hill stations of India.

During the early Victorian era "no class of society despised guidance,"[52] and there was no shortage of experts forthcoming with specialised manuals. These books dealt with a variety of subjects, and included architectural pattern books, which offered instruction and guidance on the design, construction, and decoration of a variety of dwelling types. With the expansion of the British Empire overseas, and the growing size and wealth of the middle-class the demand for guide books grew. Beyond the conventional readers – the gentry and the rich – a much wider audience required readily available knowledge. Some guide books were probably therefore written with colonial consumers in mind.

John Claudius Loudon's *Encyclopaedia of Cottage, Farm and Villa Architecture and Furniture,* (London, 1833), is a prime example of an architectural guide book of this epoch. Loudon's objective was "to improve the dwellings of the great mass of society, in the temperate regions of both hemispheres," and the designs were conceived for what "in self-governed democracies, like North America, or in newly-

Saint Stephen Church, Ootacamund.

Typical English-style bungalow, Kalimpong. This small hill station located near Darjeeling has many beautiful bungalows, many of them, like this one, inspired by the turn-of-the-century "Arts and Crafts Movement".

Bungalow, Pachmarhi.

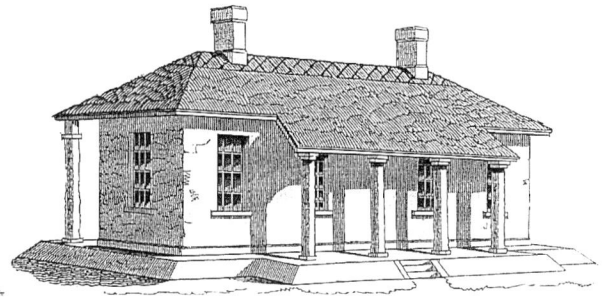

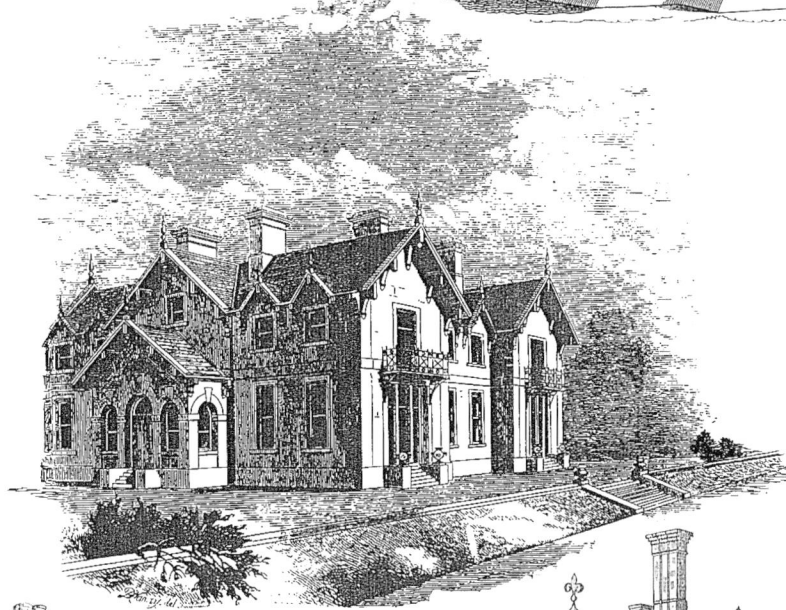

Typical cottage designs taken from various pattern or guide books which were used extensively in the colonies. After J.C. Loudon, *An Encyclopaedia of Cottage, Farm and Villa Architecture* and Robert Kerr, *The Gentleman's House*.

colonised countries, like Australia, constitute nearly the whole rural population."[53] Loudon's book, illustrated with more than 2,000 beautiful engravings, became immensely popular; copies could be found in every quarter of the British Empire and throughout the United States. After his death a new edition, issued by Mrs. Loudon, remained in circulation as late as the 1880s.

Neither Loudon's nor any of the other popular pattern books of the time provided any designs intended specially for colonial hill resorts. Still, the designs conceived were primarily for temperate areas, and could be adapted to the Indian hills. To this day copies of architectural pattern books can be found in hill station libraries. In the collection of the Nilgiri Library in Ootacamund, for example, one can find a 1869 edition of Loudon's *Encyclopaedia of Cottage, Farm and Villa*

Architecture and Furniture (Edited by Mrs. Loudon); C. Wicke's *A Handbook of Villa Architecture*, (London, no date); and J. Birch's *Examples of Labourers' Cottages*, (London, 1871). The influence of architectural pattern books was not limited to the hill resorts, as evidenced in particular by the many Wren and Gibbs inspired churches built throughout the Indian plains during the British era.

A 19th century pattern of a very particular sort inspired the building designs of Indian hill resorts. One did not build a palace in the hills, or in a mountain retreat, but a cottage. According to the Oxford Dictionary, a cottage is a dwelling-house of small size and humble character, such as is occupied by farm-labourers, villagers, miners and generally found in the country or at a resort, usually of single storey. For the Victorians, however, the type represented a much broader reality and a deeper meaning.[54]

An idyllic image of that age "was a blissful scene of a green valley in which nestled a scattered group of thatch-roofed cottages, with lattice windows and winding paths with hollyhocks and roses."[55] George Sand, a French Victorian, had gone as far as dividing people into two types: "those whose ideal dwelling-place is a palace and those whose ideal is a cottage. Most representative Victorians would have opted for the cottage over the palace, as did George Sand herself – although she happily contrived to make the best of both worlds by owning both a cottage and a chateau."[56]

In *The Gentleman's House*, (London, 1865), architect Robert Kerr noted that although the design characteristics of cottage-style buildings were not on a par with high architectural styles, cottages were extensively in vogue throughout the kingdom for many years as the common model for a small country-house. Moreover, according to Kerr, the design of a cottage was suitable to any situation:

"because it is perfectly unpretentious in the first place, and, in the second, capable of being treated with any amount of regularity or irregularity that may be thought proper. The *Scale of building* ought not to be large, because the style is essentially not *important*. The *Materials* may be economical to any

extent, but ought not to be otherwise; and the *Cost* correspondingly low. The *Ornamental character*, under good management, is simple and neat. The *Internal style* is precisely that of common use. *The Influence on plan* is simply this, – that any amount of symmetrical arrangement or of freedom therefrom is equally suitable."[57]

As late as 1905, the American architect P.H. Ditchfield, observed that the beauty of cottages is derived from their functionalism: "Frank and simple and direct, built for use, not the exploiting of empirical theory, they possess in the highest degree perfect adaptation to function, and therefore absolute beauty."[58]

For the European rulers in India, cottages, became the ideal building type for the hills: a classic rural dwelling type, with an informality of style, low-cost, flexibility of design, and adaptability to any locally available building materials. The Arcadian scene of cottages in highland splendour soon prevailed throughout the hills of India.[59] However, it is also important to bear in mind that the cottages which dotted the hills of India were not meant for modest farmhands; they belonged to the rulers of the Empire's Jewel in the Crown. In most instances what emerged was a mix of a small country-home with sweeping driveways, terraced gardens, ponds, and a touch of a cottage.

The typical Indian bungalow, which the British

Cottage, Ootacamund. In recent years, wealthy corporations and individuals have acquired such graceful cottages and converted them into guesthouses.

had already adopted widely for their use in the plains and also exported to other colonies around the world, is similar to a cottage, because of its informal layout. It also allows for the use of local building materials and a partly vernacular construction, an asset while building in remote mountain areas. An important change which was introduced, specially in the northern stations, was the elimination or considerable reduction of the wrap-around verandas. Thus, the British married these two traditions beautifully in their domestic architecture in the hills: "wooden tie beams became exposed timber framing, and fretwork eaves and canopies became ornamental carved bargeboards, often in the style of the alpine cottage."[60]

The popularity of Switzerland as a favourite alpine tourist destination among Europeans also placed an imprint on cottage designs. The *châlet* (German *sennhutte*) is basically a log-hut built with pine trunks notched at the ends to fit into one another, and a shingled-roof with overhangs. According to John Murray's *A Handbook for Travellers in Switzerland, and the Alps of Savoy and Piedmont,* London, 1854, then in its sixth edition, a pastoral Swiss valley was usually speckled with numerous chalets. The herdsmen had two or three such places of temporary abode and travellers were often disappointed to find them devoid of human habitation. But, "what an agreeable contrast to reach a well-appointed chalet of the better sort, where delicious milk, cooled in the mountain stream, fresh butter, bread, and cheese, are spread out on a clean napkin before the hungry and tired stranger!"[61] The wholesome image of the Swiss chalet was so popular then that they were readily copied in the Indian hill resorts. What is more remarkable is that, like the bungalow, the "Swiss chalets" have remained with us as an almost universal model for weekend homes and country cottages.[62]

According to George Sand "the ideal cottage must be thatch-covered – the substitution of slate roofs would be a desecration."[63] In the remote hills of India there were few expert thatchers who could build roofs capable of resisting the heavy monsoon rains, so a better alternative was found. This is when corrugated iron sheet made its appearance.

The process of hot-dip galvanising which increased the durability of corrugated metal sheets was patented by Craufurd in 1837. The credit for the first manufacture of galvanised corrugated iron sheets, in 1843 goes to John Porte in Southwork, Scotland. A year later, the Phoenix Iron Works in Glasgow went into mass production.[64] Corrugated iron sheets became popular and most of the production was earmarked for the colonies. By 1891 British production of corrugated iron exceeded 200,000 tons, with 75 percent of the production being exported.

Although very noisy during heavy monsoon

Staff bungalow, Bishop Cotton School, Simla.

Kasauli Club, Kasauli. More than 100 years old, the Club is still the centre of social life in Kasauli, and attracts members from as far as Chandigarh and Delhi.

rains and under the feet of native monkeys, the sheets were easy to transport, quick and simple to install, and highly durable. In very short order, galvanised iron sheets became the de facto roofing standard throughout the hill resorts. They did not contribute to a picture-perfect image of a Victorian village, but in the colonies, alas, finer details had to give way to pragmatism.[65]

Cottages, government offices, schools, churches and commercially-important structures such as factories for plantations, were needed in the colonies, and only mass-produced industrial products such as cast iron building components and galvanised iron roofing sheets could meet the demand effectively. The capacity of industrial mass production was well demonstrated at the Great Exhibition of 1851. In fact, a portion of the Great Exhibition held in Paxton's vast prefabricated iron and glass Crystal Palace in Hyde Park ended as a sugar store in Commercial Road, Durban; iron lighthouses were

Galvanised iron church for the diocese of Melbourne, Australia, ca. 1850. This church and other buildings were fabricated in the British Isles and shipped to the colonies around the world. After The Illustrated London News.

Utilitarian structures such as cottages and villas, light houses, and tea factories like the ones above, which were made from iron and galvanised steel sheets manufactured in the British Isles and exported throughout the colonies. Such factories, or parts of them, can still be seen in the hills of India. Collection, Centre Canadien d'Architecture / Canadian Centre for Architecture, Montreal.

Lobby, *above,* and the main Dining Room, *below,* Savoy Hotel, Ootacamund, originally a school for European children. Wood salvaged from Tipu Sultan's Lal Bagh Palace at Srirangapatam was used in the construction of this building as well as to span the roof of Saint Stephen Church, Ootacamund, *see page 63.*

exported to Barbados and Ceylon, a customs house was sent to Peru and Matthew Digby Wyatt designed an iron church for Rangoon.[66] The new government offices in Simla were constructed entirely from prefabricated iron parts which were transported up to the hills with relative ease.[67]

To cover churches, theatres, town halls, school gyms, steel and iron trussing and galvanised sheet metal technology were employed extensively. The range of trusses designed to optimise the use of expensive metal parts without sacrificing visual beauty of the building in the hills is also quite amazing.

Prior to the introduction of steel and iron, one had to rely on the use of native wood, but the supply of heavy timber, needed for large span structures, was not always assured. Early sketches and photographs of the high Nilgiri downs reveal that there were very few large trees. This may be one reason that in building Saint Stephen's Church, Ootacamund, which dates from 1829-30, the timber from Tipu Sultan's palace, plundered after the British victory over the native ruler, was hauled up with the help of bullock carts from Srirangapatam. The Superintendent of the Gun Carriage Factory at Srirangapatam was put in charge of tearing down the old Lal Bagh Palace, to ensure that the materials required for public buildings in the Nilgiris were salvaged properly and quickly.[68] Wood from the same source was also used for the nearby Mission school which is now a part of the Savoy Hotel complex. The ethics of using the spoils of the war or material recycling aside, the accomplished use of heavy timber beams has produced two beautiful buildings with simple and clean lines, especially in the interior.

The new settlers brought all the way from Australia rapidly growing eucalyptus and acacia trees. They were introduced in hills surrounding Ootacamund,

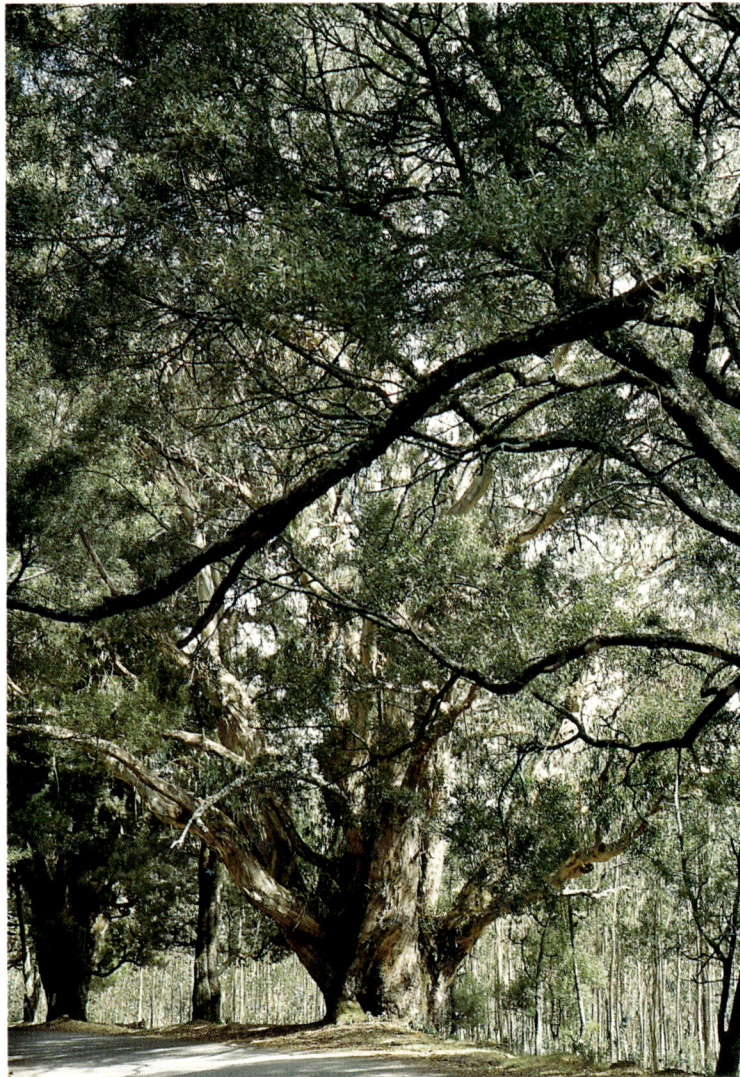

Giant eucalyptus trees, like this, dating from the 1850s and 60's, when they were brought from Australia and introduced to this region, endure in Ootacamund.

Kodaikanal and other southern stations to remedy the shortage of wood. Today, broad patches of eucalyptus trees soar up to more than 100 feet and appear as if they have always been an integral part of the landscape, but their history dates back less than 150 years.

At the settlement level, the hill resorts were conceived as, and remained, small communities. By the middle of the 19th century, although frequented regularly by various Governors-General as a vacation spot, and soon to become the summer capital of the empire, Simla was only a town of a 100 houses with a British population of 320 during the summer.[69] As late as 1881 the total number of houses was only 1,141.[70] Compared to Simla, other hill resorts were even smaller. It is only in the post-Independence era that several hill resorts, such as Bangalore and Poona, have grown into large urban centres.

The hill resorts resembled the typical villages found in the British Isles: small, with a scattering of cottages, a church, a common school, a reading room, perhaps a post office and army barracks (if the station also served as a military sanatorium). Loudon describes the attributes of an ideal village in his *Encyclopaedia*, "all cottages that are built along a road... are destructive of all picturesque beauty... Every cottage in a village should be surrounded with its own garden ground, and nothing more... Nevertheless, we are far from asserting that all the cottage gardens ought to be of the same size; on the contrary, variety will be produced by a difference in this respect, as well as by difference in accommodation and style of cottages."[71] British settlers and administrators assimilated these lessons in the hill resorts of India, and produced informal and organic communities, each one distinct from the others.

70

Unlike the Nilgiri mountains, Pachmarhi plateau is surrounded by dense jungle, with an incredible diversity of native plants, and deep ravines of breathtaking beauty.

Numerous public sites were adorned with fountains. Bandstands and statues were fairly common. Often, individuals donated funds to erect these civic refinements, which helped create a sense of belonging.

Little information is available on how these resorts were planned. In old tourist guides to individual hill resorts, however, one can often find information about land acquisition and the local building regulations. The regulations from one hill resort to another did not vary much. This may well explain why, in a given region, say from Dalhousie to Murree, the general make up of the hill resorts, remained similar. Few fairly simple, local regulations reflected the concern for picturesque beauty and variety expressed in Victorian guide books. The by-laws at the end of E.B. Peacock's *A Guide to Murree and its Neighbourhood*, (Lahore, 1883), stipulated that:

> "Ten acres is the largest extent of ground which can be sold to one person in a single plot... An acre to be the smallest extent of ground occupied by one house with out-offices, except in special cases... All public roads and thoroughfares are to be maintained, and 20 feet on either side from the centre of any public road or pathway originally traced for road are public property."[72]

Basically the whole community was organised around this thoroughfare, which was almost always located on a ridge, stretching along the crest, on either side of which the settlement was established. Over the

Memorial to Sir Vere Henry Levinge, who donated money to build a small dam to create the Kodaikanal Lake, the most important feature of the station.

Lake at Yercaud, painting by Lieut. Colonel Douglas Hamilton, ca. 1860. The British Library.

Kodaikanal Lake and its beautiful surroundings.

Boats on Yenna Lake, Mahabaleshwar.

years, as the resorts matured, the mid-section of the relatively level ridge developed into the most important institution of the hill resorts – the Mall, thereby binding the entire community together around this central element, the heart of the resort.

In southern and central Indian locations, the ridge had to be traded for the high elevation plateaus, as was the case in Matheran, Mount Abu and Pachmarhi. Nevertheless, the general resort locations, either along the high ridges or on an elevated plateau, were chosen for their relatively even grade. The level ridge, especially at high elevations, facilitated the establishment of the community, and allowed residents to move around easily, without having to negotiate great climbs or descents.

In army cantonments the parade grounds served as the central organizing space, as was the case in Sabathu and Pachmarhi. Occasionally, the centre of the community was tied to an important geographical feature such as a lake, as in Naini Tal and Mount Abu.

Lakes added much beauty to the resorts, and were rightly seen as an important amenity. Artificial lakes were created atop several hill resorts, at Kodaikanal, Mahabaleshwar, Matheran, Ootacamund, Pachmarhi, Shillong, and Yercaud. The Berijam lake at Kodaikanal was artificially created in 1867, when Sir Vere Levinge, Collector of Madurai, donated his personal retirement funds to build a small dam. The surrounding facilities such as the botanical garden, the town hall, the European club (now the Kodaikanal Club), a couple of churches, and of course the boat club, are all beautifully linked, sometimes by open clear views. A stroll around this star-shaped lake, also known as Lake Kodaikanal, is perhaps one of the most refreshing promenades. Similarly, most of the lakes in other stations look and function like an integral part of the present landscape.

As in British resorts, in the Indian hill resorts the Mall or the central portion of the station was the focus of the town. High-priced stores – emporia as they are often referred to in India – which imported items of daily use from the continent lined the market. The Mall was a place to see and to be seen. Morning and evening, gentlemen and ladies, dressed in their best, came out to take the fresh air. Other civic facilities such as the church, the court house, the post office and the town hall were located around it. The Anglican church occupied the most prominent position on the Mall. Indeed the higher areas of the ridge were always reserved for the Church of England, while other social institutions, including Protestant and Catholic churches, stood at slightly lower elevations. All the public structures fitted harmoniously into the landscape to complete a charming ensemble giving coherence and character to each resort.

With the Mall or a civic promenade at its heart the town-community generally had an effective control over the mountain ridge. Controlling the ridge was a simple and practical method for subdividing the land as the settlement grew. Furthermore, it allowed the settlers to dominate the valleys below and their watersheds. The hill resorts were situated strategically on vital ridges, which allowed the rulers to control all the important watersheds of India. Certain cantonments, located at relatively low elevations, permitted a comfortable year-round stay for the troops, who could be deployed quickly if needed in the plains.

The old map of the Darjeeling cantonment clearly indicates how the British occupied the territory, acquired from the Rajah of Sikkim. It also shows how it was now possible to control the surrounding waterways. Control of the ridge was a key determinant factor as one can see from other detailed maps of Darjeeling and its adjoining station, Hope Town. The significance of a ridge or a plateau as the command post and the generator of the settlement plan is evident from the contour maps prepared by the office of the Surveyor General of India.

Evidently, one basic function of the Indian hill resorts was then to maintain strategic control over the subcontinent. Major-General Newall, J.J.F. in his *The Highlands of India* has noted that Sir Henry Lawrence, Sir Colin G. Campbell, Robert Clive, Warren Hastings, Arthur Wellington, Thomas Munro, William Bentinck, Charles Metcalf, Edward Law Ellenborough, Marquess of Dalhousie and Charles John Canning advocated British settlements in the hills for strategic reasons.

In fact, many hill resorts served multiple functions: as summer retreats, sanatoria for sick troops, as well as defensive military outposts, and administrative and social refuge. In the early 19th century, with a series of conquests leading westward from the Gangetic plains into Garhwal and Punjab, and looking beyond to Afghanistan, Company officers recognised the strategic importance of the highlands of India. In *The Highlands of India,* published in 1882, after the key hill resorts had been established, Newall provides a wonderful analysis of all the hill regions, their colonisation and use as reserve circles and military stations.

Many hill resorts also acquired significant economic importance, especially with the growing of different types of commercial crops. The hill climate could support a variety of crops, of which coffee and tea were the most successful. With the exquisite climate of the hills, the British soon discovered that they could grow many different types of plants, especially the ones native to "home."

The English Garden and Much More

No cottage community is ever complete without its gardens. Trimmed hedges, lush growth and walks and paths lined with flowers are an integral part of any true cottage composition, as Matthew Arnold described in his pastoral *Thyrsis* (1866):

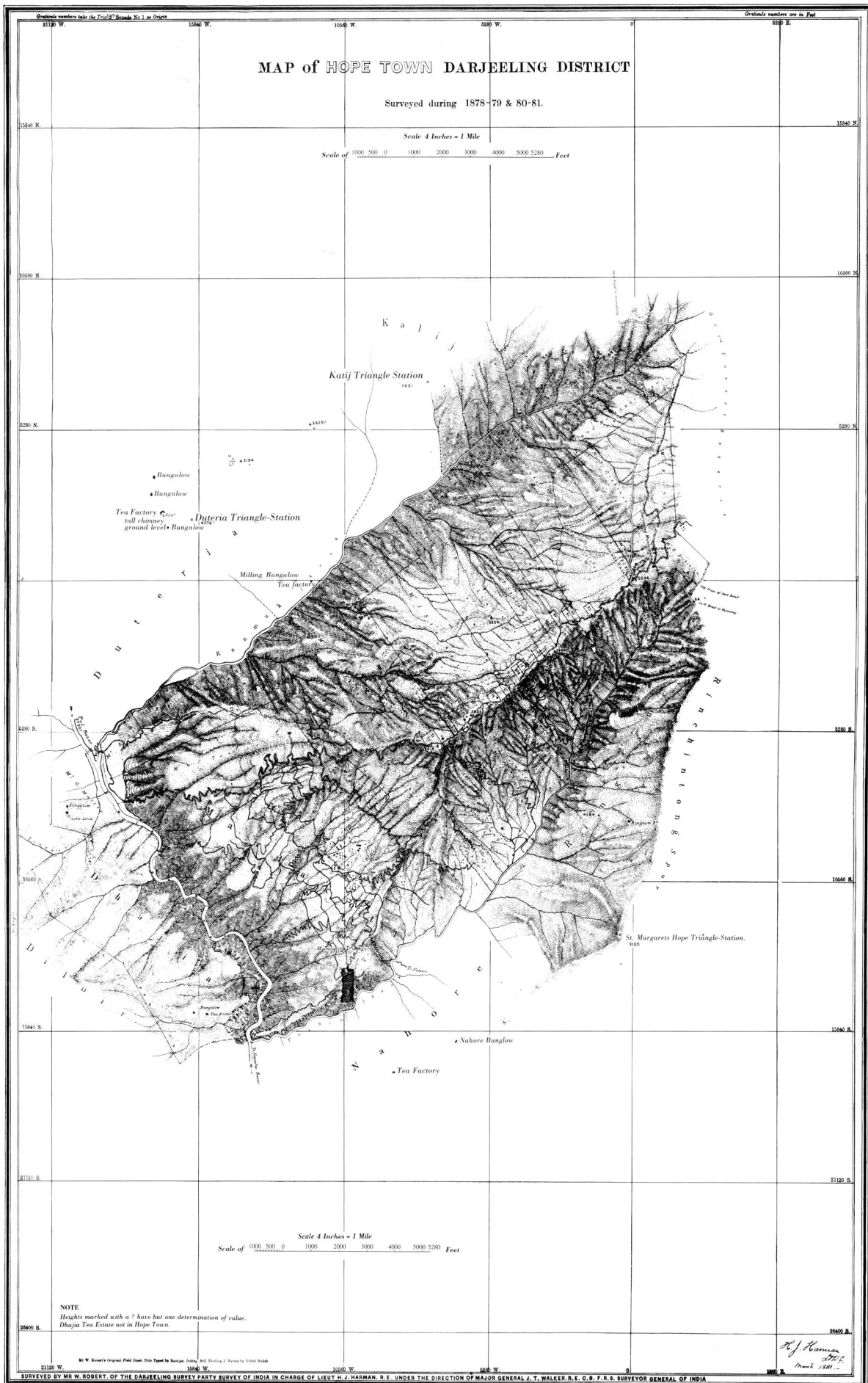

Map of Hope Town, near Darjeeling, clearly shows how important the control of the ridge was in the design of hill resorts. The British Library.

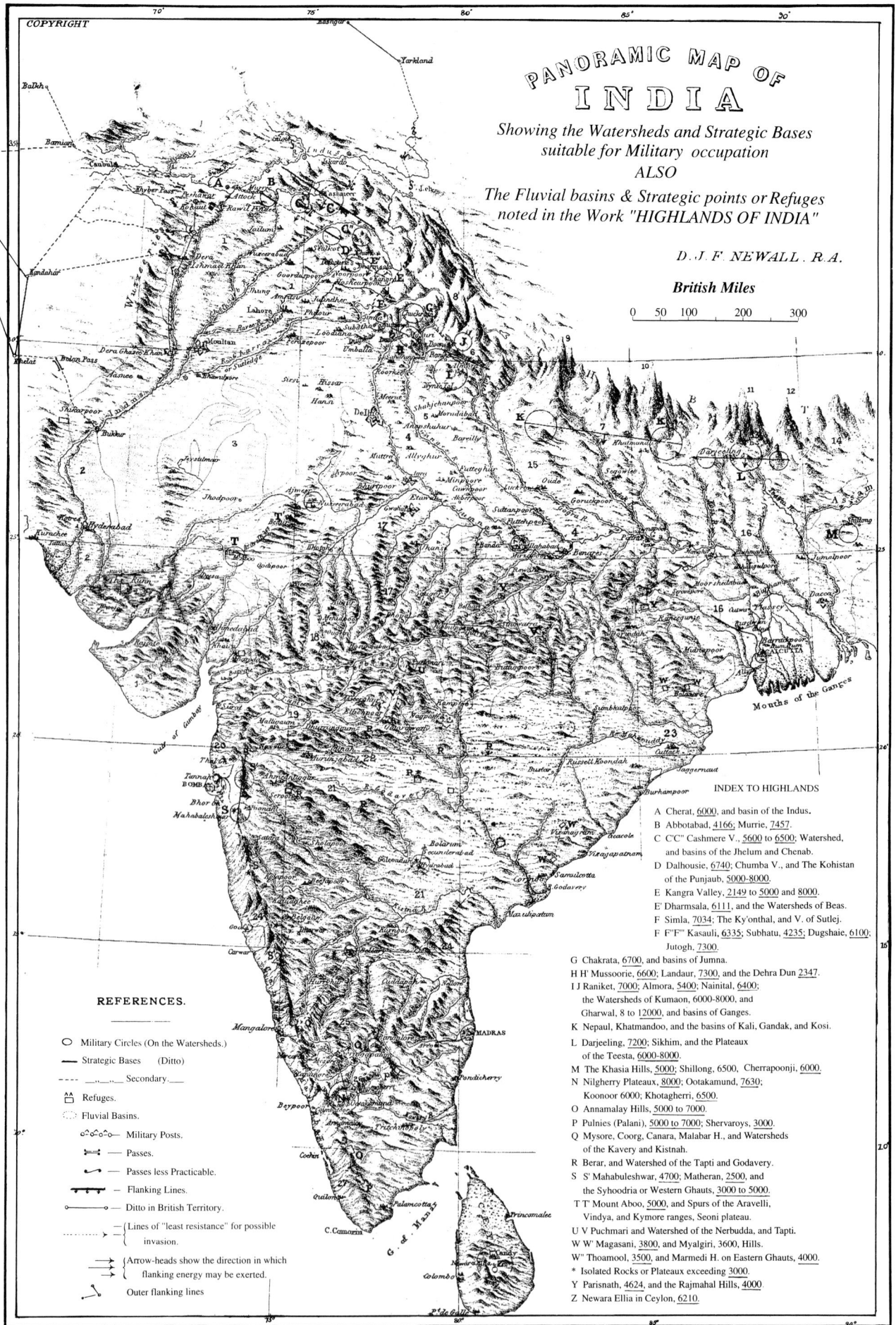

PANORAMIC MAP OF
INDIA
Showing the Watersheds and Strategic Bases
suitable for Military occupation
ALSO
The Fluvial basins & Strategic points or Refuges
noted in the Work "HIGHLANDS OF INDIA"

D. J. F. NEWALL. R. A.

British Miles

0   50   100   200   300

COPYRIGHT

Mouths of the Ganges

REFERENCES.

◯ Military Circles (On the Watersheds.)

—— Strategic Bases   (Ditto)

----- __,__ Secondary.___

⌂ Refuges.

∴ Fluvial Basins.

o⌐o⌐o⌐o Military Posts.

⊢—⊣ Passes.

•—• Passes less Practicable.

⊤⊤⊤ Flanking Lines.

o—o Ditto in British Territory.

— { Lines of "least resistance" for possible
      invasion.

→ { Arrow-heads show the direction in which
→   flanking energy may be exerted.

↘ Outer flanking lines

INDEX TO HIGHLANDS

A Cherat, 6000, and basin of the Indus.

B Abbotabad, 4166; Murrie, 7457.

C C'C" Cashmere V., 5600 to 6500; Watershed,
    and basins of the Jhelum and Chenab.

D Dalhousie, 6740; Chumba V., and The Kohistan
    of the Punjaub, 5000-8000.

E Kangra Valley, 2149 to 5000 and 8000.

E' Dharmsala, 6111, and the Watersheds of Beas.

F Simla, 7034; The Ky'onthal, and V. of Sutlej.

F F'F'" Kasauli, 6335; Subhatu, 4235; Dugshaie, 6100;
    Jutogh, 7300.

G Chakrata, 6700, and basins of Jumna.

H H' Mussoorie, 6600; Landaur, 7300, and the Dehra Dun 2347.

I J Raniket, 7000; Almora, 5400; Nainital, 6400;
    the Watersheds of Kumaon, 6000-8000, and
    Gharwal, 8 to 12000, and basins of Ganges.

K Nepaul, Khatmandoo, and the basins of Kali, Gandak, and Kosi.

L Darjeeling, 7200; Sikhim, and the Plateaux
    of the Teesta, 6000-8000.

M The Khasia Hills, 5000; Shillong, 6500, Cherrapoonji, 6000.

N Nilgherry Plateaux, 8000; Ootakamund, 7630;
    Koonoor 6000; Khotagherri, 6500.

O Annamalay Hills, 5000 to 7000.

P Pulnies (Palani), 5000 to 7000; Shervaroys, 3000.

Q Mysore, Coorg, Canara, Malabar H., and Watersheds
    of the Kavery and Kistnah.

R Berar, and Watershed of the Tapti and Godavery.

S S' Mahabuleshwar, 4700; Matheran, 2500, and
    the Syhoodria or Western Ghauts, 3000 to 5000.

T T' Mount Aboo, 5000, and Spurs of the Aravelli,
    Vindya, and Kymore ranges, Seoni plateau.

U V Puchmari and Watershed of the Nerbudda, and Tapti.

W W' Magasani, 3800, and Myalgiri, 3600, Hills.

W" Thoamool, 3500, and Marmedi H. on Eastern Ghauts, 4000.

* Isolated Rocks or Plateaux exceeding 3000.

Y Parisnath, 4624, and the Rajmahal Hills, 4000.

Z Newara Ellia in Ceylon, 6210.

Drawn & Engraved by James Wyld, 457 Strand, London.

Map of the highlands of India, from Major-General D.J.F. Newall's, *The Highlands of India.* It is very clear from this map that control of the high plateaus and watersheds was deemed essential by the British for effective rule in India.

Rose hedge surrounding the Ootacamund Club garden, is reminiscent of an English country lane.

Rolling hills surrounding Ootacamund. The gentle tops of the Nilgiris were a constant reminder to the British of the rolling downs of their own isles.

Botany gave rise not only to style but also purpose – wealth – for the Empire. Raw materials, such as these Indian cotton bales waiting to be shipped from Bombay to Manchester, ca. 1862, were collected from the colonies and processed into finished textile or other consumer items in England, and returned to the colonies to be sold at enormous profits. After the Illustrated London News.

Sweet-William with his homely cottage smell...
And open, jasmine-muffled lattices,...[73]

So along with the cottages, came European vegetation, and of course, English-style gardens.

A considerable number of plants, flowers and trees, different types of berries, magnolias, rhododendrons, oak, pine, and cedar, which are common in Europe, are also native to the Indian hills. Europeans joyously discovered these plants, and in addition soon started to grow English fruits, their own flowers and vegetables in the mild climate of the hills. After all, is not every Englishman a born gardener?

In all of the Raj writings, there is a constant referring back to English gardens, a desire to recreate a home-like setting. According to Terrell, "My mother planted English seeds – sweet peas, petunias, phlox, clarkia which by Christmas time were in full flower... The display of blooms could not have been better in any English garden."[74] While Lady Wilson was delighted to be in the hills where "from our morning-room, where we breakfast, we look out on our lilac trees, an archway covered by a mass of wistaria, and flower-beds with rows of forget-me-nots, sweet-peas, and wall-flowers. When

the time of roses has come, we shall see them everywhere, and the yellow china clusters, which will cover one side of the house, will tap on our window, and the air be full of the scent of deep crimson and yellow Gloire de Dijon roses."[75]

Since resorts were generally situated on the crest of a hill, it was not easy to bring water all the way to the top, especially for a extensive garden. For ease of irrigation, common vegetable gardens were located close to a water source. People got together to plant vegetable gardens which developed into larger undertakings. Early maps of hill resorts indicate that most of them had fair sized public vegetable patches. The military cantonments in the hills always maintained vegetable gardens, generally attended to by soldiers, and also by prisoners. Some vegetable gardens later grew into civic or botanical facilities. For example, the Ootacamund Botanical Garden was started with public subscription as a vegetable garden in 1845, but slowly developed into an outstanding public park and arboretum.

The British started the public garden projects in India in the late 18th century (1780s) with the establishment of the Calcutta Botanical Garden.[76] But they were not the first. Actually, the tradition of large pleasure gardens in India pre-dates the arrival of the British. There were magnificent gardens established by the Moguls in Agra, Delhi, Kashmir, and for that matter the Lal Bagh in Bangalore, which was originally established by HyderAli and later evolved into a Botanical Garden under the British. All these facilities were primarily for the use of the ruling elite, and their objective was to create a familiar landscape, an oasis, in a foreign land. Although conceived by the British the botanical gardens were also open to the native population. The Darjeeling and Ootacamund gardens were established, so were similar gardens in other hill stations, based on the Calcutta botanical garden.

"Botany gave style to the Empire, too, and was one of the oldest of the imperial enthusiasms. From the earliest days of British expansion navigators, explorers and settlers had been concerned to collect rare plants, transfer cuttings, experiment with smoking of rolled-up leaves or the eating of hitherto unsuspected tubers."[77] The East India Company itself had been formed to fight the Dutch intrusion in the east which had raised the price of Indian pepper in the English market from 3 shillings to 8 shillings per pound. The Company, formed with capital of £30,000, was granted a charter in 1600, and soon after, a fleet of its ships sailed for the East Indies. When the Company's ships returned home in 1603 they brought back 1,030,000 pounds of pepper, worth more than £400,000.[78] As a desperate beginning, it certainly was a lucrative venture. The trade in indigo, cotton, coffee, tea, opium and sugar was still to follow.

Exotic plants from distant parts of the world came to Kew Gardens, outside London, and went back to the colonies for commercial exploitation. From 1841 onwards, Kew Gardens was designated the State institution where all available botanical samples and knowledge resided; "Kew had its derivatives or ancillaries in most of the British possessions – part

Decorative display of strawberries. Such display techniques and distinct farming methods, such as the use of dig-hoes with long handles, employed by the farmers around Mahabaleshwar, were inherited from the Chinese prisoners kept here during the last century.

pleasure-places, part scientific laboratories, with their learned keepers and their catalogues."[79] The Agricultural and Horticultural Society of India was established in 1820, like Kew Gardens, to spread the word of good gardening practices. Soon after, from its headquarters in Calcutta, the Society actively distributed seeds and grafts of fruit trees and vines.

A wide variety of seeds consisting of cotton, tobacco, flax, cereals, grasses, carrots, turnips, cabbage and mangelwurzel were imported from suppliers in England, North America and Holland. The Society also tried to train native boys as *malis* or gardeners, "to avoid encountering the prejudices, generally entertained by adults against a system of gardening differing from what they have been accustomed to."[80] There was a great disappointment among its members when the boys who were taught how to read and write along with their gardening skills opted for clerical careers instead of the one which was chosen for them by their teachers. In any event, the Society was an influential group spreading new agricultural and gardening practices throughout India, both in the plains and in the hilly regions.

Strawberries were introduced in the Western Ghats near Mahabaleshwar and cultivated by the Chinese prisoners held there. Remarkably, the Chinese influence is still evident in the neatly decorated little piles of berries which the local farmers sell, and the Chinese-style long handled dig-hoes that they use.

Potatoes, first introduced in the Himalayas by Captain Kennedy, the founder of Simla, perhaps pre-date the founding of the Society. Today, potatoes are a popular crop cultivated throughout the lower Himalayas. In late

Following pages:
Cherry blossoms, Kulu Valley, in the early spring, perhaps the most beautiful time of the year in the Himalayas.

Botanical gardens were also used for experimental purposes. Exotic plants, such as this monkey puzzle tree, in the Botanical Garden, Ootacamund, were imported from around the Empire for research.

spring one can hear vendors yelling, in a singsong fashion on streets of large cities, *pahadi aalu lo*, advertising mountain grown potatoes.

Mr. Sullivan, founder of Ootacamund, was also an avid gardener, and was responsible for bringing "the first English apple and peach trees and strawberries, the first seeds of flowers and vegetables"[81] from England. The fruits of the British pioneers can be had even today; for, in almost all the hill stations of India, one finds a separate section in the markets of "country vegetables" vs. "English vegetables" selling, "potatoes, the snowy turnips, the rosy radishes, the big, glossy orange tomatoes, the brilliant green of the string beans, peas, artichokes, lettuce and (as a sign that the British have been here) the tiny, delicate Brussels sprouts, no bigger than a thumbnail – all washed and trimmed and arranged with art in huge vegetable still-life."[82]

The Lal Bagh botanical garden in Bangalore was the centre of botanical and horticultural research in south India. The garden, covering more than 100 acres (40.5 hectares), was under the management of an expert horticulturist trained at Kew Gardens. Its glass house was like a miniature copy of the Crystal Palace, the great pavilion built for the 1851 World Fair in London. For the benefit of the public, the military band played weekly in the garden in a specially constructed bandstand.[83] Norman Macleod, who had great difficulty preaching in Madras because of the swinging punkahs was most delighted to visit the Lal Bagh garden on the occasion of a

The glass house at the Bangalore Botanical Garden is modelled after the Crystal Palace, Great Exhibition structure which was built to house the 1851 London World Fair, *above* and General view of Lal Bagh Garden, *opposite page.*

flower show, a tradition still maintained in most hill resorts:

"Our home feeling was greatly intensified by attending a flower show... There was the usual military band; and crowds of carriages conveyed fashionable parties to the entrance-gate. Military officers and civil servants of every grade..."

"The most remarkable and interesting spectacles to me were the splendid vegetables of every kind, including potatoes which would have delighted an Irishman; leeks and onions worthy of being remembered like those of Egypt; cabbages, turnips, cauliflowers, peas, beans, such as England could hardly equal; splendid fruit- apples, peaches, oranges, figs, and pomegranates, the display culminating in a magnificent array of flowers, none of which pleased me more than the beautiful roses, so redolent of home! Such were the sights of a winter's day in Bangalore."[84]

Botanical gardens in other hill resorts were also used as public amenities as well as laboratories for medicinal and commercial purposes. Often, in special nurseries separate from the botanical gardens, the settlers first experimented with the planting of commercial crops such as tea, coffee and chincona. Chincona was named after the countess of Cinchon, a 17th century Spanish lady of Peru, who was cured of an ailment by an alkaloid medicine derived from the bark of an Andean plant, it was introduced to India from South America in 1862. The tree took her name, and was anglicised as quinine. A nursery for chincona existed at Dodabetta, just outside Ootacamund. "Mr. Broughton, an able chemist and pupil of the celebrated Professor Faraday, was employed for some years as Quinologist to Government. He lived in the Botanical gardens and successfully carried on his chemical operations, turning his strips of chincona bark into excellent quinine."[85] This facility, which was established in the latter half of the last century, remained in operation until after the Second World War. Since then

Peruvian bark tree (chincona) plantation, soon after it was introduced in the Nilgiris ca. 1860. After The Illustrated London News.

cheaper chemical substitutes have replaced chincona in the production of quinine and other medicines.

By the middle of the 19th century, the English concentrated on tea, which started to overtake all other commercial crops. Captain George Powell Thomas of the 64th regiment Bengal Infantry, who painted the *Views of Simla* published by Dickinson & Son, London, 1846, gives a very good account of the early British experiment with tea planting in the western Himalayas:

"Our first experiments in the cultivation of the Tea plant on the low hills and in the valleys of the sub-Himalayas, were made as recently as 1836. Yet, already, there are eight flourishing nurseries in Garhwal, and four in Kumaon, all of which produce Tea of a good and constantly improving quality; and in Kumaon alone, the number of plants sufficiently matured to yield Tea (though for the first three years the leaves are unfit for use) was last year 3,008,122. The quantity of Tea produced in all the nurseries under notice is steadily increasing, and it would be difficult to define the limits of its future extension and improvement. With regard to the area of production – it appears that the extension of these tea nurseries in the sub-Himalayas may proceed in any quarter at an elevation from 3,000 to 5,000 feet above the level of the sea... Such are the capabilities of the country, so cheap is human labour, so accessible is river carriage, (not to speak of railroad in prospect), and lastly, so decided has been the success of these experiments, that the belief has become general, and seems well founded, that in a few years tea will constitute by far the most important of all exports from upper India. The teas thus produced will probably be equal ere long, both in strength and flavour, to the best teas of China, and they will *certainly* be producible at one half the cost of those."[86]

Captain Thomas's rave reports and his sketches of the high life in Simla must have attracted a few planters to India. Moreover, the passage of the Charter Act of 1833 opened India for others from Britain. Until the passage of the Act, the East India Company had absolute control over the immigration of Europeans to India. The Company officials did not approve of non-officials and "used their powers of deportation frequently against people whom they regarded as undesirable."[87] The size of the European population in India had remained small until the passage of this Act. The groups which took immediate advantage of this change in rule were often the ones whom the Company had worked hard to keep out: missionaries, businessmen, and planters.

Like the pattern books, travel guides were an ideal source of information for prospective planters about the potential of specific hill resorts and their settlement practices. The numerous Darjeeling guides surely played a role in the development of the resort. The early Darjeeling guides such as Samuel Smith (1845) deal, at length, with the land, how to settle, local regulations, paper production, and includes a gardening calendar. Smith's guide also provides information on the type of schooling available for European children, with prices for special musical and painting lessons above the cost of lodging and boarding. Captain J.G. Hathorn's guide (Calcutta, 1863), contains a considerable amount of information on tea planting, and building costs. G.S. Bomwetsch's handbook (1899) contains a wonderful account of the mountain railway which connected Darjeeling with the plains but has no information about starting a tea plantation. G.P. Robertson's guide (1913) addressed to travellers, gives information about short trips outside Darjeeling, travel routes and local facilities. While the nineteenth century guides were aimed at new settlers, K.C. Bhanja's guide (1941) is similar to Robertson's, a typical aide for short-term travellers, yet it includes information about the schools and educational facilities of the station. Guide books contained plenty of domestic information. Hull and Mair's *Anglo-Indian's Vade-Mecum and Medical Guide* advises settlers on how to maintain English tastes at breakfast; a job far easier in the hill resorts than on the plains:

> "Butter is an article difficult to procure of good quality except on the hills, where it is sold by the European settlers who make dairy-keeping contribute to their support. The native tendency is to palm off buffalo butter for that made from cow's milk... Native-sold milk is largely watered..., butter... coloured with turmeric."
> "Eggs are plentiful but very small and... flavourless as compared with English ones. In making puddings, cakes, etc., allowance must be made... putting in two of every one mentioned in an English... cookery book. Many people keep English fowls by this means securing fine fresh eggs for the breakfast table... "

A note of warning is sounded too:

> " 'Country' ham and bacon may be priced low...; I would here warn the Anglo-Indian housekeeper,

that it is as a rule unfit for food, unless reared and cured by European settlers on the hills."[88]

Hill resorts matured and evolved with time. By looking at generations of guide books, we see how important stations like Simla became the centre of the colonial empire. Darjeeling and its surrounding hills took over the hill resorts of Garhwal and Kangra as the centre of the tea industry; smaller cantonment stations like Sabathu and Abbotabad grew as army cantonments. With some variations in character, the hill resorts continued to attract the colonial rulers because of one main constant element: the climate. Describing the climate of Simla, Captain Thomas wrote:

> "From March, when the sleet and snow may be said to have passed away, to the middle of July, the climate is heavenly. There is nothing like it on earth. Nothing! Nothing in Italy! Nothing in France! Nothing anywhere that I know of. Recall the fairest day, nay hour, of sunshine you have ever known in English spring, and conceive the beauty and gladness of that sunshine, brightened by continuing without a storm, almost without a shower, daily *for months together;* and deck the fruit trees and bushes in a thousand English blossoms; and spread violets and daisies, and strawberry blossoms, and wild roses, and anemones, thickly, over the bright close emerald turf; over crags amid the pine roots, and far away down amid the ferns beside the 'runnels,' and you may fancy something of what our Simla spring and brief summer are. And then, alas, come the rains!"[89]

Even rain was delectable for Lord Lytton. During an official visit to Ootacamund, where it rains more than in Simla, Lord Lytton wrote in a letter to his wife Lady Betty Balfour:

> "The Duke drove me in his ponney (pony) carriage this morning to the first stage of our journey hither. The morning was fine and for the first time I have seen Ootacamund. Having seen it, I affirm it to be the paradise, and declare without hesitation that in every particular it far surpasses all that its most enthusiastic admirers and devoted lovers have said to us about it. The afternoon was rainy and the road muddy, but such beautiful English rain such delicious English mud. Imagine Hertfordshire lanes, Devonshire downs, Westmoreland lakes, Scotch trout streams, and Lusitanian views!"[90]

To the climate, the British added imagination and determination. It was the combination of the three, which recreated the idyllic English countryside in the hills of India, and made the hill resorts a true home away from home.

Simla: The Abode of "the High and the Mighty"

Though the argosies of Asia at Her doors
Heap their stores,
Though Her enterprise and energy secure
Income sure,
Though "out-station orders punctually obeyed"
Swell Her trade –
Still, for rule, administration, and the rest,
Simla's best;[1]

From "A Tale of Two Cities" by Rudyard Kipling

A Tale of Two Cities is about Calcutta and Simla, the two administrative capitals of British India. When Kipling wrote the poem, Calcutta was the most important city in India and perhaps the second most important city of the British Empire, with its buildings, boulevards, commerce, social life modelled after the imperial city of London. However, the spectacular setting of Simla, sitting above 7,000 feet (2,154 metres) among tall deodar trees with a backdrop of the snow-capped Himalayas, dispels any doubts about Kipling's choice of Simla over Calcutta.

Kipling's poem belongs to his early career, the period between 1882 and 1889, when he worked in India as a journalist. By then Simla had clearly become an integral part of the high social life of the British living in India, and Kipling, in venerating it, was only confirming the legitimacy of their foremost resort. When composing these lines, Kipling was perhaps reminiscing about the ride that he once took as an aspiring author, along the Simla Mall, with Lord Roberts, at that time the Commander-in-Chief of the Indian army. In *Something of Myself* Kipling described this ride as "the proudest moment of my young life."[2]

The Beginning

As early as 1827, the Governor-General of India, Lord Amherst, had spent a summer in Simla, and set the tone for the future development of this town. Until Amherst's visit, the hill tract that later developed as Simla was used for hunting, and as a place to convalesce, primarily by the officers and invalids of the East India Company's army stationed in Sabathu. Situated at an elevation of 4,750 feet (1,462 metres) with a commanding view of the plains, Sabathu was strategically important as an army cantonment. It also served as the seat of the Assistant Political Agent in charge of those hill states brought under Company control after the 1814-15 Gurkha war.

The Simla ridge, which stretches from the lofty, 8,048 foot (2,476 metre) high Jakho mountain in the east to the Observatory and Prospect Hills in the west, is visible from Sabathu. Lieutenant Ross, the Assistant Political Agent in charge of Sabathu, frequented the wooded Simla ridge and was the first European to build a thatched cottage there. In the same vicinity, in 1822, Captain Charles Pratt Kennedy, who had served as the Garrison Officer under Ross and succeeded him as the

Early days of Sabathu, ca. 1860. Photograph by Samuel Bourne. The British Library.

Previous pages: View of Simla from Mashu (Mashobra), by G.P. Thomas, ca. 1840. The British Library.

Political Agent, built the first permanent structure at Simla, and called it Kennedy House.

It was Kennedy House in which Lord Amherst stayed during his visit to Simla. While it is recorded that the Governor-General and his entourage needed 1,700 coolies to transport themselves and their belongings to the town,[3] there is no account of how and where the 1,700 coolies lived. It is known, however, that in the late 1820s Simla had fewer than 30 structures,[4] and to accommodate the Governor-General's staff, half a dozen new buildings had to be erected.[5] Amherst's visit immediately placed Simla, until then an insignificant little hill settlement, on the Anglo-Indian social map.[6] "The climate of Simla soon became famous; invalids from the plains resorted there, and built houses – instead of breaking up establishments and sailing for the Cape of Good Hope, with little hope of reaching it; – and finally Simla was rendered fashionable

Roads in the Himalayas are "impracticable, except for mules and men stimulated by curiosity," wrote Victor Jacquemont in the early 19th century. More than 150 years later, communications in the Himalayas remain very difficult. The rugged landscape and vastness of the mountains render any human endeavour insignificant by comparison.

by the Governor-General, Lord Amherst, who resided there with his family for several months, and brought back to Calcutta rosy complexions, and some beautiful drawings by Lady Sarah Amherst, to attest the healthful and picturesque properties of the spot."[7]

The following year, Lord Combermere, was the first Commander-in-Chief to visit Simla. Like Amherst, Combermere stayed at Kennedy House. From the beginning of 1822 to 1830, when Victor Jacquemont stayed with Captain Kennedy, Simla had developed into a prosperous little resort. Jacquemont, Travelling Naturalist to the Museum of Natural History, Paris, undertook a journey in the British Dominions of India, Tibet, Lahore, and Kashmir under the order of the French Government during the years 1828 to 1831. The first decade of Simla's successful and rapid development and its unique social life is probably best summed up in Jacquemont's letters to his father and to Madame Victor de Tracy, in Paris. In a letter to his father, dated 21 June 1830, at Simla, Jacquemont wrote:

"This place, like Mont-d'or or Bagnères (Bagnieres), is the resort of the rich, the idle, and the sick. The officer (Jacquemont's host Captain Kennedy) entrusted with the military, political, judicial, and financial service of this extremity of the British Empire, acquired only fifteen years ago, bethought himself, only nine years since, of leaving his place in the plain, during the heats of a terrible summer, and pitching his tent under the shade of the cedar trees. He was alone in the desert; some friends came to visit him there. The situation, and climate, appeared to them admirable. Some hundreds of mountaineers were summoned, who felled the trees around, squared them rudely, and, assisted by workmen from the plains, in one month built a spacious house. Each guest wished also to have one; and now there are upward of sixty scattered over the peaks of the mountains or on their declivities. Thus a considerable village has arisen, as it were by enchantment, in the centre of the space they occupy. Beautiful roads have been cut through the rock; and at a distance of seven hundred leagues from Calcutta, and seven thousand feet above the level of the sea, the luxury of the Indian capital has established itself, and fashion maintains its tyrannical sway...

"We gallop an hour or two in the morning on the magnificent roads which he has made, often joining some elegant cavalcade, in which I meet many of my Calcutta acquaintances... At sunset fresh horses are at the door, and we take another ride, to enlist the most friendly and lively of the rich idlers and imaginary invalids whom we may chance to

Grand Masonic banquet in honour of Charles Napier in Simla, ca. 1840. After The Illustrated London News.

meet... We sit down to a magnificent dinner at half-past seven, and rise at eleven. I drink Hock, Claret, and Champagne only, and Malmsey at dessert; the others, alleging the coldness of the climate, stick to Port, Sherry, and Madeira. I do not recollect having tasted water for the last seven days."[8]

So magic was the atmosphere and the air at Simla! The social mood was even more magic, and life buoyant and elegant. Jacquemont in his letter of June 24th 1830 to Madame Victor de Tracy wrote:

"...although the road to it seems impracticable, except for mules and men stimulated by curiosity; although it must be reached by a march of several days through a thousand difficulties: nevertheless your countrywomen[9] come here and spend whole months during the summer, thereby avoiding the insupportable heat of the plains. Braving the wild and sterile solitude of the desert, they mount their horses every morning and evening in very elegant costumes, adorned with ribands, and without the omission of a single pin. They could not be better dressed in Hyde Park."[10]

The Frenchman, who on a limited budget could not have completed his trip without the generous support from his English hosts in India, had reasons to be impressed. Charles Mundy emphasised the more important practical aspects of a pure, cold atmosphere:

"We have reason to be thankful that we are here far elevated above the atmospheric strata that have hitherto been subject to the cholera, a disease now raging in Calcutta... The salubrity of this abode of Hygeia is well attested by the presence of no less than 16 ladies, who generally embrace the inconveniences attendant ...for the advantages accruing from the climate to themselves and their children. The cheeks of the latter quickly exchange their mealy, muffin-like hue – the livery of Bengal – for good healthy ruddy bronze."[11]

Governor-General Amherst made Simla fashionable, but his successor Lord William Bentinck acquired it for the British and placed it under direct British jurisdiction.[12] The British elite adored Simla and they needed to expand their pleasure ground. In 1830 the Maharajah of Patiala was asked to give four villages near Simla in exchange for seven villages around Bharauli, and the Rajah of Keonthal made to part with 12 Simla area villages in exchange for lands near Ravin.[13] The six square mile area which thus emerged formed the territory of Simla. It was surrounded by three princely states: Patiala to the north and west, Keonthal to the south and east, and Koti, which included the suburbs of Sanjauli, Mashobra, Kufri, and Naldehra, to the north-east.

The oldest known map of Simla, ca. 1830. The British Library.

The earliest known map of Simla,[14] presumably prepared soon after the British acquired the station, shows five properties along the main ridge; Kennedy House is in the middle, the Governor-General's and Captain Robert's residences are to its east, and Gorton Castle and Captain Turner's residence to its west. Not marked as such, but indicated as the Governor-General's residence, is Bentinck Castle which Lord Bentinck had built for himself on the spur. Simla was well on its way to becoming the paramount summer resort of British India.

When a Governor-General retired, or was replaced, he invariably returned to England. Consequently one might assume that building Bentinck Castle would have solved the housing needs of the ambitious Governor-Generals who followed Bentinck to Simla, but the opposite is true.

From Fort William in Calcutta the Governor-Generals of India administered an enormous business empire and vast territories, accumulating unprecedented amounts of wealth and power. As early as 1783, E. Burke, speaking in the Houses of Parliament on the East India

Company Bill, put the Company holdings in India in a European perspective. "If I were to take the whole aggregate of our possessions there, I should compare it as the nearest parallel I could find to the Empire of Germany; our immediate possessions I should compare with the Austrian dominions, and they would not suffer in the comparison. The Nabob of Oude might stand for the King of Prussia; the Nabob of Arcot I would compare, as superior in territory and equal in revenue, to the Elector of Saxony. The Rajah of Benares might well rank with the Prince of Hesse, at least; and the Rajah of Tanjore (though hardly equal in extent of dominion, superior in revenue) with the Elector of Bavaria."[15] The Governor-General controlled the above mentioned principalities, as well as many smaller possessions, their land revenues, and the entire trade of the East India Company. In today's context, such abundance of power and wealth is impressive: it could only be attained if the CEO of the world's largest multi-national corporation was simultaneously a head of state – an improbable concept.

Characteristically, between 1827 and 1862, each Governor-General visited Simla at least once during his tenure, and all but two of them chose different homes from their predecessors. Of course, these were no ordinary summer cottages. Built in an era when public accountability of Company officials was rather limited,[16] these were distinctive made-to-order retreats. The chronology of the residences built for different Governor-Generals in Simla is interesting.

As mentioned earlier, Lord Amherst stayed at Kennedy House. Lord Bentinck was so particular about residing only in his new home in Simla that, while Bentinck Castle was under construction, he spent a summer in Ootacamund in south India. Lord Auckland, who replaced Bentinck[17] chose yet another property. Initially, it was known as Government House, but soon after Lord Auckland moved in, it came to be known as Auckland House. The two Governor-Generals who followed Auckland, Lords Ellenborough and Hardinge, were satisfied with this residence. The next occupants of Auckland House were Lord and Lady Dalhousie. Although Lady Dalhousie was "charmed with the house, the place and everything about it,"[18] the Dalhousies were not content with having only one property. At various times they sojourned at Strawberry Hill, Kennedy House, and a cottage at Mahasu – the last may have been

Peterhoff, the summer residence of the Governer-General at Simla ca. 1860. After The Illustrated London News.

The main entrance, Viceregal Lodge. The Lodge is a rambling Scottish baronial building designed by Henry Irvine.

Wildflower Hall.[19] Lord Canning, who followed Dalhousie, stayed at Barnes Court,[20] and Lord Elgin, who came after, stayed at Peterhoff.

One year after the Mutiny of 1857 the administration of India was transferred from the East India Company to the Crown. The Governor-General was also made the Crown's Viceroy, and reported directly to the newly appointed Secretary of State for India.[21] The new administration regularised housing for the Governor-General and Viceroy in Simla. In 1862, Lord Elgin moved into the new official residence, Peterhoff, which remained the official Viceregal residence until 1888, when the Viceregal Lodge was built on Observatory hill. The Viceregal Lodge was in official use longer than any other residence: from 1888 until the departure of the British from India in 1947.

Places of the High and the Mighty

A number of the beautiful original residences described here have survived, and some have fared better than others. With the historical records and literature available it is possible to explore these splendid and important homes of the high and mighty.

Approaching Simla from the plains either by road or by train, the traveller first sees the Viceregal Lodge from a distance. The Lodge is an obvious structure, located at the western end of the Simla ridge, wearing an onion dome half hidden by tall deodar woods. It is the only building in Simla occupying a hill to itself, standing in absolute contrast against the crowded Simla ridge. The building exemplifies British rule in India: the Viceroy, epitome of power, stands alone, proud and aloof, overlooking crowded Simla and the mass of his subjects.

VICEREGAL LODGE, SIMLA
WEST AND EAST ELEVATION

WEST ELEVATION

SCALE OF FEET
5' 0 5' 10' 15' 20' 25' 30' 35' 40' 45' 50'

Elevation and section, Viceregal Lodge. The mechanical facilities of the Lodge, such as the power plant (the Lodge was the first Government building in India to have a full electric network), boiler room and laundry, are accommodated in a five-storey wing neatly tucked in the side of a natural slope below the main Lodge structure. The British Library.

The Viceregal Lodge, a rambling Scottish baronial building designed by Henry Irvine, architect to the Public Works Department, India, was criticised abundantly by its hosts. Lady Curzon found its appearance a trifle ludicrous – a building in which a "Minneapolis millionaire would delight."[22] Conceivably it was her criticism that prompted her husband to alter the appearance of the ostentatious Lodge; Lord Curzon had the external tower raised, because it was out of proportion, and he spent considerable sums on correcting defects in the structure. The renovations were not all that successful, as the Secretary of State for India, Lord Montague, thought it resembled "a Scottish hydro,"[23] while someone else compared it to "Pentonville Prison."[24]

It would be a mistake to take these critics at face value, because Lord Montague also admitted that he disliked mountains and the life in Simla. "Four hours round the hairpin curves is very tiring... I myself am not fond of the hills, they obscure the view, and the sight of snow-capped mountains does not please me... We went up to Government House (the Viceregal Lodge) in rickshaws, a form of conveyance which I, personally, find most distasteful."[25] Imagine arriving at the main entrance of the great Viceregal Lodge pulled by a barefoot rickshaw-wallah barely able to breathe and still remain objective about the edifice in front. Hence, in spite of these criticisms, the Lodge should be on the "must see" list of every visitor to Simla.

This palatial structure has a stately, well ordered sequence of spaces. A leisurely entry, through the south facing entrance portico with a view of extensive verandas on either side, brings the visitor into the reception hall. The hall is marked by a grand staircase, which springs from the right as one enters, and spirals up three full

EAST ELEVATION

HENRY IRWIN, M.I.C.E., C.I.E.
Architect
The Hon'ble L.M.ST.CLAIR,A.M.I.C.E.,
Executive Engineer

Following pages:
The Viceregal Lodge, Simla. Today the building serves as the home of the Indian Institute of Advanced Study.

This splendid staircase circumscribes the entrance hall of the Viceregal Lodge, *left* and the gallery of the Viceregal palace at Simla.

floors. Facing the entry to the hall and functioning almost like a magnet drawing the visitors forward is the grand fireplace which is at the top end of the gallery. The gallery is the principal space of the building, around which all major functions are organised. It is only 18 feet wide, soars through three floors of well-appointed teak panelling up to an attractive top-lit ceiling. The state drawing room, ballroom, and the wood-panelled dining room, decorated with the coats of arms of former Governors-General and Viceroys, lead to the gallery at the lower level. These beautiful spaces are designed as a set-piece to function in

concert with one another. The two floors of private bedrooms above and living suites with a wrap-around galleria unite this space exquisitely.

Verandas and terraces surround the entire building at different levels; those at the lower level link the Lodge to the magnificent grounds while the upper ones provide superb views of the lower foothills to the west, and the mid-Himalayan ranges to the north and north-east. Views of the early morning sun lighting up the snow-clad Himalayas, and colourful sunsets, which can be secured from different terraces of the Lodge, are glor-

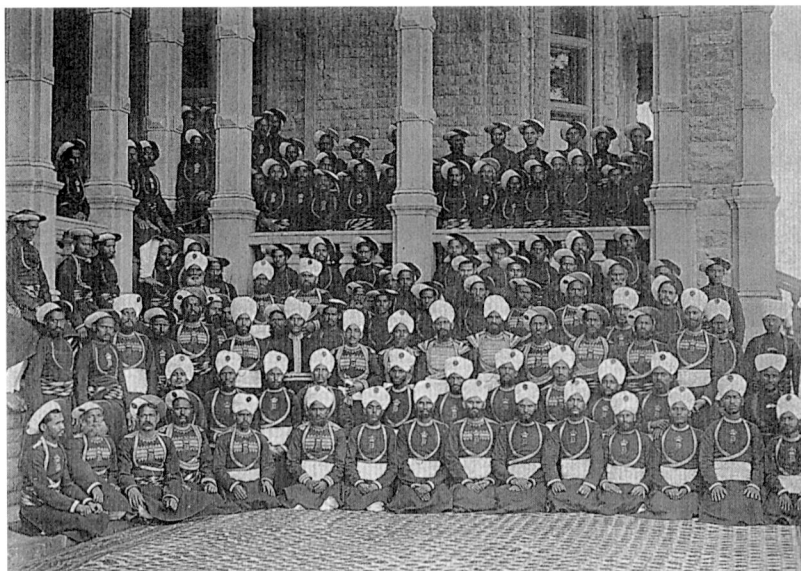

A battery of servants was required to maintain the Viceroy and his Viceregal Lodge at Simla; photograph ca. 1888.

The Retreat, Mashobra, six miles from Simla. Originally the house of Sir Hugh Rose, and later the weekend residence of the Viceroy, it is now used as the summer residence of the President of India. Photograph by Samuel Bourne, ca. 1860. The British Library.

ious. Even Lady Curzon, who found the building itself a "trifle ludicrous,"[26] was ready to live on the same views for five years.

The Viceregal Lodge was the first Government building in India to have a full electric network and its own power generation. The Lodge had extensive facilities, including kitchens, separate rooms for storing table linen, plate, china, and glass, laundry, an enormous wine cellar, a room for empty cases, boilers for central heating, running hot and cold water for bathrooms, and so on. All these facilities were accommodated in a five-storey mechanical wing arranged on the side of a natural slope below the main Lodge structure.

Following Independence, the Viceregal Lodge remained in use as the summer retreat for the President of India, renamed Rashtrapati Nivas, Hindi for the President's Residence. In the early 1960s the President of India, Dr. S. Radhakrishnan, a leading philosopher and writer, and the Prime Minister Jawharlal Nehru decided to establish an Institute for humanistic studies.[27] The Rashtrapati Nivas was to become the home of the proposed institution, and the President of India shifted his summer residence to the Retreat at Mashobra, about six miles from Simla, and it is still used as such. The newly formed "Indian Institute of Advanced Study" moved into the Lodge in 1965, and remains there to this day.

Some of the beautiful interiors of the Lodge were sacrificed to accommodate changes required for the Institute; the state drawing room, ball-room, and dining room, for example, were converted into a rather poorly conceived Institute library. Without the contingent of Viceregal servants, or Presidential resources, this large estate and the Lodge lack maintenance and animation. At the time of my visit the building needed major repairs. I was delighted to learn from the Director of the Institute, however, that they intend to restore the building.

In Simla, the splendid structures of Peterhoff and Wildflower Hall were less fortunate: both were destroyed by fire. Peterhoff was used as the residence of the Governor of the newly formed state of Himachal Pradesh, but burnt down in 1981. A new hotel building was under construction on its site at the time of my visit. Wildflower Hall, located about seven miles outside Simla, operated as a hotel until 1993. A lonely chimney, standing defiantly against the snow-clad Himalayas, is the only remnant of a once splendid edifice.

One of the most famous buildings in Simla, Barnes Court, was originally acquired as the official residence of the Lieutenant-Governor of Punjab in 1879. "Set in spacious gardens, probably no other house in Simla reproduced so convincingly the familiar landscape of an English country house."[28] This half-timbered building has a Moorish ball-room, and is enriched with decorations designed by John Lockwood Kipling, Rudyard's father, and Principal of the Mayo School of Art in Lahore.[29] An important feature of the interior decor is the extensive use of the coat of arms of the Punjab state, integrated ingeniously in the ceiling decorations, above mantelpieces, and wall friezes. The emblem bears five waving diagonal stripes, connoting the five main rivers of the region (the name *punjab*, also means five-waters, a combination of two words: *punj* = five, and *ab* = waters). The other elements on the crest, the rising sun, vine leaves, and fruit, symbolise a bright future and prosperity.

Barnes Court housed various statesmen, and visiting dignitaries. Lord Napier, Colin Campbell, General Anson, and Sir Hugh Rose lived there. After Independence it was used as the official Government Guest House. Barnes Court was also the site of the historic "Simla Peace Accord" signing between President Zulfikarali Bhutto of Pakistan, and Indian Prime Minister

The Coat-of-arms of Punjab, designed by John Lockwood Kipling, father of Rudyard Kipling, is used as decoration throughout Barnes Court, Simla.

Indira Gandhi in 1972. The room in which the accord was signed is adorned with photographs marking this historic event. In 1993, however, the Governor of Himachal Pradesh took it over as his own residence.

General neglect and inadequate maintenance diminish both the buildings and the garden. Nevertheless, Barnes Court merits a visit, though one needs special permission from the Governor's Secretariat.

Auckland House, named after its most famous resident, went through several conversions: first it was transformed into a boarding-house, then into a hotel, and finally, in 1868, into a girls' school.[30] Originally known as the Punjab Girls' School it became the Auckland House School after its move from Jakho Hill to its present premises.

Lord Auckland secured his estate in 1838 from Doctor Blake, a surgeon in the East India Company's service. After obtaining a grant of land from the Political Agent in Sabathu, Blake had built two houses in Simla: a large one,

Barnes Court, Simla, from its garden.

which Lord Auckland and his two sisters, Frances and Emily Eden, occupied, and, a stone's throw away, a smaller one in which Lord Auckland's nephew, Captain William Osborne stayed.[31] Osborne was also the Military Secretary, and for some time, the smaller house was called the "Secretary's Lodge."

Auckland House sits on Elysium Hill, named after Emily and Frances Eden. The two sisters kept journals and sketched extensively during their stay in India. In her letters to her family back home, Emily Eden described their journey through upper India, including the seven month long stay at Auckland House in Simla.

These letters were published as a two-volume set entitled *Up the Country.* In the Introduction, in a letter to her nephew Lord William Osborne, Emily Eden regretfully wrote about their sad fate: "... you and I are now almost the only survivors of the large party that in 1838 left Government House for the Upper Provinces."[32]

A large party it indeed was that took Lord Auckland and his convoy across the plains of northern India, and up to Simla. For the first leg of the journey on the Ganges river, from Calcutta to a little beyond Benares, the convoy needed two steamers and a flat. Further inland, they required "elephants, two or three hundred

The Entrance porch, *above left,* Banquet hall, *above right,* and the Living room, *below,* Barnes Court, Simla. The Living room served as the venue for the historic "Simla Peace Accord" signed between President Zulfikarali Bhutto of Pakistan, and Indian Prime Minister Indira Gandhi in 1972.

baggage camels (they are much larger beasts to *live with* than I thought), bullock carts without end, and everybody loading every conveyance with everything."[33] On land, the Governor-General and his sisters, had three private tents, each divided into bed-room, dressing room, and sitting room, and great covered passages, leading from one tent to another. Opposite the private tents were the great dining tent and the durbar tent. In spite of this elaborate network of well-furnished tents, the first evening for Emily Eden "was more uncomfortable than" she had "ever fancied," and she thought she "never had seen such squalid, melancholy discomfort."[34]

To pitch, un-pitch, pack, load, unload, unpack, and pitch again, all those tents, and to move belongings of the Auckland party required in addition to elephants, camels – the number of which had swollen to 850 by the time they reached Allahabad – hundreds of horses, bullock carts, and 12,000 people. In this way, the Auckland convoy travelled from October 1837 to March 1840. Excluding their seven-month stay in Simla their journey had thus lasted almost two years. The building of the *Titanic* and its slightly smaller sister ship the *Olympic*, which required a workforce of 14,000 people and two years, is almost equivalent in terms of the time and human resources required to keep the Auckland party on the move.[35] Looking at it all, reminded Emily Eden of the Israelites crossing the Red Sea. Its rendering, by Mrs. Trimmers at Stafford House, was described by Emily Eden as "a skimpy representation" compared to "the real thing."[36] In the end this major undertaking brought some rewards:

"Well, it really is worth all the trouble – such a beautiful place – and our house, that everybody has been abusing, only wanting all the good furniture and carpets we have brought, to be quite perfection. Views only too lovely; deep valleys on the drawing-room side to the west, and snowy ranges on the dining-room side, where my room also is. Our sitting-rooms are

"Rolled up tentwallas," by Fenny (Francis) Eden, ca. 1830. After Janet Dunbar, *Golden Interlude: The Edens in India 1836-1842.*

small, but that is all the better in this climate, and the two principal rooms are very fine. The climate! No wonder I could not live down below! We never were allowed a scrap of air to breath – now I come back to the air again I remember all about it. It is a cool sort of stuff, refreshing, sweet, and apparently pleasant to the lungs. We have fires in every room, and the windows open; red rhododendron trees in bloom in every direction, and beautiful walks like English shrubberies cut on all sides of the hills. Good! I see this to be the best part of India."[37]

It was all worth it for that "cool sort of stuff." After enduring the oppressive heat of the Indian plains Emily and her sister had finally reached the promised land, and stepped into their own garden of Eden.

An observer, with a keen sense of humor wrote: "Like meat, we *keep* better here," Emily Eden provides useful information about the housing conditions of their native servants. In her correspondence she admits that unlike the Europeans, "all native servants are, or have been sick,"[38] but it did not surprise her. Since reaching Simla they had built only "twenty small houses, and lodged fifty servants in those outhouses." However, "there were actually sixty-seven who had no lodging provided for,"[39] and as a temporary measure were housed in tents. They were eventually moved into new houses finished before the rains.

When the time came to leave, Emily Eden lamented the fact that everybody went away at the same time: not enough coolies could be raised at the last moment, and instead of 3,000 at once, they needed 1,000 three times over to move their belongings, thus prolonging their discomfort. As if offering a final parting gift, on the first day of their return trip Emily Eden wrote: "We left poor Simla at six this morning, and if I am to be in India I had rather be there, than anywhere."[40]

From the time she began writing in 1838, to 1866 when her letters were first published, Emily Eden recognised the changes which were taking place in India.

In her introductory letter all discomforts, and hardships of the tour were forgotten and as seen earlier she was concerned about "the curse of railroads."[41] Ironically, the best way to enjoy the red rhododendron blooms around Simla today is to take the train ride up from Kalka in spring. Although stripped of its glamour and surrounding foliage, Auckland House, poised and perched on the spur with a view of the Simla ridge remains magnificent today. Lady Wilson, like Emily Eden, a prolific letter writer wrote "How do we like Simla? My dear child, how do you like Life? I suppose most people would answer the same question in the same way, 'Sometimes very much. Sometimes not at all'." But on her return to Simla her attitude was much more positive:

> "We had such a cheery homecoming. The house had been dressed up to look at its best, repainted and polished, with flowers everywhere, and our chairs drawn up by the drawing-room fireplace, the tea-table set, while Komal's best scones and his crispest toast were brought in by the smiling butler, before we had time to sit down."[42]

The Secretary's Lodge, adjoining the main house, and forming an integral part of the original estate, is well preserved. The Secretary's Lodge came into prominence as the venue for signing the "Afghan Manifesto," the declaration of the first war against Afghanistan, while still occupied by William Osborne. The Afghan campaign proved to be grievous for British soldiers on the front, and also for the reputation of both Lord Auckland and Osborne, but it bypassed the building itself. Afterwards General Peter Innes purchased the Secretary's Lodge and named it Chapslee. Over the years the property has changed hands many times: General Pamberton, General Sir C.E. Nairne, Surgeon General A.F. Bradshaw, Surgeon General J. Cleghorn were its occupants, just to name a few,[43] but it has retained the name Chapslee. Since 1930, Chapslee belongs to the family of the Rajah of Kapurthala who acquired it from the heirs of Sir Arthur Ker, Manager of the Alliance Bank of Simla.[44]

The Kapurthala family resides at Chapslee, and transformed it into a hotel in 1976. Chapslee is very well maintained, richly decorated with "heirlooms such as Gobelin tapestries, rare textiles and cabinetry from the Doge's palace in Venice, chandeliers from Morano, blue pottery jardinieres from Multan, Peshwa vases, Persian carpets, marble statuary and collections of Indian object d'arts."[45] It is a fitting example of what the resorts of the Raj were all about.

Chapslee, essentially oriented east-west, sits on the crest of a small hill. The southern side of the slope accommadates a garden terrace, croquet lawn, and tennis court. This arrangement permits guests to enjoy

March of troops en-route for the plains from their hill station. This picture evokes memories of Emily Eden's descriptions of their journey through Upper India. After The Illustrated London News.

The best way to enjoy the red rhododendron blooms around Simla is to take the train ride up from Kalka in spring.

Living room, Chapslee, Simla.

Formal dining room, Chapslee, Simla.

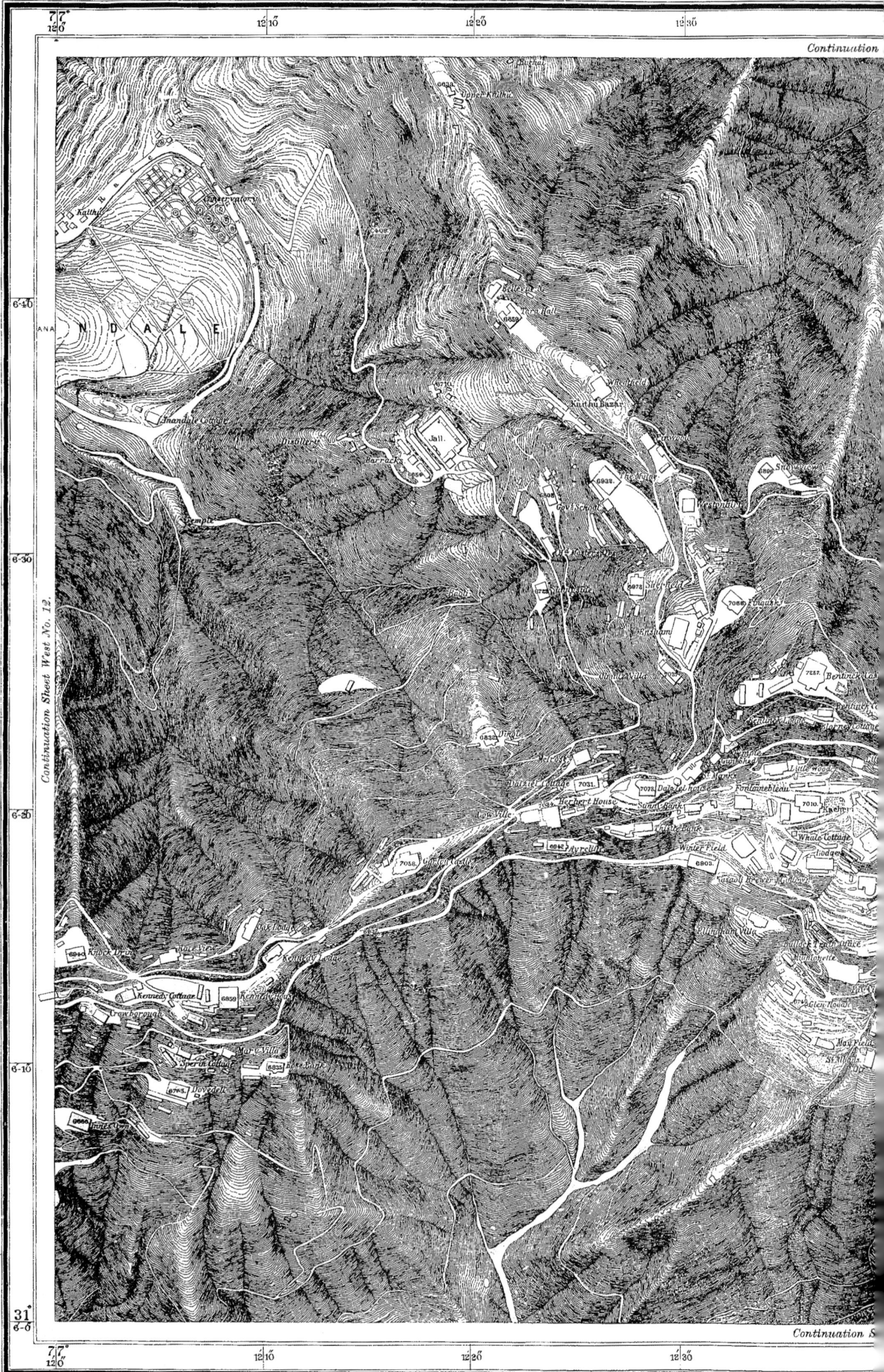

Continuation

Upper Kaithu

NDALE

ANA

Kaithu

Conservatory

Annandale Cottage

Kaithu Bazar

Wheatfield

Jail

Barracks

Summerhill

Chadwick

Summerhill

Sutcliffe

Fagu's

Chadwick

Bentinck

Little Wood

Dale Cottage

Fontannebleau

Herbert House

Sunny Bank

Dingle

Low Ville

Nychele

Whale Cottage

Winter Field

Clyde Castle

Oak Lodge

Rose Villa

Kipling Lodge

Kennedy Lodge

Kennedy Cottage

Kennedy

Craigborough

Mont Villa

Sperin Cottage

Rose Cottage

Bayrock

Continuation Sheet West No. 12.

Breakfast room, Chapslee, Simla.

Morning room, Chapslee, Simla.

the sun, while using any of the facilities, throughout the day. Yet another, and perhaps greater pleasure of Chapslee (and also of the adjoining Auckland House, however tattered) is to watch from the terrace, the sun set over the Simla ridge, and observe the Mall lights come on at twilight.

The Mall

In the heyday of their rule, British officers in their uniforms, *memsahibs* in beautiful gowns carrying elegant parasols, and proud nannies behind baby prams, populated the Mall. The Mall, a fairly level meandering esplanade that runs along the ridge, is the centre of main social activities. There, tourists mingle with uniformed school children and residents of Simla. An amazing multitude of honeymooners, the bright and beautifully clad young couples, who flock to this hill resort from all over India, stand there to be photographed.

Several generations of British couples initiated the promenade tradition when Simla was at the top of the list for attracting the socialites, especially of the amorous type. Generally the proportion of European women to men here far exceeded the ratio in the plains. Some men rejoined their wives after long absences, others flocked to meet their future spouse and others came here in search of adventure. Opportunities for romance were plenty. It was an ideal playground for courting. Among themselves, in this intoxicating vacation atmosphere the social codes of conduct were more relaxed. The ruling elite who assumed a strict official guise in public in the plains could free themselves without losing their prestige. Occasionally they indulged in gambling, drinking and licentious behaviour causing rumours of all sorts which were immortalised by gossips and story tellers like Kipling. The artist Prinsep observed: "I am very much amused at the English habits joyfully resumed by the visitors to Simla. Down in the plains they say that you always know the 'Griff' or new arrival, by his morning salutation of 'Fine day.' It is always fine in India... In Simla however, the weather is the principal topic of conversation and anxiety, for the rain occupies everyone's thoughts. No wonder! The health of Simla depends on it."[46]

As a background to these encounters were the sublime vistas of the Himalayas, the Gaiety Theatre, the bandstand which was a popular meeting point and other structures. "Our band played again yesterday at their new place, and it is a most successful attempt for the good society, very much aided by the goodness of the strawberry ice... The strawberries here are quite as fine as in England, but they last a very short time."[47] Most buildings reflected the "good society" of the British era. That social order is still visible to anyone who takes a leisurely walk along the Mall. The clump of buildings on the ridge, visible from the Chapslee terrace, are almost at the mid point, and form the core of the Mall. The important civic amenities of Simla, which comprise Christ Church, the public library, the gazebo-like bandstand, a Victorian theatre, the town hall, the general post office, and the Presbyterian Church, are clustered around the core. The Mall, which stretches for a couple of miles in either direction from the core, terminates at Barnes Court on the eastern end and the Viceregal Lodge at the western. The main bazaar is concentrated in the middle two-thirds of the Mall, while the native bazaar, a rabbit warren of streets and alleys supported precariously on the steep southern slope, cascades below it. The gracious bungalows, bearing names like Woodville, Forest Hill, Benmore Estate, Glen View, Daisy Bank, Glengarry, Hydevale and Fir Hill are scattered around Barnes Court, on the lower slopes of Jakho hill. There are others on the slopes along the western half of the Mall as well.

Large buildings, which defy the small domestic order of Simla, are concentrated at both ends of the market section of the Mall. At the eastern end are several large hotels, and to the west, hotels and a scattering of administrative buildings such as the Railway Board Building, the Army Headquarters Building, Gorton Castle, and the Telephone Exchange.

Henry Irwin designed the Railway Board and the Army Headquarters buildings, using cast iron and steel elements in combination with native wood and brick. In the Railway Board building he made remarkably judicious use of materials: precast elements to attain speed in the erection of the building frame and maximise use of native materials as infill to reduce the transporting of materials from the plains. In 1904, the Government Secretariat activities were consolidated in the recently completed Gorton Castle. This sinister looking building would serve as an ideal set for a Hollywood horror production. With its massive base of rusticated stone masonry, arched openings, turrets, and towers covered with steep pointed roofs, the building is an out-of-control Swinton Jacob. Major Chesney modified the architect's initial design as the construction progressed. The mansard-roofed Telephone Exchange with its bulky base, which was designed by James Ransome, also clashes with its surroundings. Most of these big-boned structures in Simla were built between the 1880s and the 1920s to house the Government of India Offices, but their vindication dates back to 1864.

Simla: the Summer Seat of the Empire

Before 1864, the visits of Governor-Generals and Viceroys to Simla were rationalised as official tours of duty to the northwest, a region of military importance. These visits usually coincided with the onset of the hot weather in the plains. Sir John Lawrence would end this charade. He had accepted the Viceroyalty on condition that he be allowed to spend summers in the hills on account of ill-health.[48] Sir Charles Wood, the Secretary of State, had readily accepted Lawrence's condition. Lawrence disembarked in Calcutta on January 12, 1864, and exactly three months and three days after his arrival, on April 15, with the Executive Council, he left for Simla. In the subsequent correspondence between Lawrence and Wood it is clear that the Secretary of State was hoping that the Viceroy would travel to different hill resorts across India during the summers. In fact Lawrence had suggested that the Supreme Government move to Simla for six months of the year, but Wood had replied: "with or without your Council, you are welcome to be away from Calcutta for six months,... If you like, next summer, to go and see Madras and the Neilgherries

(Nilgiris), and put some life into their proceedings, or visit Darjeeling and our enemies in Bhotan (Bhutan), or to go to Simla again, I have no sort of objection."[49] Lawrence, clearly had his mind set on Simla as the summer seat for the Government of India. Arguing in favour of Simla, Lawrence wrote:

"This place, of all Hill Stations seems to me the best for the Supreme Government. Here you are with one foot, I may say, in the Punjab, and another in the North-West Provinces. *Here*, you are among a docile population, and yet near enough to influence Oude. Around you, in a word, are all the warlike races of India, all those on whose character and power our hold in India, exclusive of our own countrymen, depends."[50]

Charles Wood, concerned about Simla being entirely cut off from the rest of India, as it was during the 1857 Revolt did not subscribe to Lawrence's ideas. Nevertheless, Lawrence prevailed and spent every spring and summer of his Viceregal tenure, from 1864 to 69, in Simla with the Supreme Government. Thus 1864 marks a turning point in the development of the station. After more than a decade Simla was officially accepted as the summer capital of the Empire, Lawrence had set a precedent and the proverbial annual transfer of the Government had started.

Lord Elgin, who preceded Lawrence, loved Dharamsala. Had he lived longer, would he have chosen Dharamsala instead of Simla as the summer capital? Elgin died while on a tour of duty near Dharamsala, and was buried in his favourite resort. A beautiful memorial marks his grave.

Lawrence's 1864 move to Simla was very modest compared to the visits of the other Governors-General. His official party included the Viceroy, the Executive Council, and the necessary secretarial and support staff, 480 persons in all.[51] Lawrence was known as a frugal and efficient administrator, who controlled the size of the annual move to Simla. His successors did not. The physical advantages of the summer move to the hills were too obvious, and year after year different departments managed to join the Government procession to Simla. In 1865 the Sanitary Commission joined the trek, in 1880 and the Surgeon General and his staff.

Thus in a couple of decades the annual move of the Government to the hills had reached amazing proportions. In 1883 the move was estimated to cost taxpayers 6,00,000 rupees. The construction of large office establishments, including the Railway Board and the Army Headquarters, commissioned during Lord Ripon's tenure, 1880-84, and completed in 1885, had cost over 1.7 million rupees.[52] The owners and managers of commercial interests and the population at large complained about such large expenses and the recurring cost of the annual migration. In Calcutta, businesses

Two views of the Mall, Simla. Looking towards the Post Office, ca. 1880, *left*, and from near the Post Office towards Christ Church and the Town Hall on the right, ca. 1870, *above*. The British Library.

which dealt with the Government on a daily basis were upset by the long-term absence of officials.

The "exodus question", as the annual shift of the Government from Calcutta to Simla was known, was widely debated: there was sustained criticism of the practice, especially by the active nationalist press. Indian newspapers printed letters and editorials criticising the move. The overall effect of recurrent public criticism during the last two decades of the 19th century and first two decades of the 20th, however, was negligible. The following incident best illustrates the attitude and approach of the British authorities in dealing – or not dealing – with this issue.

A Great Public Meeting to discuss the subject of "Exodus to the Hills" was called in the Calcutta town hall on Wednesday, July 14, 1886. The Sheriff had called the meeting after receiving a petition. The meeting received great publicity and support across India. Telegrams and letters of support were received from people of influence both European and Native from Madras, Bangalore, Benares, Allahabad, Lahore, Patna, Poona, Bombay, and also Government Assistants in Simla. The feeling of the crowd at the meeting is best summed up in Sheriff George Yule's opening speech:

"...I know of no country in the world where a similar custom prevails;[53] and were it not that we are docile people and too much occupied with our own affairs to care much what the Government does or where it goes to, the evil would have been checked long ago...No one grudged the veteran Sir John Lawrence the gratification of his wish to spend some of his time in the Hills with one or two of his trusted advisors and his Secretary, and no one would complain of a similar arrangement with his

Gorton Castle, initially designed by Swinton Jacob, and modified by Major Chesney. Its rusticated stone masonry, arched openings, turrets and flamboyant roofs would make it an ideal set for a Hollywood horror film.

successors. But it is another matter when the Legislative and every other Department of the State are removed bodily, down to its clerks and printing presses, to a remote corner of the country. The small and unobjectionable beginning of 20 years ago has developed into a general stampede, to the dislocation of business, to an unknown additional expenditure, and to the dissatisfaction of all classes and conditions of the people. (Hear, hear!)... Imagine, if you can, the condition of things in which the President, the Secretary, the Committees of the Chamber of Commerce, the Traders' Association, and all other Associations of Calcutta, Bombay, and Madras, could waft themselves and families to the Himalayas for eight months out of twelve at the Association's expense, on the plea that they would do their work better there than here. Imagine our doctors flying to the same heights, and assuring their patients, whom they leave behind, that they will be able to attend to their special ailments better from the Hills than at Chauringhi (main thoroughfare in Calcutta)

(Hear, hear!), and suggesting accordingly that their fees be capped by substantial allowances. (Hear, hear!) Imagine our High Court with all its officers joining the glorious company of runaways. (Laughter and applause)."[54]

Grievances aired at the Great Public Meeting were witty but very serious. Measures were drafted, and submitted to the Government after the Great Public Meeting to curtail the annual move. There were questions raised on the matter in the Houses of Parliament in London. What is the *minimum* proportion of the year that should be spent in Calcutta. What staff should accompany the Government, and what expenditure, in respect of the removal of that staff, should be sanctioned were questions raised by the Secretary of State.[55] The India Office started an enquiry on the duration and cost of the annual move of the Government. In the end, however, the vested interests, keen to maintain the status quo, easily stonewalled the matter. The only tangible effect of the Great Public Meeting was felt by the poor assistants in the Government Secretariat in Simla who had sent a telegram extending their confidence and support for the meeting in Calcutta. Assistants, most of

114

The Railway Board building, Simla.

them either natives or Eurasians, because of limited salaries and the high cost of living in Simla had to leave their families in Calcutta. They did not like long periods of separation, so their support for the meeting was obvious. In a reprimand, however, the assistants were summoned one by one and asked to commit in writing whether they had anything to do with the sending of the telegram. Afraid of losing their jobs, some replied "I have had nothing whatsoever to do with this matter," and the rest concurred "Nor I."[56]

From the first occupation in 1818 the Governor-General and the Commander-in-Chief regularly visited Simla at the end of their cold-weather tours. For a considerable time, from 1864 to the early 1880s, "the Government had professed to make the summer move to Simla each season for that season only, never to return."[57] All that changed under the administration of Lord Ripon who decided to build buildings for all public departments. The Viceregal Lodge was built during his successor Lord Dufferin's time. The Supreme Government, at last, had a fixed seat away from hot and sweaty Calcutta, and no amount of rumbling was going to change this.

Simla remained the seat of the Great Empire, officially for 75 years, and close to 100 years unofficially. Stories of the use of power, political intrigue, duplicity, and coercion in Simla abound. A famous romantic incident from the British era persists in the collective imagination, and is retold vividly, as if it had occurred just yesterday.

Scandal Point is at the centre of the Simla Mall. According to the popular myth, the dashing Maharajah of Patiala kidnapped the beautiful daughter of an English gentleman (the wife of a Viceroy, according to one version of the story, daughter of a Viceroy, according to another) from this point, whisking her away to Chail on horseback, and leaving the Viceregal guards gaping. It is alleged that "the incident was hushed up, the lady never complained and only the name, Scandal Point, remains to remind visitors of the story."[58] Pamela Kanwar, in her *Imperial Simla* writes ironically, "There is a touch of pity for the inept researcher hunting for documentary evidence. I have not found any for such a well-established 'fact'."[59] Like Kanwar, I have not been able to find any documentary evidence to support the tale, but still hope that proof will someday be found for this legend.

Monument to Lord Elgin, who died while on a tour of duty at Dharamsala.

Salubrious Sanatoria

When the cholera comes – as it will past a doubt –
Keep out of the wet and don't go on the shout,
For the sickness gets in as the liquor dies out,
An' it crumples the young British soldier.
Crum-, crum-, crumples the soldier . . .

But the worst o' your foes is the sun over 'ead:
You must wear your 'elmet for all that is said:
If 'e finds you uncovered 'e'll knock you down dead,
An' you'll die like a fool of a soldier.
Fool, fool, fool of a soldier...[1]

From "The Young British Soldier" by Rudyard Kipling

*H*ard indeed was the sojourn of British soldiers in India, and often short-lived. Not used to the hot weather and without immunity to tropical maladies, they frequently succumbed to cholera, malaria, typhoid, or sunstroke. "A youthful subaltern called Walter Campbell – a spirited boy of seventeen, fresh from the Highlands, who kept a careful journal of his experiences – describes the gloom that descended on his regiment when, in 1830, it received orders to embark for India: 'This news fell like a thunderbolt on many. India was to them a land of hopeless banishment – a living grave – a blank in their existence – a land from whence, if they escaped an early death, they were to return with sallow cheeks, peevish tempers, and shattered constitutions. And such, alas, was the fate of many'."[2]

In the early 17th century, when the British East India Company merchants set up their first trading posts in India they did not have many soldiers. Since these businesses, or factories as they were known, were located in native territories, they usually had a small security force, but no regular army. This situation lasted for more than a 100 years without much change.

From the 1740s onwards, however, the Company started building up its army in south India (their trading post being Fort St. George, Madras) to guard its business interests from the neighbouring French traders. Sparked by the war in Europe between France and England, the establishment of the Company's army had a most profound impact on its possessions in India. The expanding military might of the Company resulted in the phenomenal growth of the Empire. Between 1748 and 1857, the Company's affairs in India, which had started with a handful of "factories" measuring scarcely a few square miles in area, grew to a power base spread over an entire subcontinent.

The beginnings of the Company's army were humble. In 1748, the force, hurriedly put together to resist the French, comprised a small body of native sepoys and a still smaller European contingent formed of sailors who could be spared from the ships on the coast, and men smuggled from England by crimps.[3] The subsequent increase in the military establishment in India was remarkable. British troops from England joined the Company army in 1754. In two years, they were fighting alongside Lieutenant-Colonel (later Lord) Robert Clive, outside Calcutta in the decisive battle of Plassey, "on which may be said to have hung the destinies of India."[4]

By 1773 the Company's army consisted of 54,000 soldiers of which about 9,000 were European and 45,000 native. After the Maratha conquest, in 1808, the military forces were reduced to a "permanent peace-footing,"[5] but

the size of the army was 154,500, comprising 24,500 British and 130,000 native soldiers; the size of the Company's military force continued to grow unabated. On the eve of the 1857 Mutiny the East India Company had about 280,000 uniformed men on its payroll, of which 45,000 were British.[6]

Compared to the military establishment, the size of the British civilian population in India remained small, it was made up mainly of merchants, planters, and administrators. The passage of the Charter Act of 1833 increased the flow of British civilians going to India. By 1859, there were 126,000 Europeans in India, including 85,000 troops.[7] Although the total number of British soldiers was not very large, many of them died while on duty in India.

The Problems of Survival

Some 100,000 men perished in the Company's and Queen's British Armies in India between 1815 and 1855. This enormous death toll was in addition to casualties in the field. The death of so many young soldiers was not only a human tragedy for the East India Company, an army that was losing so many soldiers to disease and disability was also a serious liability. Training and bringing a soldier to India meant time, energy, and money; it was a total loss if a soldier died before completing his commission. The Company calculated that each soldier was worth £100. Hence the loss of 100,000 young and able-bodied soldiers had cost the Company £10,000,000.[8] Assuming that the value of money doubles every seven years, these losses, converted in 1995 terms, would amount to more than a trillion pounds sterling – a staggering amount.

With such large sums of money involved, the health of British soldiers remained an important concern for the colonial rulers throughout their stay in India. Numerous commissions were set up and reports prepared regarding the well-being of the military establishment.

J.R. Martin, in his "Report for Promoting the Health and Efficiency of the British Troops Serving in the East Indies," to the Court of Directors of East India House, observed, "How truly saving of the public revenues must be a well-ordered and well-directed, and well-contented Medical Corps!" He added that "In truth, the importance of an efficient Medical Establishment is so great that we cannot put a money value on it."[9] To preserve the health of British soldiers in India, Martin made two significant recommendations: first, the selection of the locality; and next in importance, the proper arrangements of barracks and hospitals.

Martin based his recommendations on medical observations made in Europe and the colonies during the first half of the 19th century: throughout the European campaigns, regardless of the climate, or whether in

The life of British soldiers in India was often short, and cemeteries, such as this one at Dharamsala are silent proof.

Holland or the Crimea, sick soldiers housed in huts fared better than those kept in barracks and general hospitals who perished in large numbers. During the great famine, the Irish suffering from typhoid who were kept in work-houses and hospitals died in larger numbers than those who were thrown along the roads and under hedges and recovered in "goodly proportions." In Jamaica, Sir Charles Metcalfe ordered special buildings in the mountains to house sick personnel, but in comparison, most humble buildings built on a pure and elevated soil with ample ventilation assured better health among occupants.[10]

Similarly, in the Indian subcontinent, during the cholera epidemics of 1817-19, "which started in 1817 in Bihar, became pandemic and spread throughout Asia with the tea caravans,"[11] soldiers living at high elevations remained free of the disease. The removal of troops from an infested district to an elevated location was followed by a speedy disappearance of the illness.[12] Moreover, there were accounts of quick recovery of civilian patients when they visited the hills in India.

In 1819, John Sullivan, the Collector of Coimbatore, and M. Leschenault de la Tour, the Naturalist to the King of France, were on a scouting trip to the plateau, later developed as Ootacamund. The Frenchman, who had been on the verge of death from fever during the ascent, recovered miraculously, fortified by the buoyant air and moderate climate.[13] This plateau had been discovered just a year before, in 1818, by two surveyors, Whish and Kindersley.[14] Upon their return to Coimbatore in the plains, the surveyors spoke to John Sullivan, of "a hidden plateau over fifty miles across and eight thousand feet up in the hills. Here, it was said, the soil was rich, the air fresh and the moors and thicket teemed with wild flowers and game."[15] The plateau was, and still is, inhabited by a native tribe called the Todas. Because of their unique ceremonies, clothing, customs, features, and language, early researchers erroneously linked Todas either to the ancient inhabitants of Sumer or to the Syrian followers of Saint Thomas who came to south India in the first century. Since Todas are often described as the lost tribe of the Israelites, the region surrounding Ootacamund is often called "the lost world."[16]

Although the Todas were an exotic tribe, the countryside and climate of the Nilgiris was perhaps closest to that of "home." Norman Macleod, journeying in India, noted that: "The sportsman, artist and invalids are sure to speak with equal enthusiasm of the Nilgherries... the rich clothing below contrasting with the wild summits above, made a most unique picture. Never before or after in India had I the pleasure of seeing such rapid interchange of light and shade. The shadow of the clouds slowly moving across the mountain side brought the Highland hills vividly before me. We remarked at the time, too, how like the Dunkeld was the broken and wooded scenery of the lower grounds."[17]

A Toda family in front of their 'mund', or hut, ca. 1870. After *Letters from India and Kashmir*.

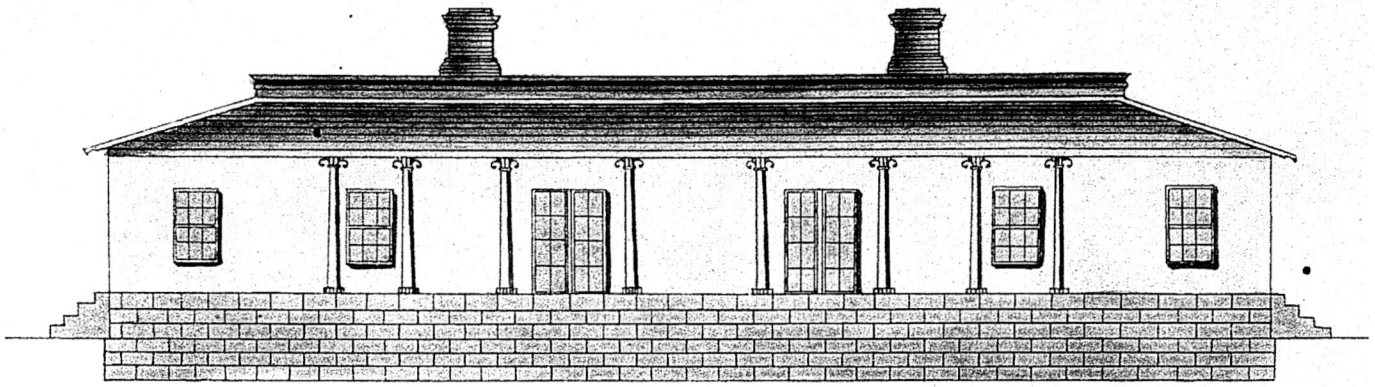

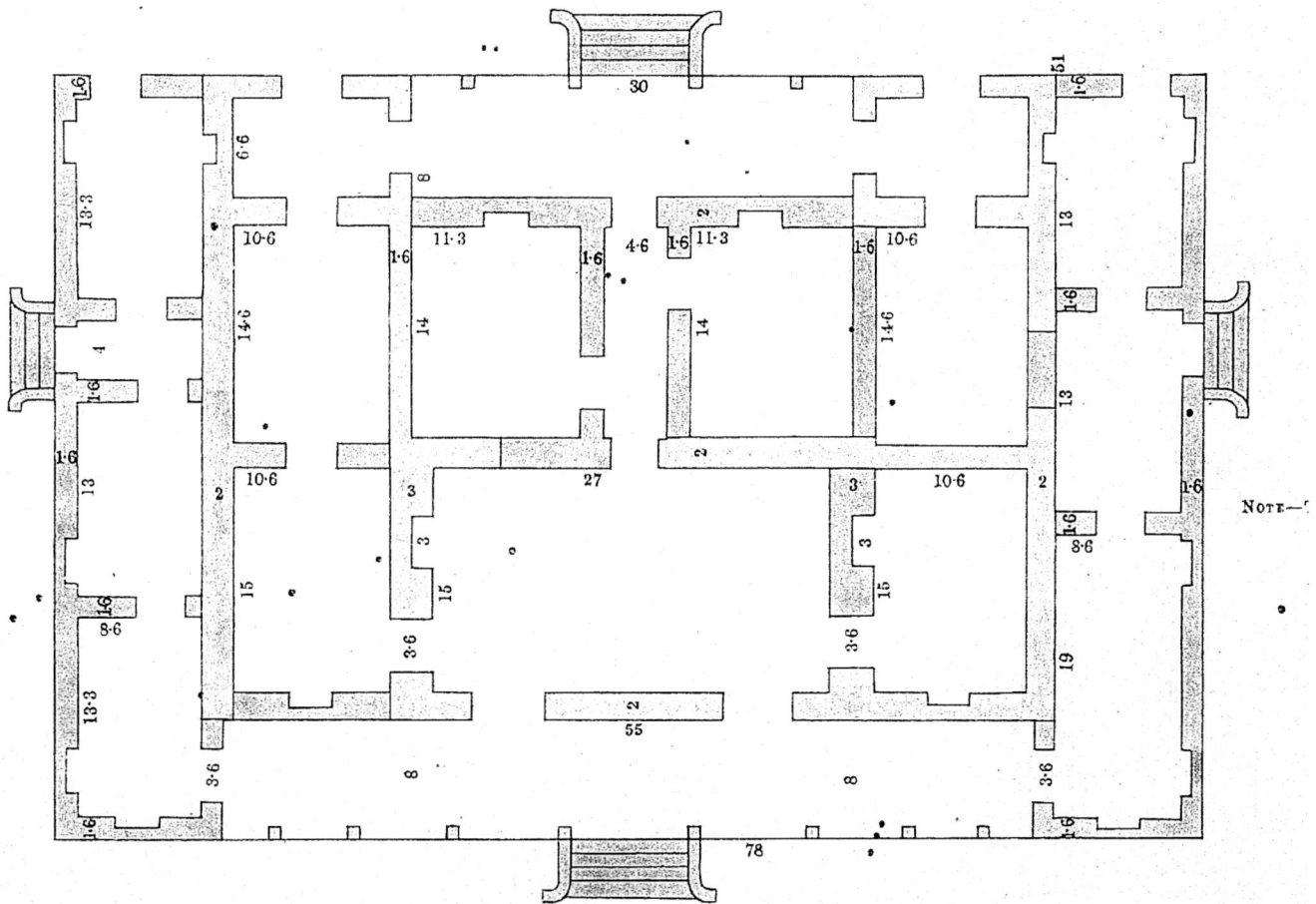

Stone House, the first permanent residence in Ootacamund, built by John Sullivan, Collector of Coimbatore, in 1823 one year after the Kennedy House was built in Simla. The Kennedy House was destroyed by fire, but the Stone House survives. After Frederick Price (Sir), *Ootacamund: A History.*

Sullivan built the first permanent house on this plateau in 1823, one year after the famous "Kennedy House" was built in Simla, and Ootacamund, the "Queen of the Nilgiris," was born. "Kennedy House" was built, destroyed, re-built, and destroyed again by fire, but Sullivan's original "Stonehouse" and its attached properties have survived. Over the years, "Stonehouse" has accommodated different users; leased to the Government as a sanatorium, it reverted to Mr. Sullivan as his residence, but later it was incorporated with the Government Secretariat Office building, and at present it is used as a college. Altered considerably over the years,

"Stonehouse," comprising several buildings spread over a spur, has retained its pioneering air. Tucked under the canopy of giant eucalyptus trees, the Sullivan estate stoically overlooks the recent commercial developments which are starting to obliterate the famous Charing Cross, renamed Gandhi Chowk, at the heart of the Ootacamund bazaar.

Geographically, like Ootacamund in the South of India, Kodaikanal was surveyed by the British in 1821, but, unlike other resorts, it was the Americans who first moved up into the Palni hills. The American Madura Mission at Madurai, founded in 1834, suffered a great loss of lives over the first ten years and in 1844, there was a "fearful attack of cholera." The Americans used to go to Ootacamund, but it was considered too far, and to Sirumalais which was found to be too low to offer protection from the disease, so they decided to purchase a boat and send the sick to Jaffna peninsula in northern Ceylon. When they approached the British officials in Madurai for help, a Mr Fane, who was familiar with the hills in the region, suggested they could establish a depot in the high Palnis – Kodaikanal basin, an ideal location because of its proximity to Madurai. In 1845 the Americans decided to build a couple of bungalows in Kodaikanal with the money set aside for the purchase of the boat to ferry invalids to Jaffna. Chandler wrote:

"The sanatorium we have chosen promises every facility for the restoration of health which is to be found on the Nilgherries or even on the Ceylon hills, and at much less expense even counting our houses at twice their cost. We are now surprised at ourselves for not knowing years ago that within our own district we had a resort which affords us nearly every facility which can be found by going further and spending more."[18]

Although established by American missionaries the physical organisation of the resort was very similar to that of the British stations. The British, too, soon recognised the benefits of Kodaikanal, and Hamilton, who surveyed the location in the 1860s wrote:

"The climate of the Upper Palnis is considered to be exceedingly salubrious and no sickness of any kind is known to be endemic or epidemic upon them. They are too lofty to be visited by the ordinary malarious fever of India, too sparsely populated to be scourged by typhus and typhoids. And having a much drier air and more equable temperature than in the Nilgiris they are said to be far better suited to children and invalids."[19]

The English and Americans worked together in harmony. They established a common church which was visited from the plains by alternating priests representing both groups. When the communities grew larger the Anglicans built another church. In the 1860s the Roman Catholics came and later established the first educational institution. The Sacred Heart College was established to train priests at Shembaganur five miles outside Kodaikanal. At the turn of the century, the Kodaikanal School was started by the American Mission for children of American missionaries working in India. The German Lutherans also started their own community and school here, but this was taken over by Swedish Mission during the First World War.

Kodaikanal owes a good deal to Sir Vere Levinge, Collector of Madurai, who retired there in 1867 instead of retiring to his native Ireland. Important municipal improvements could be made because of his administrative influence and personal donations. He built the dam and created the lake with his own funds, improved road links with the plains and imported numerous plants, including eucalyptus or blue-gum trees. Kodaikanal continues to attract the children and families of missionaries and other foreigners living in India, due to its climate and educational infrastructure.

In the early 1820s, when Kodaikanal was surveyed and Simla and Ootacamund were founded, the scientific link between germs and the spread of communicable diseases had not yet been established. It was not until the last quarter of the 19th century that this connection – germ theory – was understood by Louis Pasteur in France and Robert Koch in Germany. Martin, in his report to the Company Directors, had concluded that "the thorough ventilation through the openings and crevices of huts supplies the sick what they do not obtain in our ill-constructed Barracks and Hospitals – namely, pure air."[20] Overwhelming medical evidence linked good health to pure air. Being healthy pointed in one direction: up, up to the mountain tops, where an ample supply of fresh air was assured. Thus developed the incentive for the establishment of a series of mountain-top sanatoria across India.

As we have seen, the lower Himalayas in the North and the high Nilgiri mountains in the South were the obvious choice, offering health-restoring pure air as well as an ideal escape from the oppressive heat of the plains. The first generation of sanatoria were built in places such as Simla, and Ootacamund, as well as smaller stations like Nainital, Mussoorie and Cherrapunji.

The name Mussoorie is derived from the Mansur shrub (Cororiana nepalesis) native to this region. Captain Young of the Sirmur Battalion was the first European to visit the spot and Mr Shore, Joint Magistrate of Dun with Young built a modest structure on Camel's Back in 1823. In 1826 Captain Young built the first house, Mullingar, on Landour hill and in 1827, a convalescent depot was established at Landour, an area which developed into a large military cantonment. In 1832, Surveyor General Colonel Everest, after whom the world's highest mountain is named, opened the Survey of India office and built his home in Mussoorie. The Doon valley and Mussoorie attracted many travellers. For Charles Mundy the march through the valley "was most beautiful and reminded me of the milder and least wild regions of the Alps... On the north side of Nuhan mountain we saw for the first time... the fir-tree. It is of a beautiful species, with large spreading branches, like Scotch fir. The raspberry grows wild and eatable and the pomegranate in the sunny nooks shows its dark green leaf and beautiful bell-shaped crimson blossom."[21] The two settlements of Landour and Mussoorie started as distinct entities, but grew into one continuous town spanning a long and undulating ridge. Minturn, the American traveller found "the grandeur of the view... almost overpowering. At our feet was a dark and narrow valley, sinking almost perpendicularly for hundreds of feet, beyond were the parallel chains of the Himalayas each more distant range a little higher than those which were nearer and towering high above all the others were the magnificent peaks of snowy ranges." He noted that "Mussoorie is one of several hill stations. The others are Darjeeling, Nainee Thal (Naini Tal) and Simla... These are kept up principally as Sanatoria. Hither are sent the European soldiers, when their health becomes affected by long residence in the plains. Here, too, all children of English parents must pass the greater part of each year, that they remain in India."[22]

Due to this reason from an early date Mussoorie developed as an educational centre, MacKinnon's Seminary, The Mussoorie School, where the Savoy Hotel now functions, The Convent of Jesus and Mary, Waverly, St. George's and The Woodstock School, founded in 1854, and today one of the most sought after by the international diplomatic community of Delhi because of its American style of education, were all part of the educational community. Ruskin Bond, author and long time resident of Musoorie, has estimated in comic detail the impetus to the local economy given by the school system:

"Have you ever thought of how much the prosperity of Mussoorie of its tradespeople at least depends on these institutions? Taking only the question of food, a conservative basis estimated, with one of our poorest schools as a criterion, the domiciled schools in the station consume in their nine month term: loaves of bread 1,88,000; rice lbs. 118,800; ...vegetables lbs.162,000; and sugar lbs. 86,400. God bless the schools!"[23]

Naini Tal, also established as a sanatorium, grew quickly to become the summer seat of the Governor of the United Provinces and the headquarters of the General Officer Commanding Eastern Command. Situated at an elevation of about 6400 feet with a large lake at its centre and lofty wooded peaks surrounding it, the resort is one of the most popular in central India. P. Barron discovered it in 1839, but the area surrounding it had come under British control following the 1815 Gurkha War. Barron, a shrewd sugar merchant who recognised the potential of the place took the headman of the locality in his boat to the middle of the lake and then offered him the choice of accepting the claim of the Company or being capsized with his property intact. Barron himself relates:

"He looked very blank, said the lake was very deep and agreed to waive his claim in preference to the chance or rather certainty of being drowned if the boat were upset."[24]

In this highhanded fashion, Barron became the first Englishman to build his "Pilgrim's Cottage," near the

Construction of the Jackatalla Barracks near Ootacamund, ca. 1850. The lower Himalayas and the high Nilgiris were an obvious choice for army barracks and sanatoria. After The Illustrated London News.

Typical bungalow, Kasauli.

present Naini Tal Club and wrote several articles to publicise the location and attract other British settlers.

The entire Kumaon Hill region was made famous by the exploits and bravery of Jim Corbett, a man worshipped by the locals in his life time as "Carpet Sahib," who destroyed man-eaters and had a magical knowledge of the local flora and fauna. Jim and his sister Maggie, his life-long companion, were born, raised and spent most of their adult life in Naini Tal at "Gurney House," their ancestral home; winters were passed at the bottom of the hill in the thick jungles at Kaladhungi where the family had built another home. The Corbetts represented the best of the Raj, a family whose Indian links spanned several generations. Jim Corbett's parents and grandparents spent their lives serving the Company in India and lie buried in different parts of the subcontinent. Joseph Corbett, Jim's grandfather was only 18 when he left his native Ireland for Bengal abroad the *Royal George* in 1814. He arrived in 1815 in India with his wife Harriet, died at the young age of 33 and is buried at Meerut where his son Christopher William was born. Jim's father saw action as the Company's apothecary in military service, during the First Afghan War, and the Sikhs wars, and was decorated in the battles of Sobraon,

Aliwal and Chilianwala and the 1857 Mutiny. He later joined the Postal service and was transferred to Naini Tal in 1867. Jim Corbett's mother had even earlier links with India, dating back to 1794 when a Nestor of Limerick left Ireland for India in the service of the East India Company. Though Jim is the famous author, Maggie, like many European women, provides intimate details of life in British India:

"The journey from Mussoorie to Naini Tal had to be made by *doolie dak*. A *doolie* was a large boxlike contrivance suspended from poles and capable of accommodating a number of people. This conveyance was carried on the shoulders of eight stalwart *doolie* bearers. Travelling by day as well as by night along a road which ran... through dense jungles teeming with wild life, the journey was not accomplished without its thrills. Sometimes the *doolies* had to be put down because of a tiger in the road while strips would be torn from a bed sheet, soaked in Kerosene oil, and used as flares to frighten the tiger away. On arrival at Kaladhungi, ...the mode of travel was changed from *doolie* to the *dandy*, a sort of hammock... attached to a pole... it is hard to

Billiard room, Ootacamund Club, Ootacamund. It was in this club – perhaps on the same table – that one rainy afternoon, the game of Snooker was evolved.

imagine a more uncomfortable way of travelling. Only women and children resorted to it."[25]

Like many other British-Indian families the Corbetts left India in 1947 and spent their twilight years in Kenya. Legends and songs about the great hunter are still recounted in the little hill villages that surround Naini Tal, and Corbett's family residences both at Naini Tal and Kaladhungi are worth a visit.

As seen in the previous chapter, as early as 1824, European patients had permission from the native hill rulers to establish themselves rent-free near Simla. However, Simla, frequented by the rich and the renowned, quickly acquired sophistication and shed its sanatoria air. In the vicinity of Simla, however, emerged a series of smaller hill resorts. More relaxed and less glamorous than Simla, they served as army cantonments and sanatoria. A ring of these small stations also demarcated a clear line of defence around Simla in the years to come, facilitating its selection as the summer capital of the Empire. The hill station of Kasauli, situated 26 miles (42 kilometres) from Simla, has retained its original casual sanatorium character to the present day.

Kasauli became an army cantonment after Henry and Honoria Lawrence's nine-month-old baby daughter died of cholera in Sabathu. Henry Lawrence, the older brother of John Lawrence (the Viceroy responsible for moving the summer seat of Government from Calcutta to Simla in 1864), was a powerful person in his own right. Political agent of the North-West Frontier Province at that time, had he not been slain at Lucknow during the 1857 Mutiny, he might certainly have gone on to become the Governor-General instead of his brother. In 1841 Henry Lawrence obtained a plot of land in Kasauli and made sure that within a year the Government acquired the land for a military cantonment and commenced the construction of a road from Kalka.[26]

The Lawrences built "Sunnyside," a modest cottage, on their plot. It still stands, next to the cantonment office overlooking the Sabathu ridge (where the Lawrence daughter is buried), and the Lawrence Public School, located across a beautiful valley in Sanawar. The School, started in 1847 by Henry Lawrence,

Following pages:
Main lounge, Ootacamund Club. Trophy-studded home of the famous 'Ooty Hunt'.

primarily for orphans and children of European soldiers serving in the British army in India, was also known as the Lawrence Asylum.

Henry Lawrence chose Kasauli as a cantonment site for its high elevation and its proximity to Sabathu. The elevation of Sabathu is 4,000 feet (1,230 metres) while Kasauli is situated at 6,300 feet (1,927 metres). Moreover, Kasauli is only seven miles (12 kilometres) away by road, from Sabathu and practically looms over it. The high elevation and dense woods of deodar, oak, fir and horse chestnut render Kasauli cooler than Sabathu in summer, and officers used to frequent this hill top for hunting leopards, foxes, jungle cats and birds, riding sorties, or for picnics. Kasauli, because of its cooler climate, seemed safer and not as prone to cholera and other illnesses as Sabathu.

During the first few decades after its formal establishment in 1842, Kasauli developed primarily as an army convalescent depot, becoming a hot-weather garrison for troops from the plains and Sabathu. New barracks, large enough to accommodate four companies, and a good library were erected in 1855.[27] A hospital followed in 1856. Some residents formed the "Kasauli Reading & Assembly Rooms" in 1880, which became the "Kasauli Club" in 1889.[28] More than 100 years old and famous for its lavish "tennis teas" and gala Saturday nights, the club is still the centre of social life in Kasauli; it continues to attract members from as far as Chandigarh and Delhi.

Several hill stations could boast of having more than one club, each one serving a specific social group. The United Services Club for Military Staff, the Amateur Dramatics Club for drama enthusiasts, or the Planters Clubs which were patronised by the managers and owners of tea and coffee plantations. Each club had its nuances, but above all, their exclusive "English Only" country-club atmosphere, distinctive decor, and collections of hunting trophies set these places apart from the native population.

The Ootacamund or Ooty Club is an important landmark in that hill-station. The house occupied by it was built in 1831-32 by Sir William Rumbold and later rented by Lord William Bentinck. It was here that the game of "Snooker" was perfected by a subaltern in the Devonshire Regiment, who later rose to be Sir Neville Chamberlain; it was also here, on the walls of the Ooty Club, that the rules of Snooker were first posted in 1875. The Club also remains the meeting place of the Ooty Hunt, but gentlemen in traditional hunting "pinks" ride after jackals, not foxes, on the Nilgiri downs. The most popular event today is the August UPASI Meet (United Planter's Association of South India) when the Ooty Club plays host to planters who came with their wives from lonely, far-flung tea and coffee plantations for celebrations and business during Ooty Planter's week.

Mahabaleshwar Club, Mahabaleshwar.

In Mahabaleshwar, the Station Club, housed in a finely crafted red-stone structure, is home to unusual golf-links. Since it is impossible to keep the golf-links green during the dry months, holes are surrounded by a collar of fine, shiny black volcanic sand, instead of putting greens; the golf course itself being made up of dry golden brown grass.

Sports of all types lay at the foundation of Raj Clubs and this included sailing and boating in many hill

station lakes, the most famous being the Naini Tal Yacht Club; now named the Boat House Club, it is the home of beautiful wooden punt-like rowboats and handsome sailboats and remains a busy and popular place during the season. A special Club or Lodge was that of the Freemasons, for Freemasonry was well-established throughout Anglo-India. Michael Edwardes comments:

"There was a lodge in practically every station of consequence, and everywhere it was thought by Indians to be a house of magic. In western India, it was often known as the *Shaitankhana,* the house of the devil. In South India, the Tamil name meant 'cut-head temple,' because it was believed that part of the rite of initiation included the cutting off and restoring the initiates' head."[29]

Following pages:
The Pasteur Institute, Coonoor.

129

Clubs covered all activities. "A few evenings ago, it was proposed that at the club a band should play twice a week. A paper was sent around at once ...next morning the required number of musicians was hunted up and engaged... This is the first time that the Himalaya mountains have listened to the joyous sound of music. We have danced to music within doors, but never, until this day, have we heard a band in the open air in the Himalaya mountains... From valley to valley echo carries the sound... Back at the Club! Dinner is served. We sit down, seventy-five of us. The fare is excellent, and the champagne has been iced in the hail which fell the other night, during a storm."[30]

Clubs in these hill stations provided a refuge from life in a strange land and culture. Here the Englishman could relax, be himself and escape from the tasks of running the Empire. In many ways this is what the hill resorts also permitted him, especially smaller sanatoria like Kasauli which recaptured for the English the atmosphere of small-town England.

Gradually, Kasauli confirmed itself as a modest station with upwards of 100 bungalows. Most of these have survived along with their little wooden gates, winding cobbled paths, English cottage gardens and ivy-covered walls. Original fireplaces and well-stocked libraries in many homes are legacies from the British past as are house names such as "Killarney," "Waverley" and "Elfin Lodge." The Station Commander's residence "Gilbert House," is now used as the Flag staff house by the army, the Maharajah of Faridkot's "Belmount," has been converted into the Public Works Department Circuit House; and "St. Cloud," also known as "Ranbir Villa," was donated to the Government by the Maharajah of Patiala to establish the Pasteur Institute.

Kasauli came into true prominence as a sanatorium after the Pasteur Institute of India, modelled after the one in Paris, was established there in 1900. The Institute provided treatment to patients bitten by rabid animals.

Before the Pasteur Institute was established at Kasauli, rabies patients were often sent to Paris for treatment, but many victims died *en route.* If not treated in time, rabies causes a horrible death, characterised by choking, convulsions, and an inability to swallow liquids – hence the name hydrophobia by which the disease is also known. When a Government employee was bitten by a rabid animal the victim was given leave with pay to go to Kasauli for treatment. Several native rulers joined in this noble effort by building special facilities to house patients in Kasauli, and by allowing the patient and a companion to travel free of charge on the train routes under their control to get to Kasauli.[31]

Modelled on the Institute in Kasauli, two sister Pasteur Institutes were established: one in south India, at Coonoor in the Nilgiri mountains and another in the

eastern reaches of the Indian Empire at Rangoon, in Burma, or Myanmar as it is now known. Today, the Coonoor and Kasauli Institutes are thriving organisations engaged in biological research and the manufacture of vaccines and serums. Over the years, the physical plan of the Kasauli Institute has grown, and in the process completely transformed Ranbir Villa, the summer palace of the Maharajah of Patiala, which has been modelled on a Grecian temple, into a heap of government buildings. The main building of the Pasteur Institute in Coonoor is still intact. Its gracious onion-domed premises, located only a few 100 yards away from the botanical garden, form a charming spot atop a ridge, and are well worth a visit.

If the Pasteur Institutes played a significant role in the formation of the hill resorts of Kasauli and Coonoor, the cantonment facilities, central to many hill stations, were instrumental in the organisation of another group of resorts. Typical cantonment facilities included the parade grounds around which were arranged barracks for both single and married staff, officers housing, armoury, the mess and the club.

The Military Establishment and Sanatoria

By their nature all military establishments operate by rules, and the British army in India was no exception. For the salary and benefits of staff as well as the design of buildings, the army resorted to its rule books. For instance, Circular #89 gives information about how military facilities were planned and built. Issued by the Public Works department in 1864 as part of the proceedings of the Governor General of India in Council, it contained the general guidelines prescribed by *The Army Sanitary Commission on the Principles of Construction for Barracks for Single and Married Men*. To begin with, standard plans were issued; in addition, plans of model barracks suitable for different localities were provided. Preparation of the detailed design for barracks to be constructed, however, was left to the local officers at each station. Several rules and principles of design, however, were laid down for their guidance.[32]

The sizes of the rooms and the optimum number of occupants in each barrack were suggested, but the prescribed range was fairly broad: 16 to 20 soldiers per room and 40 to 100 soldiers for the barracks. One significant design recommendation concerning the ample amount of pure air available per soldier, however, determined all designs. For the plains, it was recommended that each soldier should have 1,800 cubic feet of space, whereas in the hill stations, depending on the elevation, this volume could be reduced to between 1,408 and 1,232 cubic feet.[33]

Barrack rooms should be kept free of anything that was likely to injuriously affect the purity of the air, and the barracks unit should comprise only the

PLANS COPIED FROM COLONEL CROMMELINS MEMORANDUM

MODIFIED PLANS PROPOSED BY THE GOVERNMENT OF INDIA

(This dotted outline shows the position in which we propose to place the blocks to leave each block open to the air at both ends.)

PROPOSED REARRANGEMENT OF MESS ROOM & SERGEANTS QRS.

A set of standard plans issued by the government for military barracks, ca. 1860. After *The Army Sanitary Commission on the Principles of Construction for Barracks for Single and Married Men.*

133

The Sanatorium, Dalhousie, *far above*, Walker Hospital, Simla, *above* and barracks, Dalhousie, *opposite page*. The basic plans of these buildings are very similar, but the choice of materials and treatment of details make each one seem different from the other.

dormitory, mess room, sergeant quarters, the water room and a day-room.[34] In addition, to ensure proper circulation of air in the barracks, strict rules were laid down with regard to the arrangement of beds. There were to be only two rows of beds in each ward.[35]

Accommodation for married military staff was organised around 8 to 10 multiple units of two rooms, measuring about 16'x14' and 14'x10'. An important feature of all types of barracks was the open wrap-around veranda, 12 feet wide at the front and on the sides and 10 feet at the back.[36]

Although the report of *The Army Sanitary Commission on the Principles of Construction for Barracks for Single and Married Men* was primarily aimed at the design of healthy *military* barracks, the words barrack and ward (referring to a hospital or a sanatorium ward) are used interchangeably throughout the document. Hence, the same standard plans, based on the Commission's guidelines, were used to build military barracks, hospitals or sanatoria in hill stations.

The general design approach of the military barracks was straightforward and deliberately kept simple to permit the use of a variety of local materials. Buildings were built entirely of wood, like the Walker Hospital in Simla and the Eden Hospital[37] in Darjeeling, or local stone and brick, like the convalescent depot at Sabathu and the barracks at Dalhousie. The outside treatment of these buildings is skilfully handled, giving a distinct identity to each structure; only upon closer scrutiny do we discover that the plans of all four facilities are basically the same. With various materials employed, roofs, verandas and decorations gave each building individual character.

The great concern about pure air also influenced domestic buildings in the hills. Travel guides, especially those produced during the second half of the 19th century, gave instructions for taking full advantage of the clean mountain air. A combination of a daily regime of exercise and sleep plus a properly designed cottage could ensure good health. For example, *A Guide to Simla*, compiled by W.H. Carey, recommended that:

"...there is not a wholesomer thing than early rising, or one which if persevered in would make a greater difference in the sensations of those who suffer from most causes of ill health, particularly the besetting disease of these sedentary times, – indigestion. The bracing, pure air which fans the cheeks of the early riser, does more in restoring health, or continuing it, than all the nauseous restoratives of *medical men*.

"Exercise is well entitled in various respects to be considered a common aid to physique ...There is no one in the way; you can walk, trot, or race as suiteth you best; your blood warms, and your spirits rise with the rapid rush through the air, and you have acquired a blithe vitality which does not desert you for the rest of the day.

Bungalow, Yercaud.

"On rising from your bed in the morning, place yourself in an erect posture, the shoulders thrown back; and while in this position inhale all the air you can, holding your breath and extending your arms as far as they will go behind your back; suspend your breath in this way as long as possible. Repeat the operation frequently.

"Every chamber (of the cottage) should have two systems of ventilation, internal and external, so that either may be employed according to the season of the year; and the health and vigour or peculiarity of the sleepers. The internal ventilation, that is, opening above the fire-places for feeble persons or for very cold weather; the external, that is, through the window, from all out-doors, for the vigorous and moderate weather.

" ...one of the pernicious errors in modern architecture, especially in the construction of private dwellings, is founded on the mischievous supposition that almost any place is good enough to sleep in. It is common everywhere to set apart the smallest rooms in the house for sleeping apartments ...let the reader remember that at least one-third of man's life is spent in bed, in sleep ...And when it is considered that air is essential to health, that without it we

cannot live two minutes, it must be of material importance whether we breath pure or an impure air for a third of our existence. A full-sized man breathes, – takes into his lungs at each breath, – about a pint of air; while in there, all the life nutriment is extracted from it, and, on being sent out of the body, it is entirely destitute of life-giving power, that if breathed into the lungs again, without the admixture of any pure air, the individual would be suffocated, and would die in sixty seconds. As a man breathes about eighteen times in a minute, and a pint at each breath, he consumes over two hogsheads of air every hour, or about sixteen hogsheads during the eight hours of sleep.

" ...(hence) no sleeping apartment, even for a single person, should have a floor surface of less than ...one hundred and forty-four square feet, and eight to ten feet high (1,440 cubic feet)... Every chamber ...have a ventilating process going on all the time, at least by having an open fireplace in it ...a little fire should be kept burning in the grate or fireplace ...this creates a draft up the chimney, and keeps the atmosphere of a sleeping room comparatively pure. In cases where an actual fire cannot be kept, an admirable substitute will be found by placing a lamp in the

A tea-planter's bungalow, Coonoor. Chimneys, and at times verandas were used to define the layouts of small bungalows.

fireplace, to be kept burning all night; this creates a draught without making much heat, and is a good means of ventilating a sick chamber when warmth is not desirable."[38]

It is remarkable that Carey's *A Guide to Simla*, published in 1870, and basically a tourist guide, regards health in such a holistic manner. The chapter, "Hints on Health," from which the above passage is taken, deals in greater detail with items such as early rising, exercise, breathing, sleep, ventilation, food, trees and health.

To sum up, a structure adequate for the hills required the prescribed minimum room sizes and a fireplace in every chamber (or more than one in large rooms) to ensure ample ventilation. Fireplaces, particularly their placement and design, became a prominent feature in domestic architecture.

According to Martin, great sums of money were lost when barracks and hospitals were placed in improper locations; the buildings for European troops at Berhampore, Bengal, abandoned after 1835 on account of unhealthiness, had cost £17,000,000 sterling.[39] Similarly, Cherrapunji had been chosen as a sanatorium for Europeans because of its contiguity to East Bengal and Assam, but without thoroughly checking its climate. The rainfall at Cherrapunji is probably the greatest in the world. The excessive dampness of the station proved to be prejudicial to the health of the invalids, and the

sanatorium was abolished in 1834.[40] A few years later, measurements showed that at Mauphlong it rains one-third less than at Cherrapunji although located only 18 miles north. If the sanatorium had been located in Mauphlong initially, great sums of money could have been saved. These experiences taught that it was not sufficient to have a well designed and properly built "healthy building" it was also crucial to place it in the right location.

Ootacamund, located in an undulating bowl which stretches for miles, surrounded by imposing blue hills and rolling green downs, with a picturesque lake lined with willow trees, seemed ideal as a health resort. But in 1825, Mr. Sullivan, cost-conscious founder of Ootacamund, suggested that sanatorium buildings should be first rented, and that only if the experiment proved successful, substantial accommodation might subsequently be provided. However, the Government could not easily obtain rental properties in Ootacamund and had to purchase a couple of bungalows. When the first detachment of invalids reached Ootacamund in May 1830, there were, in addition to "Stonehouse," which was held on a lease, three buildings: two belonging to the Madras Government, and one to Bombay, capable of holding 24 invalids. From the time the convalescent depot was first opened at Ootacamund, the various medical officers maintained very lengthy and detailed

records to determine the suitability of the station as a sanatorium. According to the medical reports the sanatorium did not prove as successful as had been anticipated. In 1834 the Government abolished the depot, removed the patients, and discharged the establishment. However, it took them several years to dispose of the properties. Ootacamund which had been declared a "military bazaar station," the equivalent of "cantonment" in 1828, ceased to be one in 1841.[41] Eventually about nine miles (15 kilometres) away in Wellington new barracks were built in 1860, and were added to in 1875.[42] Without the cantonment, Ootacamund still continued to attract important British officials and native kings. These built their summer palaces there after the Governor of Madras Presidency came to reside there in the 1860s.[43] The Government House, Ooty, now the official summer home of the Governor of Tamilnadu, remains the best preserved Government House in the hill stations, where not only the building, but artifacts, old photographs, portraits and furnishings from the British era are still well maintained.

The Faulty Science of Sanatorium Making

The creation of stations in remote and unexplored mountains was a long, laborious, and very expensive process. Many false starts were made, so over the years, the military department developed a standard evaluation method for choosing a hill station for a permanent convalescent depot or sanatorium. For example, the typical report of the committee appointed to judge the potential of Puchmurree (Pachmarhi) as a station described these points: the general features of the plateau, approaches, supposed cost of the road, healthiness of the road, the climate, especially during the hot months and in the monsoon, history of diseases such as cholera, availability of water, the soil conditions, sites for barracks, materials for building barracks, and the flora and fauna.[44]

Military surveyors and artists were sent on scouting trips to carry out physical surveys, to record the climate and general characteristics of all the mountain ranges throughout India. Lieut. Col. D. Hamilton's series of very detailed sketches and his report on the Palni mountains for the military department is a beautiful example of this type of work.[45] The series of sketches and contour maps of Mount Parisnath, credited to J.P. Steel and lithographed for the Surveyor General's office by H.M. Smith, are another such example.

The Government of Bengal's Records shed light on the time and the steps required to establish a sanatorium at Mount Parisnath. The earliest Government account of a visit to Mount Parisnath and the Jain Temples on that hill dates back to 1827. In 1858 it suggested that a sanatorium for European troops be established there, so in 1859 the suitability of the site was further tested. In 1860, once the spring water from Parisnath was approved by the Chemical Examiner, the Government issued instructions to acquire land on Parisnath Hill. The work on a small sanatorium commenced, and J.P. Steel was appointed Superintendent of the Station. In 1861 the Government of India approved the measures taken by the Government of Bengal to establish the sanatorium on Parisnath and to appoint the Superintendent with his usual allowance of 100 rupees a month.[46]

After a station was established, the surveyors recorded the physical aspects of the mountain ranges and their physiological effects. Superintendents in-charge of sanatoria, often medical officers, recorded the medical history, "exact medical topography," of the mountain climates. They noted the health of populations living at different elevations, the climate of surrounding elevated valleys, the climate of different neighbouring mountains and the meteorological observations (temperatures, diurnal variations, humidity, precipitation) of the station. They examined the human physiological systems (nervous, respiration, circulation, secretion, digestive and locomotion systems) at different elevations. They also considered the influence of mountain climates on pathology, and searched for adequate solutions for habitat, food, clothing and cultivation.[47]

Even after all these efforts the hill sanatoria did not remain free of tropical diseases. The *Report on the extent and nature of the sanitary establishments for European troops* in 1861 concluded that "the results of the various Convalescent Depots have been very disappointing."[48] Yet the army medical establishment continued to look at mountains, higher and higher mountains, for answers.

Government officials thought that to successfully complete the experiment new settlements should be established in the interior of the Himalayas. Many believed that the stations located on the mountain ranges bordering the plains, where the climate and vegetation have a tropical character, were less suited than the snowy ranges, where the climate is as bracing and healthy as that of Switzerland, with a soil equally productive, and scenery equally grand.[49] Chini (or Kinnaur), situated about 100 miles (160 km) beyond Simla, was considered for a convalescent depot. Governor-General Dalhousie spent the rainy spells of 1849-51 there. Critics complained about its inaccessibility, but he replied, "The mail will be only 46 hours from Simla, and can get there in four days, so that I am ready if wanted."[50]

Dalhousie's visit to Chini rekindled the British interest in trade with Tibet, and in the Hindustan-Tibet Road, which was commenced in 1850. As a result, the link

Opposite page:
Bungalow with a beautiful wrap-around veranda, Mahabaleshwar.

between Kalka and Simla was widened, but it never developed into a commercial road beyond Simla.[51] Since the Hindustan-Tibet road was never completed, Chini failed to develop into a full-fledged hill station and its suitability as a sanatorium was never tested.

What the authorities did not realise is that germs can be carried by an infected person into any environment irrespective of elevation. Moreover, they ignored the fact that control or spread of communicable diseases has very little to do with the location of a community per se, but more with its hygienic conditions and lifestyle. The lifestyle of the single soldiers caused considerable problems for British authorities in this regard.

Ordinary British soldiers living in India lacked the material resources for marriage, and only a few were permitted to "marry 'on the strength' of a regiment and were accordingly allowed married quarters."[52] For those who could not marry the recourse was obvious: masturbation or "mercenary love."

Great cave at the Pillar Rocks, Kodaikanal, by General Douglas Hamilton, ca. 1860. The British Library.

Pillar Rocks still remain a popular look-out and visitors' point for tourists.

However, masturbation was supposed to lead to "disorders of both body and mind" mercenary love, "to the fearful dangers of venereal diseases." Army officers regarded "homosexuality as unmanly, and it was dreaded as a threat to military discipline."[53] Frightened by the spread of venereal disease among soldiers most regiments established brothels or a *lal bazar*. Brothels, euphemistically described as "State-Licensed-Harlotry," were established in almost every hill station. "The *lal kurta*, or red jacket, was the recognised uniform of the British soldier, and this term was sometimes used as a synonym for the British cantonment, the barrack or camp area administered by the military authority. But the term *lal bazar* (bazaar) came to have special significance, as denoting the red light or brothel area."[54] Although the number of fatalities linked directly to the spread of venereal disease among soldiers is hard to establish, the annual figures of infected troops are staggering. In a survey conducted in 1886, close to 50 percent, as many as 450 troops per 1000, were reported to be suffering from venereal disease in Bengal.

For ten stations in Bengal VD infected soldiers per 1000 Troops:[55]		
1875-84	**1885**	**1886**
210.3	351	450.4

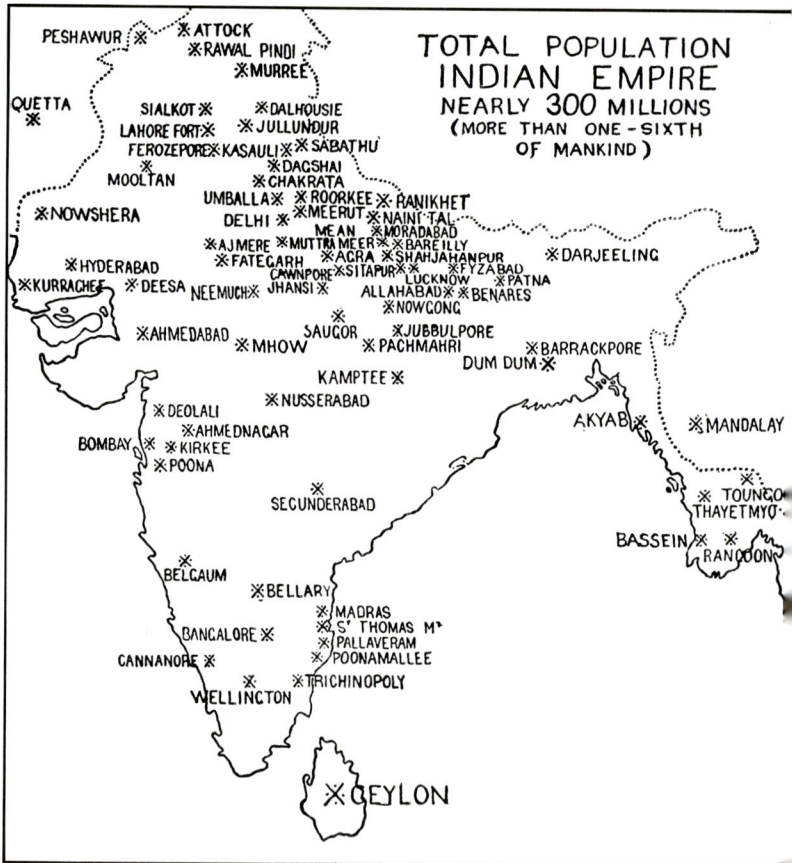

Memorial to Lieutenant Francis Reilly and his family who perished in a cholera epidemic at Dharamsala.

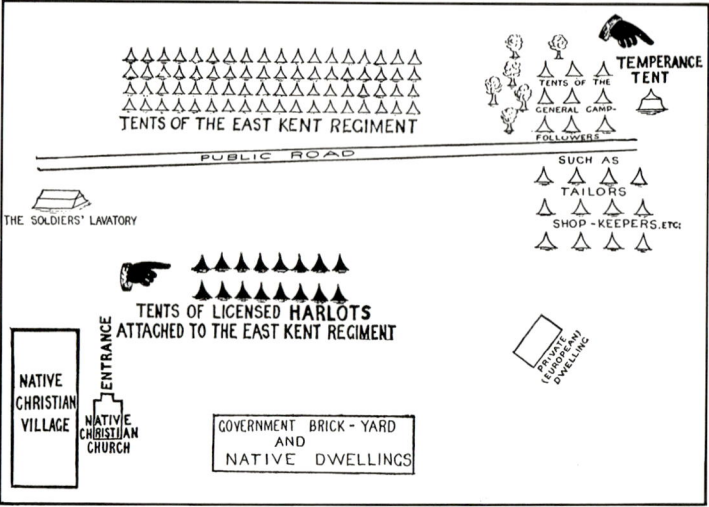

Location of 75 cantonments, most of them hill resorts, where state-licensed harlotry was permitted. After *The Sentinel*, 1888.

Map of a typical military camp, note the temperance tent on the camp side of road and the tents of licensed harlots on the other. After *The Sentinel*, 1888.

Venereal diseases did not remain the sole sickness in the hills. As the hill stations grew, hygienic conditions were compromised; as the sick came up from the plains to the hills so did tropical diseases. Undoubtedly cholera appeared in Sabathu in 1867 and 1869,[56] in Murree in 1858, in Dhurmsala (Dharamsala) or Bhagsoo in 1846, 1856 and 1857,[57] and almost all other hill stations. Often cholera had a most devastating effect. For example, in a cholera epidemic in 1875 at Dharamsala,

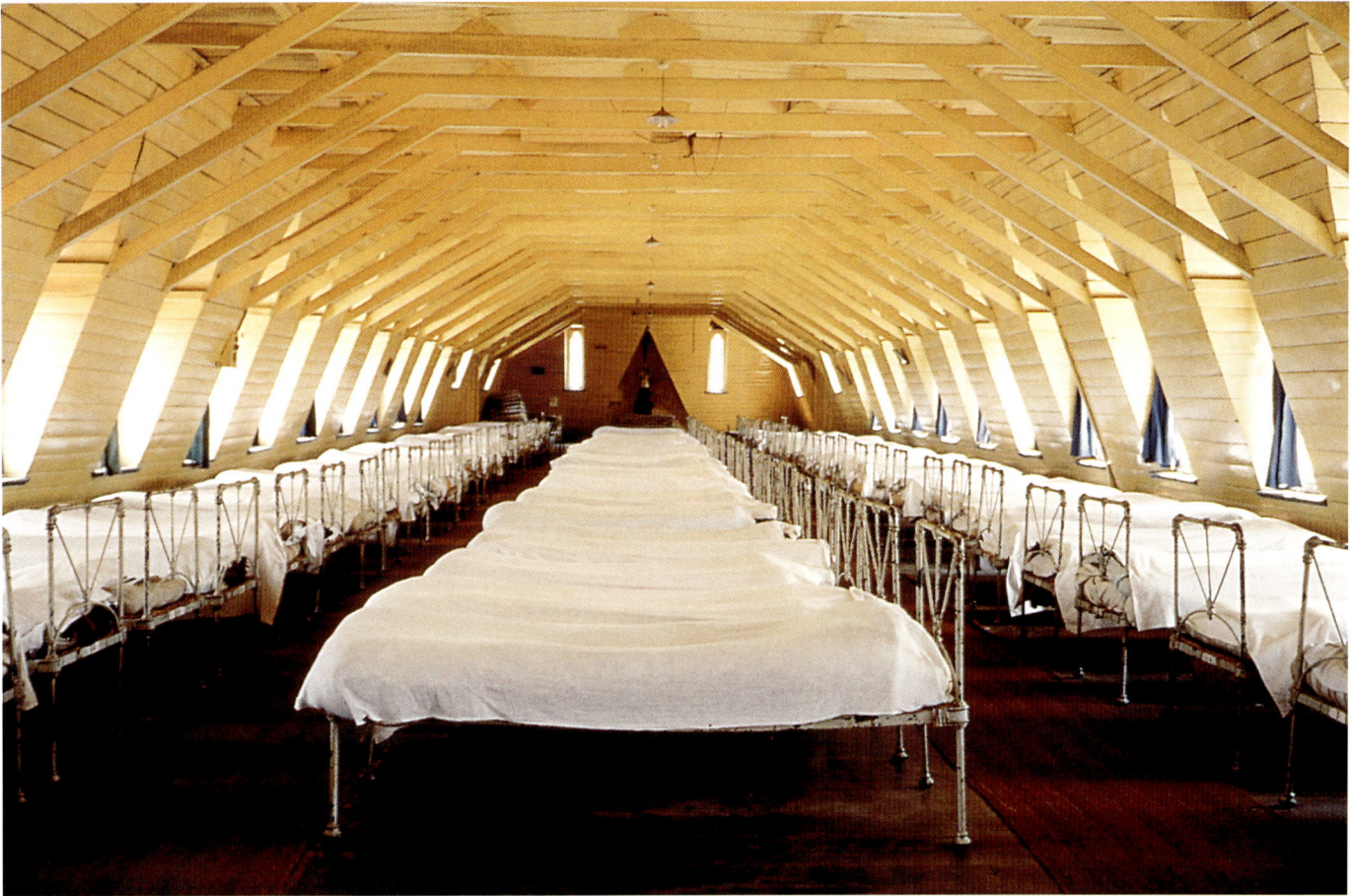

Student dormitory, Saint Joseph's College, Darjeeling. While dormitories remain crowded today, antibiotics and improved hygienic conditions prevent the spread of illness among students.

Common washroom, students dormitory, Saint Joseph's College, Darjeeling.

JESUS·SAITH·UNTO·HIM·RISE   TAKE·UP·THY·BED·AND·WALK

JESUS·TOOK·HER·BY·THE·HAND   AND·CALLED·SAYING·MAID·ARISE

+ ERECTED·BY·HIS·FRIENDS·IN   MEMORY·OF·RICHARD·JACKSON·M·D
WHO·WAS·STUNG·TO·DEATH·BY·WASPS   NEAR·THIS·PLACE·OCTOBER·1883

Lieutenant Francis Reilly lost his three children in a span of four days between July 6 to 10; he succumbed to the same malady five days later. It is impossible to imagine the suffering and anguish of his family and friends.

Even though the British perceived the hills as safe havens, these places were actually almost as susceptible to diseases as the population centres in the plains. In *Brief Account of the Past of the Lawrence Asylum* a significant number of their children is reported to have fallen sick.[58] The overcrowded dormitories, poor hygienic conditions and the lack of antibiotics must have contributed to this fact.

By the latter part of the last century, it was recognised that the hill resorts could not, and did not, offer adequate protection from tropical ailments. By then, the resorts had become an integral part of the European lifestyle in the subcontinent, and the yearly visits to the hills were well entrenched – almost embedded in the genetic code – in British officialdom. Children could get a proper education and training there. Women of means spent a good part of the hot season in the hills, and officers went up for their annual vacations.

To justify these yearly migrations the medical profession once again came to the rescue. It was argued that a hot climate always exerts an adverse influence on the European constitution, however little one may feel it. Many people remained in the hot plains for too long. Only to find out once they were sick that their change to the temperate climate, which would have reinvigorated them at the proper time, failed to produce the desired result. "It is this *change* which enables Europeans to prolong their resistance to the east; and if taken periodically and systematically, the measure of health which the individual will enjoy, will far more than counterbalance any inconvenience and expense which these changes cause."[59] There were always ready and willing medical officers to grant sick leave to the officers so that they could escape to the hills.

A stereo-typical view of women as weak and feeble creatures unable to bear the heat of the plains also perpetuated annual excursions to the hills. It was asserted that in such a climate females suffer even more than males, specially the affluent or those in easy circumstances, who are "generally torpid, and too little relieved by occupation. They have few necessities for exerting themselves; they take but little, often far too little, interest in domestic affairs; they become listless and apathetic, and they succumb to the climate sooner than men; ...But perhaps nothing produces such a beneficial effect, as regular and periodic change to another climate with a lower temperature."[60]

Along with invigorating fresh air, a change occurred in the ladies' lifestyle; the climate now allowed them to leave the house to enjoy the outdoors. They walked, hiked, rode and tended the garden, activities which improved their overall well-being and relieved them of idleness.

Even if the British soldier and his family did manage to escape the total wrath of tropical disease – real or make-believe – little did they know what hazards awaited them when they reached the hill station. The tombstones testify soberly to the harsh conditions. Consider the inexorable fate of Richard Jackson, buried in the Anglican cemetery in Pachmarhi. The marker on his grave reads:

Richard Jackson
Surgeon Major
A. M. D.
Died at Pachmarhi
24 September 1883
From the Effects of Hornet Stings
Aged 41 Years

The only consolation for his family was perhaps the beautiful stained glass window in Christ Church in Pachmarhi which immortalises his ordeal. Designed by the renowned architect Henry Irvine, a parishioner,[61] the church is a small, but beautifully crafted edifice. Its red and golden sandstone (native to the region) and a stunning set of stained glass windows give a unique glow to the interior. One of the stained glasses is a moving scene of a medical doctor helping a patient on his death-bed. Ironically, it is the same window which was donated to the church in memory of Dr. Jackson by his family and friends.

Opposite page:
Stained glass window, Christ Church, Pachmarhi. This beautiful window was donated by the family and friends of Dr. Richard Jackson who died from the effects of hornet stings.

Resorts
Then and Now

After two centuries of colonial rule, India gained its Independence on August 15, 1947. During the last five generations of their 300 year reign, the British rulers had built, cherished and patronised the hill resorts. When they left India, the heyday of the hill resorts also came to an end.

Built exclusively by and for a European clientele, the hill resorts, in fact, started to decline as early as 1925, when the recommendations of the Lee Commission allowed British officers stationed in India to spend their holidays in England. If one could go back to the true home why opt for the "home away from home?" The more sensitive Englishman realised that in many ways the bond with India was weakening. "I fear that each day we are becoming more English in India. Each year communication becomes more easy between England and the great empire in the East. Each year great facility is offered to the English official to visit his native land, and so that official becomes more and more a camper and sojourner in India. With his eyes constantly fixed on England, he does not identify himself with the people and the country, with which he has little sympathy, and is apt to regulate his conduct by the opinion of his fellow-countrymen, rather than by the interests of the Empire he is called upon to govern!"[1]

In subsequent years, various official decisions further weakened the hill resorts. In 1931, the Viceroy Lord Irwin curtailed the duration of the annual move of the government to Simla from seven months to six months.[2] More importantly, in 1939, the annual meeting of the Federal Legislature was shifted to Delhi, and with the outbreak of the World War II, in 1941, Army Headquarters, which were located around the year in Simla, were also moved permanently to Delhi.[3] Thus ended the 75-year reign of Simla as the summer capital of the British Indian Empire. Since the Presidency administrations closely followed the lead of the supreme government, the provincial summer capitals, such as Darjeeling, Mahabaleshwar, and Ootacamund, waned along with Simla. Yet British officials continued to patronise them until India's independence. Some Indian families with a large disposable income and time also maintained their summer residences in Simla and other hill resorts.

The democratic movement, especially the growing struggle for India's independence, was instrumental in undermining the high social and political standing of the British hill resorts. As the first half of the 20th century progressed, the demand for "home rule" from nationalist leaders intensified, and Indians gained an increasing share of the government administration. Led by Mahatma Gandhi, the nationalists' sentiments about the Government administration were very different from those of the British. In 1931, when Gandhi was asked where the capital of free India would be Located, he had replied, "We must go down 5,000 storeys to the plains, for

Governor's residence, Ootacamund.

Previous pages: Government House, Mahabaleshwar, garden side entry, *left,* and general view, *right.*

the Government should be among the people and for the people."[4]

It was more than a symbolic move. Gandhi was a populist who understood the Indian psyche and had a unique relationship with its masses. Gandhi, "the father of the nation," always travelled third class, explaining: "I can no more effectively deliver my message to millions by travelling first class than the Viceroy can rule over the hearts of India's millions from his unapproachable Simla heights."[5] After Independence, Simla lost its political and social clout, and along with the summer capitals the popularity of the other hill resorts also decreased. The decline was not as precipitous, however, as one might have imagined.

As the British influence diminished, and the legitimate native rulers took charge of India, the hill resorts did not change much physically. They could not. The departing foreign rulers had left behind their edifices and institutions throughout the Indian subcontinent. Other more subtle influences, however, started to alter the hill resorts' looks.

The annual infusion of the senior government bureaucrats, and their entourage stopped once the centres of power moved down to the plains, automatically altering the social and cultural make-up of the hill resorts. The small regional summer seats of Mount Abu, Naini Tal and Pachmarhi became virtual ghost towns; Pachmarhi, the most remote of the three, remains so today. This

Medical Officer's bungalow, Mount Abu.

Dak bungalow Mount Abu. More masonry used here than wood, as compared to other high elevation stations of the south or the Himalayas.

149

Main building, Government House, Pachmarhi.

Ballroom, exterior view, Government House, Pachmarhi.

Ballroom interior, Government House, Pachmarhi. This handsome top-lit room is now used as a badminton court.

situation is comparable to a single industry company town where closure of the main employment activity leaves the community without resources and purpose. Moreover, in democratic India the Government officials who still operate in these places and fine buildings do not have the same resources nor carry the pomp and grandeur of their predecessors.

The cultural vacuum created by the departing British was even more sapping than the loss of regular revenue; a whole way of life disappeared. After all, it was the Europeans and their idiosyncratic way of life – a love of the outdoors, sports and gardens; constant preoccupation with their health, eccentric demands, outrageous escapades – which added colour and gave identity to the hill resorts as true places of leisure and pleasure. The change is beautifully represented by Colonel Tusker Smalley and his wife Lucy, two main characters in Paul Scott's funny and at the same time moving classic *Staying On*. There were no passionate advocates left to protect and promote such a lifestyle and values.

During the initial decades of the post-Independence era, symbols of the British raj were treated with a certain indifference and neglect. One such symbol was the railway service linking the hills and the plains.

After Independence, the train service, another legacy of British rule in India, was an inexpensive and popular means of transportation; the rail network in India remains the most extensive and perhaps the best in the world. To maintain this rail network, in 1992 the Indian Railway was employing 1,654,066 people making it the largest single employer in the world.[6] Now a practical and inexpensive mode of transport, many trains, particularly the four rail lines linking key hill resorts to the regional metropolitan centres, have lost their opulence, charm and comfort. Little effort has been made to modernise these dainty trains, lovingly called "toy trains," but they keep on chugging. An efficient mode of transport, these trains are crowded during the high season, and often overbooked, in spite of the recent computerised reservation system.

Prior to the introduction of trains in the 1850s,[7] large parts of India were even devoid of roads. For local transport in the hill resorts, horses and *jampan*, later rickshaws, were used. A traditional *jampan* had several variations. A basic model, also referred to as a *dooli*, comprised a small wood and wicker box, in which a passenger sat, and a set of poles at two ends, which coolies carried on their shoulders; a light version of it was the *dandy*, comprising a sort of hammock, made from a *durrie*, a small cotton carpet, tied to a pole which was carried by a set of coolies. The journey up, mostly along treacherous mountain trails, was often on horse or mule back or *jampan*. The number of *jampanees*, or the sets of coolies, of course, depended on the size of the passenger.

The Fernhill Palace Hotel, Ootacamund, originally built as the Summer Palace of the Maharajah of Mysore.

If a metalled cart road was in place, passengers could make the trip lying down in uncomfortable bullock-carts or sitting in horse drawn carriages. On important routes, for example from Kalka to Simla, there were rest stops at set intervals where refreshments were served and new animals harnessed. Like the voyage from England to India on sailing ships, travel up to the hill stations was long and arduous. Therefore, as soon as work was started on rail lines to connect the four major cities, Bombay, Calcutta, Delhi and Madras, with each other,[8] proposals were made to join these four metropolitan centres with their respective networks of regional hill resorts via railways. Regardless, the trunk railway network in the plains brought the hills closer to urban centres. For example, one could get from Calcutta to Kalka, only 60 miles from Simla, on the Howrah Kalka Mail, which is still operating. Similarly, the Mahabaleshwar area became easily accessible for the Bombay crowd and Ootacamund for the Madras crowd. Other resort locations also became easily approachable via the main railway network encouraging development of new hill stations.

Rail service to the hill resorts involved complex engineering and large expenses, so it was not until the turn of the 20th century that all four links were finally in place. These trains testify to the size and wealth of the British empire. Without the vast human and material resources and control of large areas of the subcontinent, the British could not have built the extensive railway and communication networks which in turn made it possible to rule – as well as modernise – India. Today, a trip on the mountain trains can be a true delight for a railway enthusiast and provides an indulgent and historical introduction to the hill resorts and their surrounding areas.

Breakfast room, Fernhill Palace Hotel, Ootacamund. It is a true delight to enjoy a leisurely breakfast or afternoon tea in this sun-filled room.

153

Hot air ballooning, Naini Tal, ca. 1890. Europeans and their way of life – and escapades – added colour to the hill resorts. The British Library.

The Four Toy trains

The rail link between Kalka and Simla, perhaps the most ambitious of the four, is an engineering marvel of its time. The idea for it was put forth as early as 1847, but construction on the line started only in 1898. It was completed in 1903. The rail distance between Kalka and Simla was only 60 miles (98 kilometres). But as Kalka, in the foothills, is at an elevation of 2,100 feet (640 metres), and Simla at 6,801 feet (2,073 metres), the gradient of nearly half the line is 1 in 33, and the two-foot six-inch (0.75 metre) narrow-gauge line runs into a continuous succession of curves and reverse

Schooner on lake Naini Tal, ca. 1860. It is hard to imagine the effort required to haul a wooden schooner more than 6,000 feet up the rugged Himalayan terrain. The British Library.

curves with a radius of only 120 feet.[9] Moreover, to complete the line 107 tunnels (only 102 remain today),[10] aggregating five miles in length (eight kilometres), numerous lofty arched viaducts, adding up to one and three-quarter miles (2.8 kilometres) and innumerable cuts and stone walls had to be built.[11] This commercial venture was supposed to cost 8.6 million rupees, but amounted to twice the original estimate, leading the enterprise into a loss. Since a railway link was considered important for the summer capital of the Raj, the government took it over.

Nandi Hill, near Bangalore. Mahatma Gandhi loved this tiny resort of only half a dozen bungalows. He was brought here to recover after his long fasts protesting the British rule in India and his efforts to calm the violence between Hindus and Muslims.

A contemporary traveller can leave from New Delhi station early in the morning and reach Kalka before noon, where a toy-train awaits to leave for Simla. For the Victorian traveller, taking the train meant novelty and progress; for the passenger today, there is a pleasure in reliving the past, in spite of the slowness, relative discomfort and overcrowding of this anachronistic mode of transport. During the course of the journey, many details become apparent. The train is powered by a diesel engine, and not a real coal-fired steam engine. The ascent is quick, and the scenery splendid, especially after the train completes its first swing around the valley overlooking Kalka and the hazy Punjab plains with hints of its new capital Chandigarh in the far distance.

23 miles (37 kilometres) from Kalka the train stops at the handsome station of Barog. Here, in days gone by, the halt lasted an hour and a lavish lunch was served at Spencer's a beautiful restaurant.[12] Today, the stop is much shorter, allowing just enough time to get the bread *pakoras* and tea sold from a little kiosk. The original station remains unchanged, a charming mix of chalet and cottage-style building, decorated with hanging flower baskets. Actually, all the diminutive structures on the line, cabins for linesmen, attendants' cottages at level crossings, and all 20 stations, were inspired by the same chalet style.

In the late afternoon the train is in the vicinity of Simla. Before it swings around to the back (north side) of the Simla ridge to the Summer Hill station, we capture a captivating panorama of a city clinging precariously to the steep southern slopes. In *Kim*, Kipling described this dense ensemble as a "crowded rabbit warren," that has grown even more congested over the 100 odd years since the classic was first published.

To our astonishment and satisfaction the familiar landmarks are still visible: at one end, Mount Jakho; on the other, on top of Observatory Hill, the Viceregal Lodge; and in the middle, the Town Hall, the Bandstand Gazebo and Christ Church, whose distinctive gothic tower seems to crown the glory of the Mall. Two oversised government buildings, Gorton Castle and the Railway Board buildings stand near the centre, and a recent addition, the television transmission tower, looms over them. It is a tiring journey, almost six hours long, which could be completed in about half the time by automobile. However, this approach to Simla offers an effective introduction to the flora, fauna, and the landscape of the surrounding hills, and a nostalgic and sentimental journey back in time.

The first stretch of railway line in India was opened in the 1850s and ran between Bombay and Thana. Soon after, this line was extended to Poona. After The Illustrated London News.

At the eastern end of the country, the second train ride is as extraordinary and charming. The Siliguri to Darjeeling railway link, with a rise of almost 6,500 feet (2,000 metres), winding in and out among the mountains, over great crags and deep precipices, has often been described as a wonderful piece of engineering work.[13] Without heavy tunnelling or viaduct construction, the line is more a product of engineering finesse rather than force. For economy, most of the rail line was laid on an already existing cart road, built by the Public Works Department, that had already overcome the initial engineering difficulties. Great skill was required, however, to work on the existing road without exceeding the one in 25 gradient and also to assure that the proper curves needed for the fixed steel rails were somehow incorporated in the line. This was achieved through the clever use of loops, double loops and overlapping loops.

The 51 mile (84 kilometres) train ride from Siliguri to Darjeeling, like the ride from Kalka to Simla, is rather tiring, but offers many rewards. Soon after the train departs from Siliguri it passes through a superb region with lush and varied vegetation. Lofty trees rising from the tropical jungle and the famous tree-ferns start to appear. Further up are great views of the *terai*, or lower

foot hills, and the great plains beyond. At about mid-point in the journey, these vistas are spectacular. Above 4,000 feet (1,230 metres), around Kurseong station, the tea plantations, for which the region is world renowned, take over the forest until Darjeeling. The train climbs to an elevation of 7,407 feet (2,225 metres) near the Indo-Nepal border at Ghoom, also famous for its Tibetan Buddhist monastery of the Yellow Sect. From Ghoom, the train starts to descend towards Darjeeling; there lies the famous Batasia double loop which offers an exhilarating view of Darjeeling. On a clear day, with good visibility (clouds often veil the view for days together), the majestic beauty of snow-clad Kanchenjunga and its surrounding peaks fills the eye – there is hardly a vista in the eastern Himalayas to surpass this view. On another technical plane on this rare, two-foot wide gauge train, carriages are still pulled by real steam engines rather than diesel. These steam engines weigh 14 tons and are capable of pulling up 50 tons weight.

For those pressed for time, but interested in the views from the final approach to Darjeeling, there is an easier way around. A taxi can be hired near Darjeeling town hall to go to Ghoom, and one can hop back on the toy-train going towards Darjeeling. The taxi ride, usually

156

Travelling via *jampan* and *dandis.* After The Illustrated London News.

in 1950s Land Rovers kept shiny and running – one wonders how – is yet another experience of travel back in time.

Large segments of the railway between Ootacamund, elevation 7,349 feet (2,240 metres) and Mettupalayam elevation 2,000 feet (615 metres) were washed away during the heavy floods in early 1994. The authorities could not determine when the entire service would resume. The real train buff can still take a short trip between Ootacamund and Coonoor. With the superior ascending views leading into Ootacamund downs, the reverse trip is more exciting. The rolling blue mountain tops first appear on either side, then the lake and the race course, and finally Saint Thomas's Church with its large cemetery, and the town itself with distant hills beyond.

The Ootacamund–Mettupalayam trip is more comfortable than the train journeys mentioned previously. The rail gauge is wider making the carriages more stable. The train also uses a different mechanical device, an additional set of steel rails, the teeth of which break pitch and engage with the engine, allowing a much steeper (1:12.5) gradient for the line. This train also passes through an amazing array of man-made landscapes. The journey begins in a rich agricultural valley, covered with paddy fields and coconut plantations. After a quick ascent it enters the spices country; aromatic spices such as cloves,

Viaduct on the Kalka-Simla railway line. The line is an engineering marvel of its time. To complete it 107 tunnels, numerous lofty arched viaducts and innumerable cuts and stone walls had to be built. The British Library.

157

cinnamon and nutmeg are grown here. Coffee and pepper appear soon after. Around 5,000 feet elevation large patches of eucalyptus plantations and a sudden drop in the temperature signal that the tea plantations and the rolling grass-covered hills – the Nilgiri downs – which made Ootacamund so popular among the British, are not far.

Established almost 150 years ago, parts of the train service between Bombay and Poona make up the oldest stretch of the Indian railway system. The line has grown over the years, being an essential part of the network linking the most influential commercial centre of India with the southern half of the country. It has been electrified and one can practically commute between Bombay and Poona. The

Engineering works for the Siliguri-Darjeeling railway line, also known as the Darjeeling Railway. The ascent includes a complete loop and even a double loop. After W.S. Caine, *Picturesque India.*

passage of the train through the rugged Western Ghats, or the Sahyadri mountains, especially at the Khandala pass, is pleasurable, and it also required great engineering skills. Because the pass was important strategically, the British established the tiny cantonment of Khandala nearby. The original cantonment, measuring slightly less than 44 acres in area, was located close to Khandala railway station with a controlling view of the surrounding area and the railway. In recent years, Khandala has become a fashionable weekend retreat for Bombay residents; there is hardly a structure from the British era visible either from the train or when walking through the town.

Similarly, Poona has also benefited from its

A short train ride between Neral and Matheran offers magnificent views of the Western Ghats.

Often hidden by the clouds, the Kanchenjunga peak is awe-inspiring when visible.

Original steam-engines are used on the Siliguri-Darjeeling line and are lovingly maintained by railway staff.

The Coonoor-Ootacamund train skirts by the Ootacamund lake and the Catholic cemetery facing it.

proximity to Bombay. When the British took control of Poona after the final Maratha War in 1817, it was already a well established urban centre. Norman Macleod found that "Poona is very different from Bombay... in the very expanse of the plain, in the fine broad roads. There is a pleasant sense of relief. The neat, scattered bungalows, set amidst flowers and shrubs, give a fresh, healthy look, resembling very much an inland English watering-place."[14] At Kirkee, across the Mutha river from Poona, the British established a large military cantonment and also the headquarters of the Royal Bombay Sappers and Miners. Poona was the residence of the Government of Bombay during the rains, and flourished under the British. Large parts of the cantonment and numerous

outstanding buildings remain: the Sassoon Hospital, designed by John Begg, a gifted architect who was in charge of the Public Works Department in the early 1900s; the Roman Catholic Cathedral dedicated to Saint Patrick; the Church of the Holy Name, with a lofty campanile modelled on the famous Campanile at Venice; and the Deccan College, a rambling Gothic-style structure built using local grey stone. Unfortunately, in the post-Independence era, the city has overgrown into a vast metropolis overcrowding the old English charm.

Close to Poona are three hill resorts: Mahabaleshwar, Panchgani and Matheran. Even without the awesome Himalayan peaks or the lush greenery of the South, they have a charm of their own.

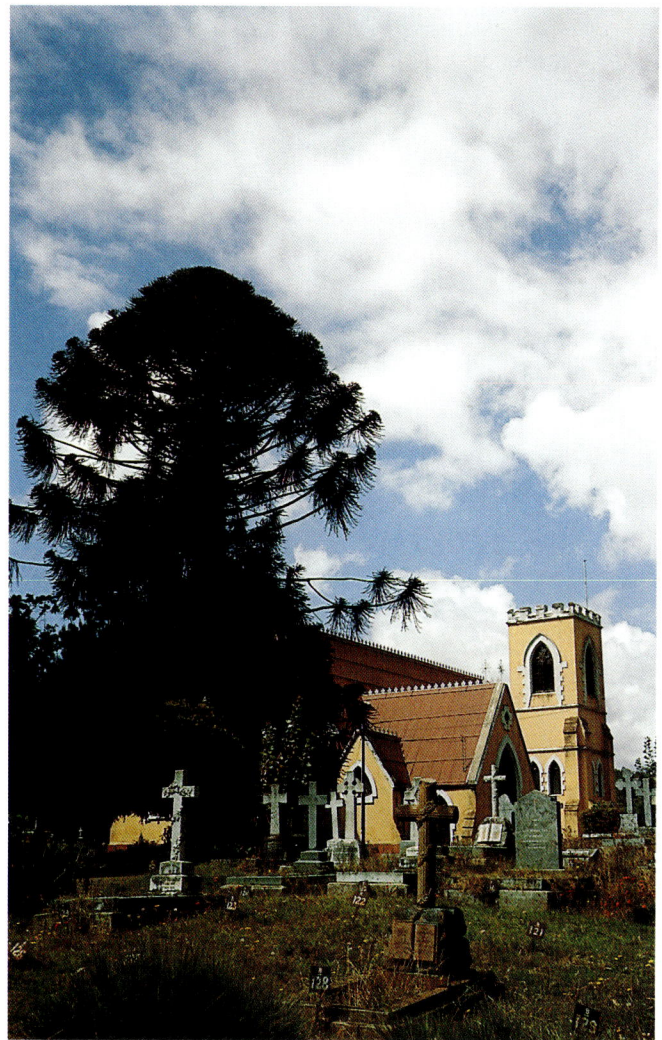

Saint Thomas' Church and its adjoining Catholic cemetery.

Mahabaleshwar, also known as Malcolm Peth, served as the principal hill station of Bombay Presidency. Founded in 1828 by Governor Sir John Malcolm, it was first identified in 1827 by General Lodwick; at Lodwick Point, a pillar commemorating the site visited by General Peter Lodwick was erected by his son. Unlike the North Indian hill stations these resorts had two seasons: April and May, and after the heavy monsoon rains, another from October to December. Few cared to remain during the monsoon storms from June to September. The Mahabaleshwar resort occupies a plateau. On a clear day, the Arabian Sea, only 30 miles due west, is visible from Bombay point. Once heavily wooded, there are still walks through tree covered patches, terminating at fine views such as at

Babington Point, Arthur's Seat and Elphinstone Points. Old Mahabaleshwar is famous for a sacred temple from which Krishna is said to rise. The station has a small lake with very rudimentary boating facilities, built by the Raja of Satara, and two waterfalls, the Yenna Falls and the Dhobi waterfalls. Most bungalows are built of stone and mud masonry with heavy columns and thick walls, covered by galvanised iron sheets painted green or rust-red and placed over wooden rafters. The red colour of the soil and the use of red stone in building give a particular glow to the houses and their surroundings. This station was used to house Chinese prisoners, who were used as labourers in the fruit and vegetable gardens and an area below Sassoon Point is still called Chinaman's Gardens. There are the remains of a Chinese cemetery too, not far from Helen's Point. A fine Holy Cross Church sits opposite the town square and the Library. The library also is a finely crafted structure with a wraparound veranda the cast-iron railings of which bear the insignia D.S.P. after D.S. Petit, a Parsi businessman who donated money to establish the library and after whom the facility is named. A legacy of the Raj are the fine strawberries grown in Mahabaleshwar and supplied not only to Bombay but the entire country.

Typical bungalow, Panchgani. Located in the vicinity of Bombay and Poona, the town has emerged as a key educational centre in western India, with close to 25 public schools. Parents or tourists who frequent this station could rent such bungalows.

Just 12 miles east lies Panchgani, founded by John Chesson in the early 1850s. It developed as a satellite of Mahabaleshwar and became popular as an educational centre for Bombay-based Europeans, Parsis and other Indian communities. Only 60 miles from Poona and 170 miles from Bombay most students come from these two cities, with parents looking for quiet and safe surroundings and seeking an old English-style education. St. Peter's School was established by the Continental and Colonial Church Office to educate the European military staff children. Today, run entirely by local staff, it still maintains the British-style house system, each House having its own House-master. Today other schools follow varied beliefs: the New Era School is run by people of the Bahai faith. As in the case of Mussoorie, education is the main source of revenue for Panchgani with about 20 well-established Public Schools each with a population of over 200 students. The direct input of about 10 million rupees per annum has a very positive multiplier effect on the local economy. Traditionally frequented by wealthy business people, in particular the Parsi community living in Bombay, a series of sanatoria were established here; many are still thriving with clients from Bombay.

About an hour south of Bombay, the Bombay-Poona trains stops at the nondescript Neral station. There, one can take a short, two-hour ride on another toy-train up to the tiny hill resort of Matheran. Matheran is a well kept secret, with an interesting history regarding its train service.

The Bombay-Poona railway line, completed in 1854, enabled visitors from Bombay to reach Neral within 90 minutes; the larger number of visitors going to Matheran in turn increased the importance of the resort. Sir Adamji Peerbhoy, a Bombay business magnate and philanthropist, once came down to Neral, only to find that all the horses and rickshaws were booked. Not a single vehicle was available to go up to Matheran, and, disappointed, Sir Adamji returned to Bombay. This is when he decided to build his own railway linking Matheran from Neral. He also resolved to visit the resort only after his own railway was ready. A scheme for the railway, submitted by Sir Adamji's son and based on the Kalka-Simla line, was approved by the Government in 1903, and the Neral-Matheran service was opened on 15th April 1907.[15]

Only 13 miles (21 kilometres) in length, the Neral-Matheran toy train run is the shortest of all the hill resort links in India. Matheran hill is only 2,625 feet (800 metres) high, but the train needs two hours to negotiate the climb, which can be completed in thirty minutes by an automobile or by an athletic five-hour hike. Sir Adamji Peerbhoy's Matheran Railway Company introduced

One-tree-hill, Matheran, ca. 1870. Hugh Pointz Malet first reached the top of the Matheran plateau via this location. The British Library.

A view of the Matheran hill, ca. 1870. After *Letters from India and Kashmir.*

The Governor of Bengal's grand and splendid summer residence and surrounding estate, Darjeeling.

several innovative ideas: a concession fare for large parties and the poor of the Hill Station, reduced rate return tickets during holidays, Christmas and Diwali (the Hindu New Year celebrated as a festival of lights); and a short notice rail service starting from Neral. Technically, it has not kept up with the times, particularly after it was nationalised. Constantly twisting and turning the train offers magnificent views, especially when it swings around Panorama Point. The commotion of various vendors getting on and off the moving train, and the movement of the adroit ticket collector from one carriage to another, from one crowded footboard to the next, add to this experience.

The train service triggered the development of Matheran, but an exceptional individual gets credit for the establishment of the resort. Hugh Pointz Malet, Collector of Thana district, was only a few years from retirement when he discovered Matheran, but he strove hard to make it into a first-rate hill resort.

Dreamer Explorer

In May 1850, on a district tour, Malet was camped near Chauk, a village situated just under the southern edge of Matheran, when he remembered an incident dating back twenty years. In 1830, Malet was having breakfast with Sir John Malcolm, Governor of Bombay,

when a report of the Commission on the two adjoining hills of Prabal and Matheran was delivered. With a view to setting up, on one or the other, a military sanatorium, the report pronounced both hills totally unfit for such a purpose, alleging deficiency in the water supply, making the project of a station unviable. Now finding himself in the vicinity of Matheran, Malet, the chief administrator of the district, made further inquiries about the area. To his surprise he found that the Officers of the Commission had made a very casual sort of investigation of Prabal at the time and, having never really visited Matheran, he decided to explore the hill for himself.[16]

Malet reached the top of the Matheran plateau via the now famous "One Tree Hill" and also visited the Bund valley, where a cool rivulet runs through the Parisnath Ravine, at the head of what is now called Charlotte Lake, Matheran's main water supply. He collected samples of the native soil, rocks, and water from springs for later examination, and returned to Chauk.[17] Convinced of the suitability of Matheran as a sanatorium, Malet obtained a grant of 500 rupees to make a passable road from Chauk, from the Government in 1852.[18]

Malet was captivated by the beauty of Matheran. In September 1850, road or no road, Malet sent ahead chickens, goats, and rabbits to the headman of Chauk to be brought up to Matheran hill. Prior to Malet's arrival, the local headman's son brought up the supplies and built a temporary structure for their use. The climb for Malet's team was not easy, especially for Mrs. Malet, who was carried on a makeshift *jampan* assembled by lashing a chair to poles. Malet and his family reached Matheran on the first of November and spent 30 days there.[19] Matheran, bypassed 20 years earlier, was again envisioned as a hill resort.

Malet had the jungle cleared at several places, creating beautiful vistas. He discovered some natural springs, and had the plateau surveyed to subdivide it for plots in the future. In 1851, three years from his retirement, Malet built the first permanent bungalow at Matheran, and invited relatives and powerful friends to do the same. So persuasive was Malet that in 1854, the year he retired and left for England, Lord Elphinstone, the Governor of Bombay, was in Matheran, making plans to build his own house on a 37 acre wooded site.[20] Matheran was rapidly becoming an influential resort.

Matheran, barely 106 miles (170 kilometres) south-east of Bombay, sits on a small plateau. The plateau stands on its own, at a distance of about 13 miles (20 kilometres), from the Sahyadris, the main chain of mountains which run along the south-western edge of the subcontinent. Surrounded by the Sahyadri mountains, which in the immediate vicinity rise to an elevation of 5,000 feet (1,540 metres) and stretch out as far as the eye can see, the Matheran plateau is insignificant. With an area of only 8 square miles (20 square kilometres), and an elevation of a mere 2,600 feet (800 metres) its proportions are paltry. Nevertheless, Matheran hill, like a young tusker separated from its herd, is most impressive in its completeness and beauty.

Amazingly, there are numerous old buildings, original bungalows built during the early years, which still stand. For example, four out of the first five bungalows to be built at Matheran remain: H.P. Malet's "The Byke," Captain Barr's "Barr Cottage," Captain Walker's "Walker Cottage," the Revenue Commissioner Fawcett's "The Hermitage," and Arthur Malet's, (Collector Malet's brother) "Stonehenge." "The Byke," converted into a luxury hotel bearing the same name, retains its original structure, but is surrounded by a series of new facilities. "Barr Cottage" has disappeared. "Walker Cottage" known as the "Tour Petit," is run as a private sanatorium by the Bai Avanbai Petit Trust. "Stonehenge," known as "Readymoney House," and "The Hermitage" are reasonably well preserved, and used as private vacation homes.

Matheran, unlike most other resorts sitting on hill crests and stretching out in either direction along the mountain ridge, sits on a relatively level plateau. Finite and minute, Matheran is and feels like an island on an open horizon. Malet made sure that Matheran, with no room to grow, developed as an exclusive hill resort.

Indeed, even today, there are only 426 plots on Matheran hill; 203 of them are for bungalows ranging in sizes from 2.24 to 90 acres and 223 are small bazaar plots, averaging about 100 square metres each and found in a closely arranged grid.[21]

Furthermore, due to its proximity to Bombay, the greatest business centre in India, Matheran attracted the powerful and financial elite of the country. At its peak, the list of prestigious visitors who frequented the station read like the Who's Who of Bombay Presidency: Lord Elphinstone, Governor of Bombay, Sir William Yardley, Chief Justice of Bombay, the Aga Khan, spiritual leader of the *Ismailis,* and business barons such as Sir Kawasji Jahangir, Sir Rattan Tata, and of course, Sir Adamji Peerbhoy, the man behind the train service. The visionary zeal and missionary persistence of Malet – typical of the colonial administrators – plus the financial commitment of its rich users, made Matheran a successful retreat.

A conversation with Shankarrao Mahadev Savant, born in 1915, the oldest surviving native of Matheran today, reveals what happened to the station after the British left. According to Savant, who at that time worked with the local Medical Officer as the Senior Compounder, "the exodus of the British in 1947 had a devastating effect on this hill station. I had to deal with members of different communities who frequented Matheran. Members of three main communities frequented Matheran; Europeans, Parsees, and *Khojas* (Ismailis followers of the Aga Khan), and a few Jews. With the departure of the Europeans, the group which had been most enthusiastic about the station, the native communities lost their interest. They just stopped coming."[22]

The enjoyment of leisure is a very personal, almost whimsical, thing. The snobbish Bombay business elite continued to patronise the exclusive resort of Matheran as long as they could mingle with the rulers. But once the British left, they had no reason to continue the charade of going up to the hill resorts. Their pledge to the place was primarily for prosperity rather than for genuine personal pleasure. Besides, most native patrons of the station could afford several homes in different locations, so they just locked up and held on to their Matheran properties after the British left. For the same reason, few properties changed hands in Matheran and it has an air of abandonment, an empty movie decor. The decline of Matheran in post-colonial times shows how primordial was the leadership role of the British in the life of the hill resorts.

Matheran, and other successful resorts of the Raj existed and flourished because of the courage, drive, vision and motivation of exceptional individuals. They include men like Captain Charles Pratt Kennedy, the pioneer of Simla; John Sullivan, who founded Ootacamund and Doctor Campbell, who transformed the

Above and below: Botanical Garden, Darjeeling. Dr. Campbell, transformed Darjeeling sanatorium into a resort, making it an integral part of the high social life and legacy of the Raj.

Cadets' dormitory, Indian Military Academy, Dehra Dun, with its luxuriant gardens, *above* and colonnaded lobby, *below*.

Darjeeling sanatorium into a resort. In the history of hill resorts, these men are often referred to as heartless administrators, but these were the entrepreneurs who created the successful resorts that became an integral part of the high social life and legacy of the Raj.

The entrepreneurial drive which created the British hill resorts and the circumstances and needs which are transforming them at present are very disparate. In terms of individual motivation, people are still trying hard to achieve something, but there are marked differences between the two situations which are worth reflecting on, especially to understand what is happening to the hill resorts today.

Resorts Today

Before returning to the plains, A.U. wrote: "At last the pleasant sojourn on the hills came to a close; and strengthened and invigorated, but with many regrets, I prepared for my return to the stifling atmosphere of the plains."[23] The British loved the hills, and made them an integral part of life in India. Today the hill resorts, sidelined during the initial decades of Independence, are becoming fashionable once again for Indians. Enough time has elapsed since the departure of the foreign rulers for a less passionate and more objective assessment – and enjoyment – of their legacy. Just as certain positive aspects of the British heritage, particularly parliamentary democracy, civil administration and language have

Forest Research Institute, Dehra Dun, main building with imposing entrance porches, *above* and finely vaulted brickwork, *opposite page.*

become an integral part of modern India, likewise the hill resorts have become part of Indian life and culture.

For instance, the hill resorts have retained their role as the prime educational centres of India. Their role as ideal places to send children for a good education seems to have grown in the recent years. A number of new schools have opened up in resorts like Dehra Dun, Mussoorie, Ootacamund and Panchgani.

The educational and research institutions created by the British, such as the Indian Military Academy (modelled after Sandhurst), and the Forest Research Institute, Dehra Dun, or the Thomson Engineering College (now Central Building Research Institute), Roorkee, are thriving. In addition, the Government has established several new institutions such as the prestigious Indian Administrative Service Training facility with beautiful views of the snowy Siwalik mountain chain in the upper Himalayas at Mussoorie.

India has the world's largest cinema industry. In a curious way Indian cinema has played a significant role in promoting the hill stations through the scenic beauty of mountains. The love songs and honeymoon sequences in Indian films use Kashmir or other alpine locations as the standard backdrop. From this a honeymoon in the hills has become an essential part of life for the growing Indian middle-class, estimated to be 200 million people. With the political unrest in Kashmir, young honeymooners and holiday seekers alike now flock to other, calmer hill resorts.

Unlike European tourists, who went to the hill resorts for the entire season, most contemporary tourists are short-term, two-to-seven day visitors, their large numbers making up for short visits. Unlike the British, these temperamental tourists do not have the commitment or vested interests in the hill resorts as places to live. They do not attach the same aesthetic or sentimental value to the landscape and nature. The tendency of the short-term visitors is to try to get the most out of their visit. Local tour guides and services oblige by rushing tourists between scenic spots and "important" locations in mini-vans. Unfortunately this type of automobile and human traffic places dreadful pressures on the local ecology.

Matheran is the only hill resort in India that has resisted the assault of the automobile, which has preserved the original character of the station. While on the plateau one either walks, rides on horse back, or takes a rickshaw. All roads on the plateau are between 15 to 25 feet (five to seven metres) wide and are earthbound macadam made from the local laterite stones and red earth. Most of these primitive roads, built during the British rule, survive. Pedestrians enjoy the tranquil long walks on red-earth paths, covered with a canopy of dark green leaves and nut brown branches – a true delight. The spirit of the original British hill station, with charming bungalows, beautiful walks terminating at different viewpoints, and captivating vistas to be enjoyed at a specific time of the day, like sunrise or sunset, lingers on. Rugged trails with magnificent views, reminiscent of the Grand Canyon, forest trees and brushwood of endless variety, birds and butterflies in abundance – nature is intact – because Matheran is still free of automobile traffic.

Only once did some brave American troops (stationed here during the Second World War) actually drive a car up to Matheran, but the Government soon after prohibited the use of motor vehicles.[24] There is not an inch of asphalt-covered road on Matheran but it is not certain how long the local authorities will be able to resist the invasion of the automobile.

The old government summer seats, of Darjeeling, Ootacamund and Simla, which have comfortable and well-established facilities, and stations accessible from the large urban centres in the plains, like Dehra Dun, Khandala, Mussoorie, Panchgani are the prime tourist and educational destinations. But they are changing quickly. The large volume of automobile traffic and tremendous amount of new construction, which is occurring in these resorts, is a result of the growing tourist

At the beginning of the 20th century, Chamba was described as the most Italian looking town in the Himalayas. Although overcrowded now, the town has not lost its original charm; view of the town from a distance, *above* and its alpine surroundings, *right*.

trade and population pressures. The new construction – hotels, holiday resorts, commercial developments, private bungalows, apartments – is sometimes done by large builders and hotel chains, but most of it is individual enterprise. What is lacking is an overall view of the development, a coherent vision of the town.

In the past, this vision, if not always formally elaborated, was understood and respected by a resort community. Administrators and residents alike held common values. They established, developed and nurtured a community having a vested interest in its exclusivity and charm. When permitted to acquire properties in hill resorts, influential natives and princes followed the same rules of conduct. The British influence went even further.

In places such as Chamba, capital of the Himalayan hill state of the same name, native rulers worked closely to develop a unique blend of a European and Indian hill town. So successful was the blend that Murray's Handbook of India described it as "the most Italian-looking town." The progressive Rajah of Chamba also built a hospital, a "residency" (guesthouse) to house distinguished visitors and a museum; in addition he donated money to build a church for the Scottish regiment

Bungalow, Kalimpong, near Darjeeling.

Bungalow of the Governor's Aide-de-camp, Darjeeling.

Bungalow, Pachmarhi.

Church, Darjeeling.

The Nilgiris form the Pillar Rocks, Kodaikanal.

stationed there and a hydro-electric power station for the town. Even today, Chamba remains one of the most charming towns in the Himalayas.

In the British hill stations, of course, there was always a native part of the town juxtaposed in every hill resort and occupied mainly by servants and traders. They were required but did not matter much in the general scheme of things. Moreover, since most of the superior officers at all levels of government, national, state and municipal, were British they set up plans and allocated funds to reinforce these European communities.

For example, there were guidelines which made funds available from the government for the construction of churches when the community grew to a given size and could raise matching funds. The minister would be supported by the ecclesiastical department of the government. *Chowkidars* and gardeners were hired from the same departmental funds to care for European cemeteries. The government paid for the gravestones of officers who died on duty, in addition, friends and relatives contributed freely to build beautiful memorials in memory of their loved ones. In secular and democratic India, the ecclesiastical department ceased to exist. Churches and cemeteries lost the qualified staff and caretakers and deteriorated.[25]

The above programmes may seem, and up to a point were, like a welfare undertaking. However, they were essential to maintain a sense of community among Europeans, and to preserve their faith and morale in a foreign land. With regard to the administration and upkeep of the hill resorts the government maintained tight control on fiscal affairs. After all, the hill resorts were like private clubs, or exclusive resorts, patronised by expatriates, and the government chose not to contribute much towards their maintenance. Residents of the hill resorts were expected to, and did, pay for most of their local services. To maintain the quality of services and their privileges, this high caste elite paid dearly. Pets, peons, pleasure yachts and properties, nothing was spared from municipal taxes.

For example, following the cholera epidemic of 1891-92 in Naini Tal, a request was made for funds to improve the water supply and drainage system of the town. The government did not approve the loan until the local authorities revised their tax structure. The municipal government had to increase the conservancy tax on large buildings, raise the toll on carts and animals entering the town, double the tax on servants and dogs, levy new taxes on boats and yachts, and demonstrate that they could carry the additional fiscal burden. Similarly, when the local administrators of Ootacamund asked the national government to pay for some of their conservancy charges this request was turned down. For this minor expense, involving bullock carts for refuse removal, the municipal government bore the burden from its own tax revenues.

Koyna valley from the terrace of the Bohemia bungalow, Mahabaleshwar.

The indigenous urban settlements throughout India were overcrowded and lacked a modern infrastructure – piped water and sanitation facilities – which resulted in frequent epidemics. By contrast, the hill resorts were quick to develop a modern infrastructure, and efficient city managers strove to keep them healthy and safe from the outbreak of epidemics. Rings of check points were often set up to prevent the entry of people infected with cholera and the plague, in particular, into hill resorts. To the English mind, the hill resorts were beacons of clean healthy and superior living, to be held up as examples of model towns for the Indians living in the plains. The hill resorts epitomised the European way of life, and it was for that sense of exclusion, that the homesick and chauvinistic British did not mind bearing the high tax burden.

In spite of the leadership role they enjoyed under the British, the hill stations, went through a very unsettled period in the last 50 years. For example, immediately after Independence, Simla was chosen as an interim administrative centre for the state of Punjab. The post-Independence partition of India resulted in the division of the Punjab state; the western half including the capital Lahore, went to Pakistan, and the eastern half, left without an administrative headquarters, to India. Simla was used as the capital of Punjab until 1956, when the seat of the government was shifted to the newly built state capital of Chandigarh. In 1972, Simla was again chosen as a capital of the newly-created mountain state of Himachal Pradesh, and remains so today.

Other resorts like Ootacamund and Darjeeling have also been subjected to coming and going of different governments – administrators and resources – making it difficult to plan properly for a long-term future.

The physical needs of increasing tourist traffic, natural population growth and rural migration – the pressures of urbanization – in most stations have been overlooked. Simla was designed to accommodate about 25,000 people comfortably. Its population had quadrupled in 1991 and it is estimated that it will reach 150,000 by the year 2001. Since 1947 there has not been a significant addition made to meet the water or other infrastructure demands and community needs. Today, Simla is experiencing serious municipal problems.

Municipal Tax Bill for 1896.

Office Home Department 3.   Municipal Office,
Simla,   7.   1896.

Serial No.	PARTICULARS.	No.	Rate.	Amount of Tax		
			Rs.	*Rs.*	*a.*	*p.*
1	*Four-wheeled vehicles drawn by horses, ponies or mules*		50			
2	*Two-wheeled vehicles drawn by horses, ponies or mules*		25			
3	*Two or three-wheeled vehicles drawn or propelled by men, excluding Children's perambulators*		8			
4	*Horses, ponies, mules or donkeys used for driving or riding*		4			
5	*Horses, ponies, mules or donkeys used for burden*		2			
6	*Dogs*		2			
7	* *Menial and domestic servants. Payable by the master or employer on menial and domestic servants residing or working for gain as such within the limits of the Municipality*	34	2	68	.	.
		Total ...		68	.	.

This tax is due on all servants whether residing in the compound or not.

On return of this bill to the Municipal Office, with the amount due, a proper receipt will be granted. Bills not paid within ten days are placed before the Municipal Committee. *vide* note on reverse.

Secretary
Municipal Committee.

Nothing – pleasure yachts, properties – and nobody – pets, peons – was spared municipal taxes. A tax receipt for servants and dogs, Simla. The National Archives of India.

But all is not lost. In some stations, the long-term residents of the community are starting to consider the local development issues seriously. A national heritage movement to conserve the fragile ecology of the hill regions is gaining momentum. In Kodaikanal for example, the Palni Hills Conservation Council has managed to pass legislation protecting the Kodaikanal lake as well as the surrounding hills. They are running seminars, training courses and newsletters for the rural populations of the surrounding areas. Their courses about improved agricultural practices, and land, soil and water conservation in the fragile hill ecology are noteworthy. There are similar groups active in parts of the Himalayas as well.

Conservation groups have catalogued important landmarks to protect significant buildings. In the Indian context, however, the number of historical monuments is so overwhelming that authorities cannot allocate enough resources to protect them.

A synergy of ideas, circumstances, individuals, and lifestyle, centred around the natural beauty of a place, brought into being the hill resorts of India. Two generations after the departure of the British, hill resorts like Kalimpong, Kodaikanal, Matheran, Ootacamund, Pachmarhi and Yercaud, have remained fairly intact. Almost 50 years of neglect have permitted slow decay and melancholy to surround these stations, but if anything, the passage of time has added other layers of beauty and meaning. Hopefully, the local communities will prize and succeed in preserving this unique heritage to be enjoyed in the next millennium.

Endnotes

Introduction

1 Nora Mitchell, *The Indian Hill Station: Kodaikanal* (Chicago: University of Chicago, Department of Geography, Research Paper No. 141) 87 lists the following 96 Indian resorts, divided into 11 geographical groups

A) Kashmir group: 6,000'
1) Srinagar, 5,230'
2) Gulmarg, 8,500'
3) Kilinmarg, 8,750'
4) Sonamarg, 7,200'
5) Pahalgam, 8,000'
6) Achhabai, 6,000'
7) Verinag, 6,100'
8) Yusmarg, 8,000';

B) Dalhousie group:
9) Dalhousie, 6,680'
10) Bani Khat, 6,000'
11) Bakioh, 5,550'
12) Balun, 6,500'
13) Dharamkot, 6,200'
14) Bharwani, 3,890'
15) Chail, 7,400'
16) Dharmasala, 7,200'
17) Chamba, 6,000'
18) Kulu, 3,500'
19) Kangra, 2,500';

C) Simla group:
20) Simla, 7,200'
21) Mahasu, 8,200'
22) Mashobra, 7,500'
23) Narkanda, 9,000'
24) Kotgarh, 6,000'
25) Sonawar (Sanawar), 5,000'
26) Jutog, 7,000'
27) Sabathu, 4,500'
28) Solon, 5,500'
29) Dogshai (Dugshai), 6,000'
30) Kasauli, 6,400'
31) Chakrata, 6,880';

D) Mussoorie group:
32) Mussoorie, 6,500'
33) Landaur, 6,000'
34) Kedarnath, 12,000'
35) Badrinath, 10,000'
36) Dehra Dun, 1,800'
37) Lansdowne, 6,000';

E) Naini Tal group:
38) Naini Tal, 6,400'
39) Ranikhet, 6,000'

40) Baijnath, 5,000'
41) Kausani, 7,000'
42) Aalmora, 5,000'
43) Bhim Tal, 5,000'
44) Mukteshwar, 6,000'
45) Bageshwar, 6,000'
46) Bhowali, 6,000'
47) Choubottia, 6,500';

F) Darjeeling group:
48) Darjeeling, 7,150'
49) Lebong, 5,000'
50) Jalaphar, 7,520'
51) Ghoom, 8,000'
52) Kurseong, 4,860'
53) Kalimpong, 3,930';

G) Assam group:
54) Shillong, 5,000'
55) Cherrapunji, 4,450'
56) Jowai, 4,300'
57) Haflong, 2,500';

H) Northeast Deccan group:
58) Ranchi, 2,140'
59) Hazaribagh, 1,750'
60) Parasnath, 2,000'
61) Madhupar, 2,100';

I) Central and Northwest group:
62) Pachmarhi, 3,500'
63) Chikalda, 3,660'
64) Taragath, 2,860'
65) Mount Abu, 3,820'
66) Saputara, 3,000'
67) Khuldabad, 2,730';

J) Bombay group:
68) Poona, 1,800'
69) Khandala, 2,000'
70) Lonavala, 2,800'
71) Matheran, 2,460'
72) Purundhar, 4,470'
73) Mahabaleshwar, 4,500'
74) Panchgani, 4,380'
75) Amboli, 3,000';

K) Southern group:
76) Ramandurg, 3,500'
77) Horsley Hills, 4,100'
78) Madanapalle, 2,250'
79) Nandidurg, 4,850'
80) Bangalore, 3,000'
81) Kenmangudi, 4,000'
82) Biligiri, 4,000'
83) Yercaud, 4,830'
84) Palmaner, 2,250'
85) Ootacamund, 7,400'
86) Kotagiri, 6,500'

87) Coonoor, 6,000'
88) Wellington, 6,500'
89) Coimbatore, 1,300'
90) Kodaikanal, 7,300'
91) Munnar, 4,500'
92) Alwaye, 600'?
93) Pirmed, 3,500'
94) Periya, 4,500'
95) Courtallam, 1,450'
96) Ponmudi, 3,000'.
The list includes a few places which were not established by the British, such as Srinagar in Kashmir; Hindu pilgrimage places such as Badrinath and Kedarnath, some very small stations and also a few new ones which were established after India's Independence, such as Saputara and Yasmurg. However, it does not include the hill resorts of Pakistan, such as Abbottabad or Murree. It is only a partial list. Eighty is an often cited number in the old literature and has been taken as a reasonable count in this work.

2 *The Compact Edition of the Oxford English Dictionary,* 2 vols. (Glasgow, Oxford UP, 1971) I:286.
Oxford defines hill as a natural elevation of the earth's surface. After the introduction of the word mountain, "hill" was restricted to lesser heights but the discrimination has remained largely a matter of local usage.

3 Flora Annie Steel, *The Garden of Fidelity, Autobiography of Flora Annie Steel 1847-1929* (London, Macmillan, 1929) 30.

4 Governments of most Presidencies established their own hot weather seats in the hills: Assam and East Bengal, Shillong; Bengal, Darjeeling; Bombay, Mahabaleshwar and Poona; Central Provinces, Pachmarhi; Madras, Ootacamund and United Provinces, Naini Tal.

5 Mollie Panter-Downes, *Ooty Preserved: A Victorian Hill Station*

in India (London: Century, 1985) 6-7.

6   A. Hirsch, *Handbook of Geographical and Historical Pathology,* I (London, The New Sydenham Society, 1833) 440.

7   Panter-Downes, *Ooty* 7-8.

8   Lady Wilson, *Letters from India* (Edinburgh, William Blackwood and Sons, 1911) 46.

Cultural Antecedents

1   Rudyard Kipling, *Rudyard Kipling Complete Verse,* Definitive Edition, (New York, Anchor-Doubleday, 1989) 31-32.

2   Gen. Godfrey Charles Mundy, *Journal of a Tour in India,Pen and Pencil Sketches in India* (1838; London, John Murray,1858) 158.

3   The two phrases "Mountain Gloom" and "Mountain Glory" were first used by John Ruskin, but not together, as Marjorie Hope Nicolson did in her book *Mountain Gloom and Mountain Glory: The Development of the Aesthetics of the Infinite* and I have borrowed them here.

4   Alan Corbin, *The Lure of the Sea: The Discovery of the Seaside in the Western World 1750-1840,* trans. Jocelyn Phelps, (Berkeley, University of California, 1994) 6.

5   Arguably, the history of British hill resorts dates back to 1786, when Francis Light acquired Penang for the East India Company in the Malacca Straits. In 1805, Penang was made the fourth Presidency of India along with the other three: Bengal, Bombay and Madras. Penang island, in particular George Town harbour and the surrounding hills rising to the elevation of 2,470 feet (760 metres), remained important until 1832, when Singapore was made the capital of the Straits. By this time, however, a number

of new hill resorts were established throughout India, and Penang declined. Its stagnation lasted until the 1920s, when a funicular railway brought new life to the hill station. For further information about Penang and other resorts of Malaya consult: Robert Aiken, *Imperial Belvederes: The Hill Stations of Malaya* (Kuala Lumpur, Oxford UP, 1994).

6   Corbin, *Lure* 25.

7   John Ruskin, "Of the Novelty of Landscape," *Modern Painters,* 4 vols., (1856; Kent, George Allen, 1888) III:150-151.

8   For further discussion on this topic consult: Marjorie Hope Nicolson, *Mountain Gloom and Mountain Glory: The Development of the Aesthetics of the Infinite* (Ithaca, Cornell UP, 1959).

9   Keith Thomas, *Man and the Natural World: Changing Attitudes in England 1500-1800* (London, Allen Lane, 1983) 260.

10   Vidya Dehejia with an essay by Allen Staley, *Impossible Picturesqueness: Edward Lear's Watercolours, 1873-75* (Ahmedabad, Mapin, 1989) XII. William Hodges made his first overseas trip between 1772-75 to the South Seas with Captain Cook. Following that historic tour, from 1780-83 Hodges visited India on his own, making him the first European professional landscape artist to do work in the subcontinent, to be followed by Thomas and William Daniell, who worked in India between 1785-1793.

11   Gillian Wright, *Introduction to Hill Stations of India* (Hong Kong, Odyssey, 1991) 112.

12   Thomas Sutton, *The Daniells: Artists and Travellers* (London, Theodore Brun, 1954) 15. According to Sutton, the Daniell team left England on *Atlas,* but she was bound, not for India but

for China and arrived in Whampoa on August 23rd, 1785. The uncle and nephew pair must therefore have come from Whampoa to Bengal in a country ship arriving in Calcutta in late 1785 or early 1786, so the exact duration of their stay in Calcutta is difficult to determine. However, this stopover gave them an opportunity to add sketehes from China to their portfolio of work.

13   Serinagur, which the Daniell team visited in Garhwal region, was washed away in 1904, (Sutton, *Daniells* 50) and should not be mistaken for Srinagar in Kashmir; an error often made.

14   Sutton, *Daniells* 50.

15   N. R. Ray, *A Descriptive Catalogue of Daniells Work in the Victoria Memorial* (Calcutta, Victoria Memorial, n.d.) 2.

16   Sutton, *Daniells* 21.

17   Ray, *Descriptive* 3.

18   Robert B. Minturn, Jr., *From New York to Delhi, By way of Rio de Janeiro, Auftralia (Australia) and China* (New York, D. Appleton, 1858) 203.

19   Lieut. George Francis White, *Simla and Mussooree (Mussoorie) Himalaya Mountains,* 2 vols., (1836; Shimla, Minerva Book House, 1991) I-39.

20   White, *Simla* II:iii.

21   This is a summary list of folios depicting the mountain scenery of India: Richard Barron, *Views in India, chiefly among the Neelgherry (Nilgiri) Hills* (London, 1837); Lt. Col. James Fullerton, *Views in the Himalayas and Neilgherry (Nilgiri) Hills* (London, 1848); Lt. Col. Douglas Hamilton, *Sketches of the Shevaroy Hills* (London, 1865); Major E. A. McCurdy, *Three Panoramic Views of Ootacamund* (London, 1830 ?), and *Views of the Neilgherries, or Blue Mountains of Coimbetoor(Coimbatore)* (London,

1830); Alicia Eliza Scott, *Simla Scenes Drawn from Nature* (London, 1846); W. L. L. Scott, *Views in the Himalayas* (London, 1852); Capt. George Powell Thomas, *Views of Simla* (London, 1846).

22 Mundy, *Journal* viii.

23 Mundy, *Journal* 85.

24 Mundy, *Journal* 92, 139.

25 General Douglas Hamilton, *Records of Sport in Southern India* (London, R. H. Porter, 1892) IX.

26 A.U., *Overland, Inland, and Upland, A Lady's Notes of Personal Observation and Adventure* (London, Seeley, Jackson, Halliday, MD CCCL XXIII) 222-25.

27 Thelma and Victor Tate (retired English coffee planter, born and raised in India, is the oldest surviving resident of Yercaud), Executive-members of the Club, personal interview, 28 and 29 January, 1994.

28 David Robertson, "Mid-Victorians Amongst the Alps," *Nature and the Victorian Imagination*, 113-136, ed., U. C. Knoepflmacher and G. B. Tennyson, (Berkeley, University of California, 1977) 113-136.

29 Margaret Drabble, ed., *The Oxford Companion to English Literature* (1932; Oxford, Oxford UP, 1985) 1006-7 Quoting Ruskin's *Modern Painters*, I (1843), who cited Turner's work: "When you can look no more for gladness, and when you are bowed down with fear and love of the Maker and Doer of this, tell me who has best delivered this His Message unto men!"

30 Dehejia, *Impossible* 31.

31 Hope Nicolson, *Mountain* 3.

32 Robertson, "Mid-Victorians Amongst the Alps," *Nature*, 113-136, ed., Knoepflmacher and Tennyson, 116.

33 Leslie Stephen, *The Playground of Europe* (London, Longmans & Green, 1871) 39.

34 Stephen, *Playground* 60.

35 Hope Nicolson, *Mountain* 12.

36 William Wordsworth, *Guide to the Lakes*, intro., Ernest De Selincourt, (1835; London, Henry Frowde, 1906) 146, (my emphasis).

37 Emily Eden, *Up the Country: Letters Written to her Sister from the Upper Provinces of India*, 2 vols., (London, Richard Bentley, 1866) I:v-vi, (my emphasis).

38 Drabble ed., *Oxford Companion* 153, 855, 970 and 1084.

39 George D. Bearce, *British Attitudes Towards India 1784-1858* (London, Oxford UP, 1961) 252-53.

40 Bearcce, *British* 250-51.

41 Wilson, *Letters* 38-9.

42 A.U., *Overland*, 283.

43 Edward J. Buck, *Simla: Past and Present* (Calcutta, Government of India Central Printing Office, 1905) 22.

44 Frederick Price (Sir), *Ootacamund: A History*, Compiled for the Government of Madras, (Madras, Superintendent Government Press, 1908) 26.

45 Sir Walter Scott in *The Surgeon's Daughter* dealt with India, this novel opens in his native Scotland and closes in the land of Tipu Sultan (in the southern state of Mysore) painting a typically romantic view of India. The hero of Tennyson's *Locksley Hall* was also involved in a complex emotional struggle in India.

46 There are a couple of obscure reasons why the Nilgiri Library in Ootacamund fared better than the ones in other resorts: The first, even after India's independence a small contingent of Europeans had chosen to stay on in Ootacamund permanently. The second, Miss Kathleen Myers, the dedicated librarian, who was among those who had chosen to remain in India. Not only did she look after the Nilgiri Library for many years, but the traditions which she established are still in place. As a visiting researcher, once credentials were established, I was granted unrestricted access to the collection and the best personal assistance by the current staff.

47 James Morris, *The Pax Britannica*, 3 vols., (London, Folio Society, 1992) I:162.

48 J. K. Stanford ed., *Ladies in the Sun, The Memsahibs' India* 1790-1860 (London, Gallery 1962) 20.

49 For a quick account of William Hickey's journey consult: Stanford ed., *Ladies* 18-35, however, for a more detailed description of his journey Hickey's biography is a better source.

50 Morris, *Pax Britannica* I:162-63.

51 Morris, *Pax Britannica* I:162.

52 Stanford ed., *Ladies* 21.

53 Stanford ed., *Ladies* 34.

54 Kipling, *Complete* 32-33.

55 John Lang, *The Himalaya Club*, Household words. A weekly Journal conducted by Charles Jickens, no: 365 Saturday, March 1857. Rpt. Ruskin Bond, *Mussoorie and Landour; Days of Wine and Roses*, (New Delhi, Lustre Press, 1992) 266.

56 Eden, *Up the Country* I-209-10.

57 Eden, *Up the Country* I-180-81.

58 Eden, *Up the Country* I-182.

59 Wilson, *Letters* 14.

60 Kenneth Ballhatchet, *Race, Sex and Class Under the Raj, Imperial Attitudes and Politics and their Critics, 1793-1905* (London, Weidenfeld & Nicolson, 1980) 144.

61 For further information on race relations and the colonial physical planning consult: Anthony King, *Colonial Urban Development: Culture, Social Power and Environment* (London, Routledge, 1972).

62 Morris, *Pax Britannica* I:221.

63 Mundy, *Journal* 325-26

64 A.U. *Overland,* 97-100 and 228-9.

65 Based on Nora Mitchell's classification, (*Indian Hill-Station*, 6) hill resorts could be grouped in three broad categories:

1) The administrative and political types: Simla the national summer capital and the summer seat of the Punjab Presidency; Darjeeling, Mahabaleshwar, Naini Tal, Ootacamund, Pachmarhi, and Shillong, summer seats of other Presidencies; plus other official administration stations: Army Head Quarters, Simla; Army Northern Command in Murree, The Easten Command in Naini Tal,

2) Military Cantonments: Among other stations, half of them were used as military cantonments, such as Chakrata, Dalhousie, Dehra Dun, and so on, and

3) Regional Stations: The remaining smaller sanatorium stations functioned as regional and specialised resorts, some were used by railway staff, whereas some were established by missionaries.

66 Bernard Darwin, "Country Life and Sport," *Early Victorian England 1830-1865,* I:245-296, 2 vols., (London, Oxford UP, 1934) I:271.

67 Carey William H., *A Guide to Simla, with Information on Neighbouring Sanatoria* (London, Wymand, 1870)

68 The list of schools in the hill resorts is very large, specially since almost every religious order, Anglicans, American Protestants, Catholics, opened their network of schools in different locations throughout India. Stations like Mussoorie and Darjeeling had more than ten schools each, many still survive. Here are a few examples: Mussoorie: Convent of Jesus and Mary, 1845; St. George's College, 1853; Woodstock School, 1856; Darjeeling: St. Paul, 1864; St. Joseph, 1888; Simla: Bishop Cotton School, 1866; Convent of Jesus and Mary.

69 Panter-Downes, *Ooty* 7.

A Home Away From Home

1 Kipling, *Complete* 82.

2 Morris, *Pax Britannica* II:36-37.

3 The first YMCA was established in 1844 as a response to unhealthy living conditions among factory workers in England by the humanitarian Sir George Williams. They spread very quickly into the New World and in the colonies, including the hill resorts.

4 Mark Bence-Jones, *The Viceroys of India* (London, Constable, 1982) 1. Lord Amherst is supposed to have made this remark in Kennedy House at Simla with reference to his 1815 diplomatic mission to establish trade links with China, which proved unsuccessful. However, this expression has remained with us.

5 Indian labourers were taken to the islands of Ceylon (Sri Lanka), Fiji and the Caribbean to work on plantations; to Australia and Canada to look after farms and to work in the lumber industry; and parts of Africa to build new railway lines.

6 Bernard S. Cohen, *An Anthropologist among the Historians and Other Essays,* Introduction by Ranjit Guha, (Delhi, Oxford UP, 1987) 521 Quoting "Extracts from the Governor-General's Notes from an official dispatch to be forwarded to the Court of Directors, with respect to the Foundation of a College at Fort William, 10 July 1800" Reproduced in Ghosal, Appendix I, pp. 469-86.

7 Bence-Jones, *Viceroys* 7.

8 Philip Davies, *Splendours of the Raj: British Architecture in India 1660-1947* (London, Dass Media with John Murray, 1985) 68.

9 Bence-Jones, *Viceroys* 8 However, Davies, *Splendours* 69, puts the price of the Government House at £167,359; unfortunately, I have not been able to verify their original sources.

10 Bence-Jones, *Viceroys* 8.

11 Michael Edwardes, *Bound to Exile: The Victorians in India* (London, Sidgwick & Jackson, 1969) 12.

12 Edwardes, *Bound* 4.

13 Cohen, *Anthropologist* 513

14 Edwardes, *Bound* 4

15 George Chesney (Sir), *Indian Polity: The System of Administration in India* (Delhi, Concept, 1976) 273-274.

16 Edwardes, *Bound* 4.

17 Stanford, ed., *Ladies* 3.

18 Stanford, ed., *Ladies* 3.

19 According to Cohen, *Anthropologist* 513-14: as per the Act of 1784 and the Charter Act of 1793, posts paying £500 a year to £1,500 were to be filled with

officers actually resident in India for at least three years; those posts paying £1,500-£3,000 a minimum of six years; £3,000-£4,000 minimum nine years; and £4,000 and above minimum of 12 years. (no Indian could hold a post paying more than £500 a year since no Indian was a Company servant within the meaning of the Acts).

20 Edwardes, *Bound* 3.

21 Cohen, *Anthropologist* 545.

22 Charles Allen ed. in association with Michel Mason,*Plain Tales from the Raj, Images of British India in the Twentieth Century* (London, Andre Deutsch, 1975) 42.

23 Allen, ed., *Plain* 34

24 Cohen, *Anthropologist* 644. Cohen mentions one significant exception. If an Indian habitually wore European clothes in public, he would be allowed to wear shoes in the presence of his English masters on occasions of western- style rituals, such as the Governor-General's levee or a ball.

25 Thomas R. Metcalf, *An Imperial Vision: Indian Architecture and Britain's Raj* (London, Faber & Faber, 1989) 22

26 Metcalf, *Imperial* 22.

27 Val. C. Prinsep, *Imperial India, An Artist's Journal* (London, Chapman & Hall, 1879), 342.

28 Edwardes, *Bound* 5.

29 C.S. Peel, "Home and Habits," *Early Victorian England*, 1830-1865, ed., G.M. Young, I:77-152, 2 vols., (London, Oxford UP, 1934) I:111.

30 Edwardes, *Bound* 6.

31 Edwardes, *Bound* 6.

32 Edwardes, *Bound* 6.

33 Edwardes, *Bound* 7.

34 Allen, ed., *Plain* 46.

35 *Yesterday's Shopping: The Army &*

Navy Store's Catalogue 1907, Introduction to the 1969 facsimile by Alison Abdurgham, (1907; Devon, David & Charles, 1969) n. p.

36 The original, 1907 catalogue had 1282 pages. The introductory pages added to the 1969 reprint are not numbered making the facsimile of *The Army & Navy Store's Catalogue 1907*, a few pages thicker.

37 Edwardes, *Bound* 158-59.

38 Allen, ed., *Plain* 42.

39 Metcalfe, *Imperial* 6.

40 Sten Nilsson, *European Architecture in India 1750-1850* (London, Faber & Faber, 1968) 76.

41 Nilsson, *European* 77.

42 Davies, *Splendours* 104.

43 Bence-Jones, *Viceroys* 24.

44 Norman Macleod, *Peeps at the Far East, A Familiar Account of a Visit to India* (London, Strahan, 1871) 121.

45 Anthony Sattin, ed; *An Englishwoman in India, The Memories of Harriet Tytler* (New York, Oxford UP, 1986) 14-15.

46 Davies, *Splendours* 82-83

47 Government of India, Selections from the Records of the Government of India (Military Department), *Report on the Extent and Nature of the Sanitary Establishments for European Troops in the Bengal, Madras and Bombay Presidencies* (Calcutta, Military Department Press, March 1861) 10-15.

48 Most resorts were established in the Presidencies which were directly under British control. Often, formal transfer of titles or long term leases were signed with the native rulers if the land was under their control, as was the case with Darjeeling, Mahabaleshwar or Simla, for

example. In areas where there were no native claims, for example Kodaikanal, land distribution was controlled by the British. Only the stations in the state of Kashmir were under the direct control of the local Maharajah.

49 Government of India, Sikkim's Cessation of Darjeeling, (Foreign Department PC, April, 6, 1835, No. 100-104), National Archives of India, New Delhi.

50 Government of India, Europeans Settle Darjeeling, (Foreign Department PC, December, 27, 1837, No. 99-100), National Archives of India. New Delhi.

51 Ransome James, *Government of India Building Designs: A Collection of Building Designs of Government Buildings Issued from 1903 to 1907, under the Advise of Mr. James Ransome, F.R.I.B.A., while Consulting Architect to the Government of India* (Simla: James Ransome, 1907).n.p.

52 A.E. Richardson, "Architecture," *Early Victorian England, 1830-1865*, ed., G.M. Young, II:177-248, 2 vols., (London, Oxford UP, 1934) II:237.

53 J.C. Loudon, *An Encyclopaedia of Cottage, Farm, and Villa Architecture and Furniture* (London, Longman, Brown, Green, & Longmans, 1842) 1-8.

54 According to the Compact Edition of *Oxford English Dictionary* (Glasgow: 1971) the term cottage has also been in vogue as a particular designation for small country residences and detached suburban houses, adopted to a moderate scale of living, yet with all due attention to comfort and refinement. While in this sense, the name is divested of all associations with poverty, it is convenient, inasmuch as free from all pretension and shows restraint.

In this sense, the appellation *cottage orné (ornee)* was generally used, especially when the picturesque was aimed at, which was the case in the hill resorts.

55 George H. Ford, "Felicitous Space: The Cottage Controversy," *Nature and Victorian Imagination,* 29-48 ed., U. C. Knoepflmacher and G. B. Tennyson, (Berkeley, University of California, 1977) 29.

56 Ford, "Felicitous Space: The Cottage Controversy," *Nature,* 29-48, ed., Knoepflmacher and Tennyson, 30

57 Robert Kerr, *The Gentleman's House: or How to Plan English Residences, from the Parsonages to the Palace* (London, John Murray, 1865) 374-75.

58 Ford, "Felicitous Space: The Cottage Controversy," *Nature,* 29-48, ed., Knoepflmacher and Tennyson, 41.

59 Since houses in hill resorts were inspired by the notion of the cottage, a large percentage of them were named cottage this or that: The 1872-73 North-West Provinces Revenue Survey map of Cantonment and Settlement of Naynee Tal (Naini Tal) lists 207 properties, including churches, hotels and government buildings. The majority of homes, 36 in all, are named cottages, two are called cots, while the rest are called house, lodge, hall, view, villa, and so on. Similarly, a 1856 survey map of Malcompeth, the name by which Mahabaleshwar was referred to then, lists 87 properties of which 22 are named cottages, most with English names such as, Belvedere Cottage, Fern Cottage, Primrose Cottage, Spring Cottage, Violet Cottage, Woodwind Cottage, and so on.

60 Davies, *Splendours* 115.

61 *A Handbook for Travellers in Switzerland, and the Alps of Savoy and Piedmont* (London, John Murray, 1854) l.

62 Most of this book was written in one such "Swiss chalet" located in the Laurantian hills of northern Quebec.

63 Ford, "Felicitous Space: The Cottage Controversy," *Nature,* 29-48, ed., Knoepflmacher and Tennyson, 30, quoting George Sand, *Promenades au tour d'un village* (Paris, 1888) 66-67.

64 Davies, *Splendours* 109-110.

65 Fortunately Tennyson never visited India; the sight of faulty cottage copies, covered with corrugated metal sheets, would have caused him great anguish. Tennyson, an avid admirer of the beauty of English cottages, noticing in his native village the transformation of roofs, from thatch to slate, had in *Locksley Hall Sixty years After* (1866) lamented: Yonder lies our sea village–Art and Grace are less and less: Science grows and Beauty dwindles–roofs of slated hideousness!

66 Davies, *Splendours* 110.

67 Davies, *Splendours* 110.

68 Price, *Ootacamund* 69-70.

69 Pamela Kanwar, *Imperial Simla: the Political Culture of the Raj* (Bombay, Oxford UP, 1990) 24.

70 Vipin Pubby, *Simla Then and Now: Summer Capital of the Raj* (New Delhi, Indus, 1988) 22, quoting the *Simla District Gazetteer* - 1888-89.
The settlement grew with extraordinary speed: From 30 houses in 1830, to upward of 100 in 1841, and 290 in 1866, which reached up to 1,141 by 1881. For a detailed account of Simla's early development also see Buck, *Simla.*

71 Loudon, *Encyclopaedia* 1191.

72 E.B. Peacock, *A Guide to Murree and its Neighbourhood* (Lahore, W. Ball, 1883) n.p.

73 Ford, "Felicitous Space: The Cottage Controversy," *Nature,* 29-48, ed., Knoepflmacher and Tennyson, 30.

74 Richard Terrell, ed. George Roche, *Childhood in India, Tales from Sholapur* (London, The Radcliffe Press) 39.

75 Wilson, *Letters,* 321 (Letter dated 1905).

76 Edward W. Ellsworth, *Science and Social Science Research in British India, 1780-1880* (New York, Greenwood, 1991) Ch. 6.

77 Morris, *Pax Britannica* I:170-171.

78 Arnold Wright, *Early English Adventurers in the East* (London: Andrew Malrose, 1917) 37-54.

79 Morris, *Pax Britannica* I:171.

80 Government of India, *Report from the Agricultural and Horticultural Society,* (Home Department, Public, October 28, 1859, No. 43-44, 1-11), National Archives of India, New Delhi.

81 Panter-Downes, *Ooty* 30.

82 Panter-Downes, *Ooty* 83-84.

83 Glen Hicken, *The Barnson Blue-Book of Bangalore & Adjacent Surroundings* (Bangalore, Good Shepherd Convent Press, 1930).

84 Macleod, *Peeps* 146-47.

85 Geofry, *Ooty and Her Sisters or Our Hill Stations in South India* (Madras, Higginbotham, 1881).

86 George Powell Thomas, *Views of Simla* in accompanying notes (London, Dickinson, 1846).

87 Edwardes, *Bound* 12-13.
Up to 1813, the opinion prevailed that "a large influx of Europeans into our Indian territories must prove dangerous to the peace and security of those invaluable possessions." Letter of Court of Directors, H.E.I.C. to Lord Liverpool, 27 May 1813. As British control in India

improved, however, a decided change in the views of the Indian Government seems to have taken place. In 1829 Sir Charles Metcalfe wrote "that it is a matter of regret that Englishmen in India are excluded from the possession of land and other ordinary rights of peaceable subjects," and he expressed his belief that these restrictions impeded the prosperity of our Indian Empire. Again, in 1830. Lord Bentinck wrote that, "I feel most anxious that the state of the law should be so amended as to oppose no obstacle to the settlement of British subjects in the interior."

88   Edmund C.P. Hull and R.S. Mair, *The European in India, Anglo-Indians Vade-Mecum and Medical Guide to Anglo-Indians.*(London, Henry S. King & Co. 1871) 89-93 Hull Lived in southern India and Ceylon on plantations, Mair served as the Deputy Coroner at Madras.

89   George Powell Thomas, *Views of Simla* in accompanying notes (London, Dickinson, 1846).

90   Price, *Ootacamund* 63.

Simla: The Abode of "the High and the Mighty"

1   Kipling, *Complete* 75.

2   Rudyard Kipling, *Something of Myself: For My Friends Known and Unknown* (London, Macmillan 1937) 57.

3   Kanwar, *Imperial* 16.

4   Pubby, *Simla*, 22, quoting the *Simla District Gazetteer - 1888-89*

5   Kanwar, *Imperial* 16.

6   Pat Barr & Ray Desmond, *Simla: A Hill Station in British India* (New York, Charles Scribner's, 1978) 8.

7   Mundy, *Journal*, 108.

8   Victor Jacquemont, *Letters from India: Describing a Journey in the British Dominions of India, Tibet, Lahore, and Cashmeer (Kashmir)*, 2 vols., second edition, (1832; London, Edward Churton, 1835) I:234-37.

9   Madame Victor de Tracy was an Englishwoman married to a Frenchman.

10   Jacquemont, *Letters* I:250-51.

11   Mundy, *Journal*, 115.

12   Lord Bentinck was also instrumental in acquiring, from the Rajah of Sikkim, the hill tract which developed into a very successful resort in the eastern Himalayas – Darjeeling.

13   Following is the list of villages obtained by the British: Kainthu, Paghog, Cheog, and Aindari from Patiala; and Panjar, Sirian, Dharam, Phagli, Dillen, Kiar, Bamnoi, Pagawaag, Dhar, Kanlog, Kilian, and Khalini from Keonthal.

14   The exact date of the map, from the British Library's Oriental and India Office Collections, is not ascertained, however, it can be dated around 1830. Note the location of two key buildings: Kennedy House, and to its east the Governor-General's residence. The only other Governor-General's residence, to be located next to Kennedy House, was Peterhoff, but it was to its west, and did not come in use until 1862. Other residences of Governor-General's were built far from Kennedy House: Auckland House on Elysium Hill and Barnes Court near Chota Simla. Considering these historical facts, it could be safely assumed that, the building indicated as the Governor-General's residence on the map is Bentinck Castle, and the map can be dated between 1830 and 1838, when Auckland House became the official residence of the Governor-General.

15   Countess of Minto, ed., *Lord Minto in India: Life and Letters of Gilbert Elliot, First Earl of Minto, from 1807 to 1814* (London, Longmans & Green, 1880) 8.

16   Lord Wellesley was the only Governor-General to be recalled from duty in 1805, for his extravagance. It was alleged that he had incurred the colossal expense of £167,359 on the Government House in Calcutta while keeping the Company in the dark about it.

17   Sir Charles Metcalfe who served between Bentinck and Amherst was only a pro-tempro Governor-General.

18   Rajah Bhasin, *Simla: The Summer Capital of British India* (New Delhi, Viking-Penguin, 1992) 32.

19   Bhasin, *Simla* 32.

20   Bhasin, *Simla* 36.

21   Lord Canning was serving as the Governor-General during the 1857 Revolt (the Mutiny or the First War of Independence) and was appointed the first Viceroy in 1858.

22   Kanwar, *Imperial* 53.

23   Kanwar, *Imperial* 53.

24   Davies, *Splendours* 117.

25   S. D. Waley, *Edwin Montagu, A Memoir and an Account of his Visits to India* (Bombay, Asia Publishing House, 1964) 155.

26   Kanwar, *Imperial* 53.

27   Grewal J.S., *Rashtrapati Nivas, Shimla* (Shimla, Institute of Advanced Study, n. d.) n.p.,

28   Barr & Desmond, *Simla* 74.

29   Davies, *Splendours* 120.

30   M. M. Kaye, *The Sun in the Morning* (London, Viking, 1990) 192.

31   Bhasin, *Simla* 13.

32   Eden, *Up the Country* I:v.

33   Eden, *Up the Country* I:31.

34 Eden, *Up the Country* I:32.

35 "To the Bottom of the Sea, Titanic: Death of a Dream," *The Gazette,* Television Times, 23 July, 1994, Montreal.

36 Eden, *Up the Country* I:54.

37 Eden, *Up the Country* I:177-78.

38 Eden, *Up the Country* I:184-85.

39 Eden, *Up the Country* I:184-85.

40 Eden, *Up the Country* I:259.

41 Eden, *Up the Country* I:v-vi.

42 Wilson, *Letters* 302, (1904) 349, (1906)

43 Buck, *Simla* 33.

44 Kanwar, *Imperial* 102-103.

45 *The Chapslee Experience,* (Brochure from Chapslee Hotel, no publication detail), n.p..

46 Prinsep, *Imperial India,* 253.

47 Eden, *Up the Country* I: 197.

48 R. Bosworth Smith, *Life of Lord Lawrence,* 2 vols., (London, Smith & Elder, 1883) II:419.

49 Smith, *Life of Lord* II:425.

50 Smith, *Life of Lord* II:426.

51 Government of India, (Home Department, Public, December 1864, 41-47 (A)). National Archives of India, New Delhi,

52 Kanwar, *Imperial* 54.

53 A country with two capitals is Bolivia: La Paz is its administrative capital and Sucre, the constitutional capital.

54 *The Exodus to the Hills: Proceedings of the Great Public Meeting at the Town Hall, Calcutta, Wednesday, July 14th 1886* (Calcutta, W. Newsman, 1886) 17-19.

55 Government of India, Removal of the Government of India and Local Governments to Simla and Other Hill Stations, (Home Department, Public, February 1889, No. 214-218). National Archives of India, New Delhi,

56 Government of India, Movement of the Government to the Hills, (Home Department, Public, May 1887, No. 102-103), National Archives of India, New Delhi.

57 Chesney, *Indian Polity* 141.

58 Wright, *Introduction* 97.

59 Kanwar, *Imperial* 5.

Salubrious Sanatoria

1 Kipling, *Complete* 414

2 Panter-Downes, *Ooty Preserved* 6-7.

3 The East India Company lost Fort St. George, Madras, to the French in 1746, this could have left the Company without any real presence in south India. However, following the 1748 Treaty of Aix-la-Chapelle, Madras was returned to the British while the French retained their interests around Pondicherry. In 1748 the Nizam-ul-Mulk, *Souhbadar* of the Deccan died; a three year long war of ascension followed involving again both the foreign interests. The military skill and daring of Robert Clive enabled the British to win this conflict, and establish control over the Coromandel coast, which later formed the core of Madras Presidency.

4 G.R. Gleig, *The Life of Robert, First Lord Clive* (London, John Murray, 1848) 82.

5 Chesney, *Indian Polity* 213.

6 Chesney, *Indian Polity* 209-217.

7 Wright, *Introduction* 15.

8 Government of India, *Report on the Extent and Nature of the Sanitary Establishments for European Troops in the Bengal, Madras and Bombay Presidencies ,* Selections from the records of the Government of India (Military Department), (Calcutta, Military Department Press, March 1861) 121.
The estimates used in the Report were based on the investigations carried out by Sir Alexander Tulloch in the War Office in London for the Directors of the East India Company.

9 Government of India, *Report on the Extent* 122.

10 Government of India, *Report on the Extent* 122.

11 Mitchell, *Indian* 30.

12 Wright, *Introduction* 15.

13 Price, *Ootacamund* 128.

14 The earliest recorded encounter between Europeans and Todas, natives of this region, dates back to the seventeenth-century when Portuguese explorers discovered this spot. The next European to visit the region was Dr. Buchanan in 1800 who was followed by two surveyors Keys and Macmahon, who came to map out the wild Nilgiris in 1812. It was only after these visitors that Whish and Kindersley visited the Ootacamund area.

15 Davies, *Splendours* 124.

16 It has been established that Todas are the native tribal inhabitants of the high Nilgiri plateau. Their unique lifestyle, which includes: animal worship, hut-type structures which they inhabit, clothing with specially woven patterns, hand-made silver jewellery, a language which is unlike any other regional language, polyandrous lifestyle, had led early researchers to link them to the ancient inhabitants of Sumer. For the same reasons, they were also thought to be the Syrian followers of Saint Thomas who came to south India in the first century.

17 Norman Macleod, *Peeps* 114.

18 *Mitchell, Kodaikanal* 106; quoting John S. Chandler, *Seventy-five years in the Madura Mission,* (Madurai, American Mission, 1909) 89-90.

19 Mitchell, *Kodaikanal* 95, quoting J.H. Nelson, *Madura Country Manual,* Part V (Madras, Government Press, 1869) 92.

20 Government of India, *Report on the Extent* 122.

21 Mundy, *Journal,* 85-102.

22 Robert B. Minturn, *From New York to Delhi* p. 205-208.

23 Bond, *Mussoorie* 48.

24 G. Wright, quoting *Barron.*

25 Maggie Cobett, Quoted by D.C. Kala *Jim Corbett of Kumaon.* From Ruby Beyts unpublished notes.

26 The Kasauli Club Centenary Sub-Committee, *Kasauli and One Hundred Years of the Kasauli Club* (New Delhi, Service Press, 1980) 6.

27 Government of India, *Report on the Extent* 58.

28 Kasauli Club, *Kasauli* 9.

29 Edwardes *Bound* 182.

30 John Lang, "The Himalaya Club" in *Household Words.* A weekly journal conducted by Charles Jickens, No 365 March, 1957 rpt. in Ruskin Bond, *Mussoorie and Landour* p. 269.

31 Government of India, Proposal to Lower Railway Fairs to Kasauli for Rabies Treatment at Pasteur Institute, (Home Department, Medical, April 1905, No. 42-43), National Archives of India, New Delhi.

32 Government of India, "Remarks by the Army Sanitary Commission on the Principles of Construction for Barracks for Single and Married Men, "The Proceedings of the Governor General of India in Council, of 16th December 1864, Circular No. 89 of 1864, Public Works

(Calcutta, Public Works Department, 1864) 2.

33 Government of India, "Remarks by the Army Sanitary Commission on the Principles of Construction for Barracks for Single and Married Men," *Proceedings* 5.

34 Government of India, "Remarks by the Army Sanitary Commission on the Principles of Construction for Barracks for Single and Married Men," *Proceedings* 6.

35 Government of India, "Remarks by the Army Sanitary Commission on the Principles of Construction for Barracks for Single and Married Men," *Proceedings* 5.

36 Government of India, "Remarks by the Army Sanitary Commission on the Principles of Construction for Barracks for Single and Married Men," *Proceedings* 9

37 Eden Sanitarium (now Eden Hospital) started as a convalescent home for Europeans in 1883. Soon after an operating room was added, and over the years other facilities were added, today it functions as the main hospital of Darjeeling.

38 Compiled by W. H. Carey, *A Guide to Simla: With a Descriptive Account of the Neighbouring Sanatoria: Subathoo (Sabathu), Dugshaie, Sunawur (Sanawar), Kussowlie (Kasauli), Kotegurh, Chini, etc., etc., etc.* (Calcutta, Wyman, 1870) 167-68.

39 Government of India, *Report on the Extent* 122.

40 Government of India, *Report on the Extent* 86.

41 Price, *Ootacamund* 168-70

42 *A Handbook for Travellers in India,Burma and Ceylon* (London, John Murray, 1938) 631.

43 Government of India, (Home

Department, Political, May 17, 1861, (No. 34-36, 1-3 (A)), National Archives of India, New Delhi.

44 Government of India, Medical Charge of the Station of Pachmarhi, (Home Department, Medical, August 1878, 70-75), National Archives of India, New Delhi.

45 Lieut. Col. D. Hamilton, *Report on the Pulni (Palni) Mountains to Accompany the Series of Sketches* (Madras, Graves & Crocein, 1864).

46 Government of India, "Papers Related to a Sanatarium Upon Mount Parisnath, "Selection from the Records of the Government of Bengal, No. XXXVII, (Calcutta, 1861), I-IV.

47 Government of India, *Report on the Extent* 125-27.

48 Government of India, *Report on the Extent* 74.

49 Government of India, *Report on the Extent* 74.

50 Kanwar, *Imperial* 27.

51 Kanwar, *Imperial* 28.

52 Ballhatchet, *Race, Sex and Class* 4.

53 Ballhatchet, *Race, Sex and Class* 10.

54 Ballhatchet, *Race, Sex and Class* 11.

55 Ballhatchet, *Race, Sex and Class* 53.

56 Norman (Sir) Henry Wyle, *Notes on Station of Sabathoo (Sabathu)* (Agra, Military Department, 1873) 5.

57 Government of India, *Report on the Extent* 49.

58 Lawrence Military Asylum, *Brief Account of the Past ten Years of Existance of the Institution* (Sanawur [Sanawar], Lawrence Military Asylum, 1858) 59-62.

59 Hull and Mair, *The European in India & Medical Guide* (London, Henry S. King, 1871) 218.

60 Hull and Mair, *European* 216-18.

61 Notes from *The Church Records* and personal interviews with Father Benjamin Lal, January 2 to 6, 1994, Pachmarhi. The Church was designed by Henry Irvine, who was one of the parishioners; the work on it started in 1880 and completed in 1882, with the exception of the south transept which was completed in 1909, and the tower which was completed in 1923.

Resorts Then & Now

1 Prinsep, *Imperial India* 347.

2 Kanwar, *Imperial* 237.

3 Bhasin, *Simla* 218.

4 Kanwar, *Imperial* 237, quoting *The Tribune*, 17 May 1931.

5 Bhasin, *Simla* 207. Although Gandhi criticised the annual British move to the hills he visited them often, especially Panchgani, and his favourite Nandi Hill, a tiny resort near Bangalore where he was taken to recover from his long fasts.

6 *Guinness Multimedia Disc of World Records,* (Grolier Electronics, 1995).

7 Commercial trains started running in England in the 1830s, soon after, the service was introduced in India. The first commercial run was between Bombay and Poona which became fully operational in 1854, parts of this stretch, the Bombay-Thana route, began running in the early 1850s.

8 Chesney, *Indian Polity* 300.

9 *A Handbook for Travellers in India, Burma and Ceylon,* (London, John Murray, 1938) 324.

10 Wright, *Introduction* 105.

11 Barr & Desmond, *Simla,* quoting, Buck, *Simla.*

12 A.P. Agarwala, ed., *Holiday Resorts of Himachal Pradesh: A Traveller's Guide, 1991* (New Delhi, Nest & Wings, 1991) H-107.

13 L.S.S. O'Malley, *Darjeeling: Bengal District Gazetteers* (1907; New Delhi, Logos, 1989) 140.

14 Macleod, *Peeps* 65.

15 Vishnu Dabake, *Handbook to Matheran* (Poona, Pratibha, 1938) n.p.

16 A.K. Oliver, *The Hill Station of Matheran* (Bombay, Times of India, 1905) 6.

17 John Smith, *Matheran Hills: Its People, Plants, and Animals* (Edinburgh, Maclachlan & Stewart, 1871)

18 Gulbai Faramji Patak, *Matheran* (Bombay, Quere Hind, 1891) 5. Note the book is in Gujarati.

19 Patak, *Matheran,* 5-6

20 Oliver, *Hill Station* 14.

21 Town Planning and Valuation Department, Maharashtra State, Urban Research Cell, *Maharashtra State, Town Directory, District Raigad* (Pune, Government of Maharashtra, 1986) 45-57

22 Mahadev Savant, Personal interview, 29, November, 1993.

23 A.U., *Overland,* 248.

24 Owen C. Kail, *The Hill Station of Matheran* (Bombay, Thacker, 1947) (IOR # T15908).

25 Two umbrella associations, the Church of South India, and the Church of North India, have taken over the management of these properties and have managed to salvage many important buildings, but a lot more needs to be done for a proper turn around.

Bibliography

Agarwala, A.P. ed., *Holiday Resorts of Himachal Pradesh: A Traveller's Guide.* New Delhi, Nest & Wings, 1991.

Aiken, Robert. *Imperial Belvederes: The Hill Stations of Malaya.* Kuala Lumpur, Oxford Uni. Press, 1994.

Allen, Charles. ed., in association with Michael Mason. *Plain Tales from the Raj, Images of British India in the Twentieth Century.* London, Andre Deutsch, 1975.

A.U., *Overland, Inland, and Upland, A Lady's Notes of Personal Observations and Adventure.* London, Seeley, Jackson & Halliday, 1873.

Ballhatchet, Kenneth. *Race, Sex and Class Under the Raj, Imperial Attitudes and Politics and their Critics, 1793-1905.* London, Weidenfeld & Nicolson, 1980.

Barr, Pat and Ray Desmond. *Simla: A Hill Station in British India.* New York, Charles Scribner's, 1978.

Barron, Capt. Richard. *Views in India, Chiefly among the Neelgherry Hills.* London, Robert Havell, 1837.

Bearce, George D. *British Attitudes Towards India 1784-1858.* London, Oxford Uni Press, 1961.

Bence-Jones, Mark. *The Viceroys of India.* London, Constable, 1982.

—— *Palaces of the Raj.* London, Allen & Unwin, 1973.

Bhanja, K.C. *Darjeeling at a Glance* Darjeeling, 1942.

—— *Wonders of Darjeeling and the Sikkim Himalaya.* Darjeeling, author, 1943.

Bharucha, P. *Mahabaleshwar, The Club 1881-1981.* Bombay, Asian, 1981.

Bhasin, Raja. *Simla: The Summer Capital of British India.* New Delhi, Viking-Penguin, 1992.

Bhatia, H. S. ed., *European Women in India, Their Life and Adventures.* New Delhi, Deep & Deep, 1979.

Bond, Ruskin and Ganesh Saili. *Mussoorie and Landour: Days of Wine and Roses.* New Delhi, Lustre Press, 1992.

Brochure from Chapslee Hotel, "The Chapslee Experience". n.p., no date.

Buck, Edward J. *Simla: Past and Present.* Calcutta, Government of India Central Printing Office, 1905.

Burton, Isabel. *AEI: Arabia Egypt India, A Narrative of Travel.* London, William Mullan, 1879.

Burton, Richard. *Goa and the Blue Mountains.* 1851; Berkeley, University of California, 1991.

Caine, W.S. *Picturesque India: A Handbook for European Travellers.* London, George Routledge, 1890.

Calvert, J.C. *Vazeeri Rupi, The Silver Country of the Vazeers in Kulu: Its Beauties, Antiquities, and Silver Mines.* London, E. & F. N. Spon, 1873.

Carey, W.H. *A Guide to Simla With a Descriptive Account of the Neighbouring Sanitaria: Subathoo (Sabathu), Dugshaie, Sunawur (Sanawar), Kussowlie (Kasauli), Kotegurh, Chini, etc., etc., etc.* Calcutta, Wyman, 1870.

Chesney, Sir George. *Indian Polity: The System of Administration in India.* Delhi, Concept, 1976.

Cohen, Bernard S. *An Anthropologist among the Historians and Other Essays.* Delhi, Oxford Uni. Press, 1987.

The Compact Edition of Oxford English Dictionary, 2 vols., Glasgow, Oxford Uni. Press, 1971.

Corbett, Jim. *Man-Eaters of Kumaon.* New York, Oxford Uni. Press, 1946.

—— *Jungle Lore.* London, Oxford Uni. Press, 1953.

Corbin, Alain. *The Lure of the Sea: The Discovery of the Seaside in the Western World 1750-1840.* (trans. Jocelyn Phelps). Berkeley, University of California, 1994.

Dabake, Vishnu. *Handbook to Matheran.* Poona, Prathiba, 1938.

Darwin, Bernard. *Early Victorian England 1830-1865,* ed., G.M. Young. I:245-296, 2 vols. London, Oxford Uni. Press, 1934.

Davies, Philip. *Splendours of the Raj: British Architecture in India 1660-1947.* London, Dass Media with John Murray, 1985.

—— *The Penguin Guide to the Monuments of India,* 2 vols., London, Viking, 1989.

——*Darjeeling and Its Mountain Railway.* Calcutta, Darjeeling Himalayan Railway Company, 1921.

Dehejia, Vidya. with an essay by Allen Staley, *Impossible Picturesqueness: Edward Lear's Indian Watercolours, 1873-75.* Ahmedabad, Mapin, 1989.

Drabble, Margaret. ed., *The Oxford Companion to English Literature.* 1932. Oxford, Oxford Uni. Press, 1985.

Duguid, J. *Letters from India & Kashmir.* London, G. Bell , 1874. (Written 1870; illustrated and annotated 1873).

Dunbar, Janet. *Golden Interlude, The Edens in India 1836-1892.* London, John Murray, 1955.

Eden, Emily. *Up the Country: Letters Written to her Sister from the Upper Provinces of India,* 2 vols. London, Richard Bentley, 1866.

Edwardes, Michael. *Bound to Exile: The Victorians in India.* London, Sidgwick & Jackson, 1969.

Ellsworth, Edward W. *Science and Social Science Research in British India, 1780-1880.* New York, Greenwood, 1991.

The Exodus to the Hills: Proceedings of the Great Public Meeting at the Town Hall, Calcutta, Wednesday, July 14th 1886. Calcutta, W. Newsman, 1886.

Fullerton, Lieut.-Col. James. *Views in the Himalayas and Neilgherry Hills.* London, Dickinson, 1848.

The Gazette. Montreal, Television Times, 23 July, 1994.

Geofry (pseud). *Ooty and Her Sisters or Our Hill Stations in South India.* Madras, Higginbotham, 1881.

Gleig, Rev. G.R. *The Life of Robert, First Lord Clive.* London, John Murray, 1848.

Grewal, J.S. *Rashtrapati Nivas, Shimla.* Shimla, Institute of Advanced Study, n. d.

A Guide to Ootacamund and Its Neighbourhood. Madras, Lawrence Asylum, 1889.

Guinness Multimedia Disc of World Records. Guinness Publishing, Grolier Electronics, 1995.

Guthrie, K.B. *Life in Western India.* 2 vols. London, Hurst and Blackett, 1881.

Hamilton, General Douglas. *Records of Sport in Southern India,* etc. ed., Edward Hamilton. London, R.H. Porter, 1892.

Hamilton, Lieut.-Col. Douglas. *Report on the Pulni Mountains to Accompany the Series of Sketches.* Madras, Graves & Cookson, 1864.

—— *Sketches of the Shevaroy Hills.* London, 1865.

—— *A Handbook for Travellers in India, Burma and Ceylon.* London, John Murray, 1938.

—— *A Handbook for Travellers in Switzerland, and the Alps of Savoy and Piedmont.* London, John Murray, 1854.

Hicken, Glen. *The Barnson Blue-Book of Bangalore & Adjacent Surroundings.* Bangalore, Good Shepherd Convent Press, 1930.

Hirsch, August. *Handbook of Geographical and Historical Pathology.* London, The New Sydenham Society, 1883.

Hull, Edmund C.P. and R.S. Mair. *The European in India and Medical Guide.* London, Henry S. King, 1871.

Jacquemont, Victor. *Letters from India: Describing A Journey in the British Dominions of India, Tibet, Lahore, and Cashmeer.* 2 vols. London, Edward Churton, 1835.

Kail, Owen C. *The Hill Station of Matheran.* Bombay, Thacker, 1947.

Kala, D.C. *Jim Corbett of Kumaon* New Delhi, Ankur, 1979.

Kanwar, Pamela. *Imperial Simla: the Political Culture of the Raj.* Bombay, Oxford Uni. Press, 1990.

—— *The Kasauli Club Centenary Sub-Committee, Kasauli and One Hundred Years of the Kasauli Club.* (article) New Delhi, Service Press, 1980.

Kaye, M. M. *The Sun in the Morning.* London, *Viking,* 1990.

Kerr, Robert. *The Gentleman's House: or How to Plan English Residences, from the Parsonage to the Palace.*   London, John Murray, 1865.

Kincaid, Dennis. *British Social Life in India, 1608-1937. (*1938; Port Washington). New York, Kennikat Press, 1971.

King, Anthony D. *The Bungalow: The production of a Global Culture.* London, Routledge & Kegan Paul, 1984.

—— *Colonial Urban Development: Culture, Social Power and Environment.* London, Routledge & Kegan Paul, 1976.

Kipling, Rudyard. *Rudyard Kipling Complete Verse* (Definitive Edition). New York, Anchor-Doubleday, 1989.

—— *Something of Myself: For My Friends Known and Unknown.* London, Macmillan, 1937.

Knoepflmacher, U.C. and G.B. Tennyson, ed. *Nature and the Victorian Imagination.* Berkeley, University of California, 1977.

Lawrence Military Asylum. *Brief Account of the Past ten years of the existence of the Institution.* Sanawar, Lawrence Military Asylum, 1858.

Letters From India and Kashmir. London, George Bell & Jons 1874

Loudon, J.C. *An Encyclopaedia of Cottage, Farm, and Villa Architecture and Furniture.* London, Longman, Brown, Green, & Longmans, 1842.

McCurdy, Major E.A. *Three Panoramic Views of Ootacamund.* London, Smith, Elder, 1830.

—— *Views of the Neilgherries, or Blue Mountains of Coimbetoor.* London, Smith, Elder, 1830.

Mackenzie, Colin. *Life in the Mission, the Camp, and the Zenana, or Six Years in India.* 2 vols. New York, Redfield, 1853.

Macleod, Norman. *Peeps at the Far East, A Familiar Account of a Visit to India.* London, Strahan & Co., 1871.

Metcalf, Thomas R. *An Imperial Vision: Indian Architecture and Britain's Raj.* London, Faber & Faber, 1989.

Minto, (Countess) ed. *Lord Minto in India: Life and Letters of Gilbert Elliot, First Earl of Minto, from 1807 to 1814.* London, Longmans & Green, 1880.

Minturn, Robert B. Jr., *From New York to Delhi, By Way of Rio de Janeiro, Australia and China.* New York, D. Appleton, 1858.

Mitchell, Nora. *The Indian Hill Station: Kodaikanal.* Chicago, University of Chicago, (Department of Geography, Research Paper No. 141), 1972.

Morris, James. *The Pax Britannica.* 3 vols. London, Folio Society, 1992.

Morris, Jan and Simon Winchester. *Stones of Empire: The Buildings of the Raj.* Oxford, Oxford UP, 1983.

Mundy, Gen. Godfrey Charles. *Journal of a Tour in India., Pen and Pencil Sketches in India, 1838.* London, John Murray, 1858.

Nature and Victorian Imagination 29-48, ed. U.C. Knoepflmacher and G.B. Tennyson. Berkeley, University of California, 1977.

Nicolson, Marjorie Hope. *Mountain Gloom and Mountain Glory: The Development of the Aesthetics of the Infinite.* Ithaca, Cornell Uni. Press, 1959.

Nilsson, Sten. *European Architecture in India 1750-1850.* London, Faber & Faber, 1968.

Oliver, A.K. "The Hill Station of Matheran"(article). Bombay, Times of India, 1905.

O'Malley, L.S.S. *Darjeeling: Bengal District Gazetteers, 1907.* New Delhi, Logos, 1989.

Panter-Downes, Mollie. *Ooty Preserved: A Victorian Hill Station in India, 1967.* London, Century, 1985.

Patak, Gulbai Faramji. *Matheran.* Bombay, Quere Hind, 1891, *(in Gujarati).*

Peacock E.B., *A Guide to Murree and its Neighbourhood.* Lahore, W. Ball, 1883.

Price, Sir Frederick. *Ootacamund: A History.* Madras, Superintendent Government Press, 1908.

Prinsep, Val C. *Imperial India: An Artist's Journals.* London, Chapman and Hall, 1879.

Pubby, Vipin. *Simla Then and Now: Summer Capital of the Raj.* New Delhi, Indus, 1988

Ransome, James. *Government of India Building Designs: A Collection of Building Designs of Government Buildings Issued from 1903 to 1907, under the Advise of Mr. James Ransome, F.R.I.B.A., while Consulting Architect to the Government of India.* Simla, James Ransome, 1907.

Ray, N.R. *A Descriptive Catalogue of Daniells Work in the Victoria Memorial.* Calcutta, Victoria Memorial, n.d..

Roche, George. *Childhood in India: Tales from Sholapur,* presented and edited by Richard Terrell. London, Radcliff, 1994.

Ruskin, John. *Modern Painters*, 4 vols. Kent, George Allen, 1888.

Sattin, Anthony, ed., *An Englishwoman in India. The memories of Harriet Tytler.* New York, Oxford Uni. Press, 1986.

Scott, Alicia Eliza. *Simla Scenes Drawn from Nature.* London, Dickinson, 1846.

Scott Paul. *Staying On.* London, Mandarin, 1995.

Scott, W.L.L. *Views of the Himalayas.* London, n.p., 1852.

Smith, John. *Matheran Hills: Its People, Plants, and Animals.* Edinburgh, Maclachlan & Stewart, 1871.

Smith, R. B. *Life of Lord Lawrence.* 2 vols. London, Smith & Elder, 1883.

Stanford J. K. ed., *Ladies in the Sun, The Memsahibs' India 1790-1860.* London, Gallery, 1962.

Steel, Flora Annie. *The Garden of Fidelity, Autobiography of Flora Annie Steel 1847-1929.* London, Macmillan, 1929.

—— *The Complete Indian Housekeeper and Cook.* London, Chadwyck-Healey, 1888.

Stephen, Leslie. *The Playground of Europe.* London, Longmans & Green, 1871.

Sutton, Thomas. *The Daniells: Artists and Travellers.* London, Theodore Brun, 1954.

Thomas, Capt. George Powell. *Views of Simla.* London, Dickinson, 1846.

Thomas, Keith. *Man and the Natural World: Changing Attitudes in England 1500-1800.* London, Allen Lane, 1983.

Town Planning and Valuation Department, Maharashtra State, Urban Research Cell. *Maharashtra State, Town Directory, District Raigad.* Pune, Government of Maharashtra, 1986.

Waley, S.D. *Edwin Montagu: A Memoir and an Account of his Visits to India.* Bombay, Asia Publishing House, 1964.

White, Lieut. George Francis. *Views in India, chiefly among the Himalaya mountains, taken during tours in the direction of Mussooree, Simla, the sources of the Jumna and Ganges etc. in 1829, 31, 32 with notes and descriptive illustrations.* London, n.p., 1835.

—— *Simla and Mussooree Himalaya Mountains.* 2 vols., (1836). Shimla, Minerva Book House, 1991.

Wilson Lady A.C. Macleod. *Letters from India.* Edinburgh, William Blackwood and Sons, 1911.

Wordsworth, William. *Guide to the Lakes.* London, Henry Frowde, 1906.

Wright, Arnold. *Early English Adventurers in the East.* London, Andrew Melrose, 1917.

Wright, Gillian. *Introduction to Hill Stations of India.* Hong Kong, Odyssey, 1991.

Wyle, Sir Norman, Henry. *Notes on Station of Sabathoo (Sabhathu).* Agra, Military Department, 1873.

Yesterday's Shopping. The Army & Navy Store's Catalogue (1907), Introduction to the 1969 facsimile by Alison Abdurgham. 1907. Devon, David & Charles, 1969.

Young, G. M. ed. *Early Victorian England, 1830-1865,* 2 vols. London, Oxford Uni. Press, 1934.

Government Documents

Government of India. *Europeans Settle Darjeeling.* (Foreign Department PC, December, 27, 1837, No. 99-100). New Delhi, National Archives of India.

Government of India. (Home Department, Political, May 17, 1861, No. 34-36, 1-3 (A)). New Delhi, National Archives of India.

Government of India. (Home Department, Public, December 1864, No. 41-47 (A)). New Delhi, National Archives of India.

Government of India. *Medical Charge of the Station of Pachmarhi.* (Home Department, Medical, August 1878, 70-75). New Delhi, National Archives of India.

Government of India (Military Department). *Selections from the Records of the Government of India* Calcutta, Military Department Press, March 1861.

Government of India. *Movement of the Government to the Hills.* (Home Department, Public, May 1887, No. 102-103). New Delhi, National Archives of India.

Government of India. *Proposal to Lower Railway Fares to Kasauli for Rabies Treatment at Pasteur Institute.* (Home Department, Medical, April 1905, No. 42-43). New Delhi, National Archives of India.

Government of India. *Remarks by the Army Sanitary Commission on the Principles of Construction for Barracks for Single and Married Men: The Proceedings of the Governor General of India in Council, of 16th December 1864, Circular No. 89 of 1864, Public Works.* Calcutta, Public Works Department, 1864.

Government of India. *Removal of the Government of India and Local Governments to Simla and Other Hill Stations.* (Home Department, Public, February 1889, No. 214-218). New Delhi, National Archives of India.

Government of India. *Report from the Agricultural and Horticultural Society.* (Home Department, Public, October 28, 1859, No. 43-44, 1-11). New Delhi, National Archives of India.

Government of India. *Selection from the Records of the Government of Bengal,* (No. XXXVIII, I-IV). Calcutta, 1861.

Government of India. *Sikkim's Cessation of Darjeeling.* (Foreign Department PC, April 6, 1835, NO. 100-104). New Delhi, National Archives of India.

Index